Who Rules the World

Who Rules the World

*Divine Providence
and the Existence of Evil*

Hans Schwarz

FORTRESS PRESS
MINNEAPOLIS

Contents

Preface

When I told the publisher that I was working on a book manuscript on theodicy, he responded, "This is the perennial issue." Indeed, as long as we live on this earth, this issue will not go away. Are we indeed lonely wanderers in the immensity of the universe, about whom nobody cares, or is there someone above and beyond ourselves who is in control of our destinies and of the history of this world? These are questions that confront every one of us sooner or later.

As the German philosopher Friedrich Nietzsche confessed in his work on Zara-thustra, the world has become cooler. After two atrocious world wars, the misery that humans inflict on each other has not lessened. Whether we look at the civil wars in Iraq, Syria, or southern Sudan and natural disasters—such as earthquakes in Fukushima, floods in Mozambique, and tropical monster storms in the Caribbean—misery seems to abound. We seem to be kidding each other when we say that we are in control of our affairs and the world around us. To the contrary, we seem to have become helpless victims of our own evil doings and of the ravages of nature. If we ever had control of our destiny, we certainly have lost it by now. Of course, with some kind of evolutionary mentality, we could comfort ourselves by saying that this is the way nature proceeds. Civilizations come and go, and so do living species. Only the fittest will survive.

When we look at the Bible, this sentiment seems to be confirmed. In the Old Testament, we find many Psalms of lament in which people in their misery cry out to God. In the New Testament, we find Jesus helplessly hanging on the cross, deserted by even his most intimate disciples. The Bible does not hide the depth of human misery and despair. But even in Psalm 22, the Psalm that Jesus presumably prayed when he was hanging on the cross, we read, "He [God] did not hide his face from me, but heard when I cried to him" (Ps 22:24). And after Jesus's crucifixion and death, we read of his glorious resurrection to new and imperishable life. Yes, the Bible concedes that there is much misery and evil in this world. But it also affirms the prospect of total redemption from the evils and imperfections we encounter in this world. Whether this justified hope, justified on the account of Christ's resurrection, amounts to a theodicy, meaning a justification of God's way of doing things, I leave that up to the judgment of the readers of this text. Yet it is my hope that after reading, one can conclude that God is indeed in control of the affairs of this world even if God allows for freedom for both humans and nature.

This text on theodicy also allowed me to incorporate and considerably update some things I had written earlier on divine providence (*Creation*, Eerdmans, 2002) and on Augustine and on Luther (*Evil*, Fortress, 1995). At this point, I also want to thank again Dr. Terry Dohm, who once more improved my style; Frau Jutta Brandl-Hammer and Frau Andrea Bauer, who secured books from various libraries and were always available when needed; and above all, my wife, Hildegard, who has selflessly supported me over the years when I was sitting at my desk to work on yet another manuscript.

—Hans Schwarz

Abbreviations

ABD   Freedman, David Noel, ed. *Anchor Bible Dictionary*. 6 vols. New York: Doubleday, 1992.

ACW   *Ancient Christian Writers*. 66 vols. New York: Paulist, 1946–2015.

ANF   Roberts, Alexander, and James Donaldson, eds. *The Ante-Nicene Fathers*. 10 vols. 1885–87. Reprint, Peabody, MA: Hendrickson, 1994.

CD   Barth, Karl. *Church Dogmatics*. Edited by Geoffrey W. Bromiley and Thomas F. Torrance. Translated by Geoffrey W. Bromiley. 4 vols. in 12 parts. Edinburgh: T&T Clark, 1936–62.

ELW   *Evangelical Lutheran Worship*. Minneapolis: Augsburg Fortress, 2006.

FaCh   *Fathers of the Church*. 127 vols. Washington, DC: Catholic University of America, 1947–2013.

HDT   Andresen, Carl, ed. *Handbuch der Dogmen- und Theologiegeschichte*. 3 vols. Göttingen, Germany: Vandenhoeck & Ruprecht, 1982–84.

Inst   Calvin, John. *Institutes of the Christian Religion*. Translated by Henry Beveridge. Edinburgh: Calvin Translation Society, 1845–46.

LW   *Luther's Works*. American ed. vols. 1–30: St. Louis: Concordia; vols. 31–55: Philadelphia: Fortress; vols. 56–: St. Louis: Concordia, 1955–.

MPG   Migne, J.-P., ed. *Patrologia Graeca*. 217 vols. Paris, 1844–64.

NIB   Keck, Leander E., ed. *The New Interpreter's Bible*. 12 vols. Nashville: Abingdon, 1994–2004.

NPNF FS   Schaff, Philip, ed. *Nicene and Post-Nicene Fathers*. First Series. 14 vols. Reprint, Grand Rapids, MI: William B. Eerdmans, 1979.

ST   Aquinas, Thomas. *Summa Theologica*. Translated by Fathers of the English Dominican Province. 5 vols. New York: Benzinger Brothers, 1911. Rev. ed., London: Benzinger Brothers, 1920. https://tinyurl.com/y5gfp6mf.

TDNT   Kittel, Gerhard, and Gerhard Friedrich, eds. *Theological Dictionary of the New Testament*. Translated by Geoffrey W. Bromiley. 10 vols. Grand Rapids, MI: William B. Eerdmans, 1964–76.

TDOT   Botterweck, G. Johannes, Helmut Ringgren, and Heinz-Josef Fabry, eds. *Theological Dictionary of the Old Testament*. Translated by David E. Green and Douglas W. Scott. 16 vols. Grand Rapids, MI: William B. Eerdmans, 1975–2008.

TRE   Müller, Gerhard, ed. *Theologische Realenzyklopädie*. 38 vols. Berlin: Walter de Gruyter, 1977–2007.

WA   *D. Martin Luthers Werke: Kritische Gesamtausgabe [Schriften]*. 73 vols. Weimar: Hermann Böhlaus Nachfolger, 1883–2009.

WATR   *D. Martin Luthers Werke: Kritische Gesamtausgabe [Tischreden]*. 6 vols. Weimar: Hermann Böhlau Nachfolger, 1912–21.

Introduction

After graduation from high school, I worked in a factory for a couple of months to earn some money before entering university. When my supervisor, a nice and caring person in his fifties, found out that I was going to study theology, he responded, "I do not believe in God." To my surprised question of "Why?" he explained, "If you read in the newspaper all the horrible things which happen in the world every day, you cannot believe in God almighty." The German dramatist and writer of poetry and prose Georg Büchner (1813–37) was perhaps right when he called suffering "the rock of atheism."[1] Indeed, innocent suffering has driven some people to despair. Others, such as my supervisor, have doubted on account of all the evil in this world that there is a God. And discerning minds since the beginning of humanity have tried to reconcile their belief in God with the factuality of evil. In the Old Testament, the whole book of Job is primarily devoted to this issue.

Even Charles Darwin was not so much challenged in his belief in God by his discovery of evolution. Much more vexing to him was the reality of cruelty in nature. He wrote, "There seems to me too much misery in the world. I cannot persuade myself that a beneficent & omnipotent God would have designedly created the Ichneumonidæ [i.e., parasitic wasp] with the express intention of their feeding within the living bodies of caterpillars, or that a cat should play with mice."[2] And then he concluded that this whole subject is too profound for the human intellect.

If God is indeed the creator of the world, why does God allow so much bad to happen in his creation? Is God not totally in control, or is he not a good God but someone who plays dice with the created order and the life that moves around? The issue of theodicy, meaning an answer to the question of why a good God permits manifestations of evil, is of existential import for virtually everyone whether believer or unbeliever. Here the issue raised is not only of God's omnipotence but also of his benevolence. This means we must try to find out whether the God we trust in is really in control of the affairs of this world. Since humans often think they are in control, the respective spheres of influence between the human and the divine must also be demarcated. Often, the issue of evil has been understood in the dualistic fashion, meaning that there are two opposing powers: a good God and an evil anti-Godly power. If this were true,

---

1. Georg Büchner, *Dantons Tod*, act 3, part 1, line 16, in 3/1, *Georg Büchners Dichtungen*, ed. Henri Poschmann (Frankfurt: Deutscher Klassiker Verlag, 1992), 58.
2. Charles Darwin, "Letter to Asa Gray" (May 22, 1860), in *The Correspondence of Charles Darwin*, ed. Frederick H. Burkhardt, vol. 8, 1860 (Cambridge: Cambridge University Press, 1993), 224.

it is important to know who will in the end gain the upper hand or whether the struggle between good and evil will continue forever.

Though we do not want to close our eyes to other important areas in which the issue of theodicy has been raised, we will confine ourselves primarily to the Christian context. Otherwise, our considerations would exceed the limits of what most inquisitive readers want to read.

I Good and Evil in the History of Religions

When we look around in the vast arena of the world religions, we find basically two approaches to the issue of theodicy, a dualistic one and a fatalistic one. The first one is essentially an apology of God, the gods, or the divine claiming in so many words that the divine cannot be the cause of negativity. The causes of evil must be sought somewhere else. In this dualistic approach, the godhead is excused of being the cause of evil, since there is a clash between the forces of good and evil. In the fatalistic view, both good and evil are contained in one supreme power. The godhead is then often considered so supreme and powerful that human beings have no choice but to accept whatever is meted out to them, implying to some extent that it is their fault if they find themselves in a precarious situation.

The Dualistic Approach

Plato

It might be strange that we start our survey of positions on theodicy with a philosopher. Yet Plato (427–347 BCE) is not only the "father" of Western philosophy but also a mighty influence on Christian theology. When we peruse the works of Plato, we will notice that in his philosophy, he wanted to elucidate what is true and then guide humans on the way to the good in private as well as public life. Life for him was perceived as the whole web of being, which, for him, also included the divine or the gods. Since in Greek mythology the gods were not always portrayed as spotless examples for humanity, Plato tackled in many of his writings the issue of theodicy.

Throughout his works, Plato defended the positive aspect of God and the gods by talking about divine guidance and providence. In his dialogue *Timaeus*, Plato explains,

> God desired that all things should be good and nothing bad, so far as this was attainable. Wherefore also finding the whole visible sphere not at rest, but moving in an irregular and disorderly fashion, out of disorder he brought order, considering that this was in any way better than the other. [. . .] When he was framing the universe, he put intelligence in soul, and soul in body, that he might be the creator of a work which was by nature fairest and best. Wherefore, using the language of probability, we may say

that the world became a living creature endowed with soul and intelligence by the providence of God.[1]

God brought harmony and order into the universe. To that effect, God also created reason and soul so that by God's providence, the universe is a living creature and can conduct itself in a reasonable way.

Yet God is also considered to be the creator, as we read in Plato's *Laws*: "God, as the old tradition declares, holding in his hand the beginning, middle, and end of all things that is, travels according to his nature in a straight line towards the accomplishment of his end" (Nom. 715–16). Plato explains, "Now God ought to be to us the measure of all things and not man" (Nom. 716). Since God is the supreme Lord, humans should follow God's example and precepts. If we abandon that example, we end up in confusion and mischief. Therefore, we cannot blame God for evil. "For few are the goods of human life, and many are the evils, and the good is to be attributed to God alone; of the evils the causes are to be sought elsewhere, and not in God" (Rep. 379c). "But that God being good is the author of evil to any one is to be strenuously denied, and not to be said or sung or heard" (Rep. 380b). Therewith God is vindicated of all evil. God is neither the cause nor the executor of evil, since he is good. "The divine is beauty, wisdom, goodness, and the like" (Phaedr. 246d). This means that the divine or God or the gods are good. To that effect, we can trust God. We read in the *Republic* (381c), "Then it is impossible that God should ever be willing to change; being, as is supposed, the fairest and best that is conceivable, every God remains absolutely and forever in his own form." Gods are not tricksters who appear at one time in this shape and mood and another time in another one. Since "God and the things of God are in every way perfect" (Rep. 381b), God is in every respect perfect. The gods "are just," and just people are then friends to the gods (cf. Rep. 352a). For Plato, there is nothing wrong or bad in the gods.

His vindication of God as the author of bad or evil things then proceeds in the following way: Since God is good and no good things can be harmful, that which is not harmful can do no harm. That which can do no harm can do no evil and cannot be the cause of evil. "The good is not the cause of all things, but of the good only" (Rep. 379b). Since God is good, God cannot be the cause of everything, especially if it is not good. Some other causes must then be sought for that which is not good.

When people surmise that God created the world but then withdrew from it, Plato counters that they do not look at the whole picture but only judge things from their own standpoint. They should also consider life on this earth, the stars, the moon, and the seasons. "Since a soul or souls having every sort of excellence are the causes of all of them, those souls are Gods, whether they are living beings and reside in bodies, and in this way order the whole heaven, or whatever be the place

---

1. *Timaeus* 30a. The quotations from Plato are from *The Dialogues of Plato*, trans. Benjamin Jowett (Chicago: Encyclopedia Britannica, 1996). Bracketed ellipses are mine throughout.

and mode of their existence" (Nom. 899c). Plato assumes here that everything in the universe is ensouled and "full of gods" that enable the universe to exist and to move. All things are full of gods. Therefore, it is wrong to argue that gods exist but do not pay attention to human affairs. The gods "are perfectly good, and that they care of all things is most entirely natural to them" (Nom. 900c). Therefore, "The Gods care about the small as well as about the great" (Nom. 900c).

For Plato, evil is not a category in its own but something that later is called a privation of the good. Humans are responsible for moral evil. "God is never in any way unrighteous—he is perfect righteousness" (Theait. 176c). Yet Plato knows that injustice remains often unpunished in this life. He then assumes that once this life has ended, those who executed injustice will live "in the likeness of their own evil selves" (Theait. 177a). Whatever does not even out in this life will even out in the hereafter. When we ponder these thoughts of Plato, we might find here some affinity to the Judeo-Christian heritage. There is the creator who brought forth the world and imprinted on it his laws. Yet there is evil and imperfection that, however, cannot be attributed to this creator. Those who succumbed to evil will bear its consequences forever in life beyond this one. We might not be wrong calling these thoughts a philosophical theology. It is not surprising then that, according to our knowledge, Plato was the first person to use the term *theology*.[2]

Zoroastrianism

Roughly around the same time as Plato composed his works, there lived in north-eastern Iran a priest and prophet by the name of Zarathustra, or Zoroaster, according to the Greek transcription. The dates for his life vary considerably from the second millennium to the sixth century BCE. Most likely, Zoroaster lived around 600 BCE. His teachings developed into Zoroastrianism, which was already an old religion when it was first recorded. From the sixth century BCE to the seventh century CE, it became the official religion of ancient Persia and its distant subdivisions. Zoroaster's training for the priesthood began very early, and he became a priest probably around the age of fifteen, which was when, according to Old Iranian reckoning, a boy reached adulthood.[3] As we gather from the Gathas (the poems attributed to Zarathustra), he gained knowledge from other teachers and personal experience on his travels when he left his parents at just twenty years old. By the age of thirty, he experienced a revelation when he saw a shining Being, who revealed himself as Vohu Manah (Good Thought) and taught him about Ahura Mazda (Wise Spirit), the uncreated creator. Zoroaster soon became aware of the existence of two primal spirits, Ahura Mazda and Angra Mainyu (Hostile Spirit),

---

2. Cf. *The Republic*, 379a, in *Dialogues of Plato*. Referring to the representation about God in "poetry, epic, lyric or tragic," Plato uses the Greek term for *theology*.
3. For the following, cf. Mary Boyce, *A History of Zoroastrianism*, vol. 1, *The Early Period* (Leiden, Netherlands: E. J. Brill, 1975), 184.

with opposing concepts of *Asha* (truth) and *Druj* (lie). Thus he decided to spend his life teaching people to seek the truth.[4] He received further revelations and saw a vision of the seven Amesha Spenta, meaning the divine sparks or archangels of Ahura Mazda. Zoroaster's teachings were collected in the Gathas and the Avesta.[5] He taught about free will and opposed the use of the hallucinogenic haoma plant in rituals (Yasna 48:10), polytheism, overritualizing religious ceremonies, and animal sacrifices. He also objected to the oppressive class system in his home country.

Similar to Mohammed many centuries later, Zoroaster completely rejected the religious tradition of his geographic environment. At the center of his religious devotion was the god Ahura Mazda, or Ormuzd. This god was the creator of heaven and earth, without image, and the lawgiver of the whole cosmos. Loyalty to Ahura Mazda excluded the worship of any of the old Iranian gods. Yet Zoroaster did not advocate a strict monotheism, since according to his teachings, there existed an insurmountable opposition between almighty Ahura Mazda and Angra Mainyu, or Ahriman, the manifestation of everything evil. This cleavage resulted in an ethical and metaphysical dualism, "the strictest antithetical dualism known in the history of religion."[6] Zarathustra expresses this dualism in the following way: "I will tell forth the two Wills at the world's beginnings, of whom the Bounteous one speaks thus to the Hostile one: 'Neither our thoughts, nor our pronouncements, nor our intellects, nor our choices, nor our words, nor our deeds, nor our moralities, nor our souls, are in accord'" (Yasna 45:2).[7]

Once these spirits or "gods" made their initial ethical choice, they separated themselves and the world into a sphere of light and a sphere of darkness.[8] The incompatibility of both gods is, for Zarathustra, the basis of his ethical demands. Though the ethical demands remain mostly in the realm of social ethics (the liberation of the suppressed peasants and herdsmen), the actual goal of ethical realization lies in the eschaton. Already here and now, the village will prosper through righteousness, and those who adhere to good thought and right actions "will be the Promoters of the regions" (Yasna 48:12). The continuous realization of the good requires a meaningful and active life involved in peaceful work. Characteristic for Zoroaster's doctrine is a twofold outcome of history: an eternity of bliss and an eternity of woe allotted respectively to good and evil people in another life beyond the grave. After death, the soul of the deceased must cross the Chinvat Bridge, "the Arbiter's Crossing" (Yasna 46:10), which stretches over hell, an abyss of molten metal and fire. For those good people, the bridge grows broader and broader for easier transit and subsequent ascent into heaven, where the pious soul will live

---

4. Martin Litchfield West, *The Hymns of Zoroaster: A New Translation of the Most Ancient Sacred Texts of Iran* (London: Bloomsbury, 2010), 19–20.
5. West, 24.
6. So Günter Lanczkowski, "Iranische Religionen," in TRE, 16:251.
7. The Yasnas are quoted according to West, *Hymns of Zoroaster*.
8. Cf. Friedrich Heiler, *Die Religionen der Menschheit in Vergangenheit und Gegenwart* (Stuttgart, Germany: Reclam, 1959), 428.

in eternal joy. But for the wicked, the bridge will narrow itself to a razor's edge, and they will fall off the bridge and will forever reside in hell, where there will be eternal torment and suffering. There is also some kind of intermediate state for those whose good and bad deeds are held in strict balance.

Zoroastrian religion also knows of a judgment and completion of the whole world: "At the last bend of creation [. . .] where Thou comest with Thy bounteous will mindful in dominion" (Yasna 43:5.6). Then the "sphere of lies" will collapse, and the final judgment will take place. The Mindful Lord judges the people wisely and accurately so that no one can deceive him. This judgment also results in a transformation of the world. The Saoshyans, or savior, will come and bring the present world to its end. The dead will be resurrected, and both the wicked and the good will have to pass through a flood of "molten metal" (Yasna 51:9). The righteous will pass without harm and enter the new world. The wicked will either be purified or burned, and the evil spirits will be burned. After this worldwide purification in the last days of the present crisis, Ahura Mazda's sovereignty will be complete, and together with him, the good will enjoy a new heaven and a new earth. Not all ideas that we know from the Iranian religion go back to Zoroaster. Some are later developments of the Avesta, the sacred book of Zoroastrianism or Parsism, but most have their roots in his teachings. Zoroaster's teaching about individual judgment, heaven and hell, the resurrection of the body, the Last Judgment, and life everlasting for the reunited soul and body, among other things, may have had a catalytic influence on Judeo-Christian eschatology and later even on Islam. They helped further their understanding of eschatology.

Similar to the ideas of Plato, we encounter in Zoroastrianism a creator who made everything and who is the cause of the good. Then an inexplicable dualism arises, a dualism between good and evil to which humanity is subjected. After a final judgment, there is a twofold outcome of history. While the omnipotence of one God is maintained, this God does not rescue everything and everyone from the fangs of evil. This is true for most other religions in which there is either punishment or reward for the believer depending on his or her life performance.

Manichaeism

Another important dualistic outlook is presented by Manichaeism. It is a dualistic system interspersed with Christian, Gnostic, Zoroastrian, and other elements. It was founded in Persia in the third century CE and is based on a primeval conflict between light and darkness. Its founder was the prophet Mani (216–77), who lived in Mesopotamia, present-day Iraq, and it was widespread in the Roman Empire and in Asia, surviving in eastern Turkestan until the thirteenth century. Mani's father had a vision that led him to join a group of baptizers at the lower Euphrates River. Mani too had revelations that convinced him to be the successor of Jesus and the representative of God as well as of humans at Judgment Day. In his missionary endeavors, he sought close contact with baptizer communities and journeyed as far as India. He became friends of the Iranian king Shapur I the Great († 270), who favored Zoroastrianism but tolerated Manichaeism and Christianity, and of his son Hormizd I. But under Hormizd I's brother, Bahram I, who succeeded Hormizd (who had reigned only a year), the fortunes turned. Zoroastrians considered Manichaeism a heresy, and Mani was sentenced to death. Manichaeism was relatively well established by that time and was supported by numerous priests under a hierarchy of religious leaders that included twelve apostles and seventy-two bishops. Yet the Zoroastrian clergy had nearly all of them put to death or at least punished. This persecution, however, could not exterminate Manichaeism. Even Augustine in faraway Italy had been a follower of Manichaeism for nine years until he converted to Christianity in 387. It was the main rival of Christianity in replacing traditional paganism. But what did Mani actually teach?

The starting point for Mani was the existence of humanity in the world, an existence characterized by a dualism of good and evil, which we know from Zoroastrianism as the opposition of light and darkness.[9] This dualism is also present in Judaism and Christianity and especially pronounced in gnosticism and in the Qumran community. From the beginning of the world, there are, according to Mani, two kingdoms: the realm of light and the realm of darkness. The first realm, or world, is ruled by the Father of Greatness together with his five Shekhinas (divine attributes of light): knowledge (*nus*), thought (*ennoia*), insight (*phronesis*), sensibility (*etymisis*), and consideration (*logismos*). In the second realm, or world, there is a continuous battle, and it is ruled by the King of Darkness. Its worlds are that of smoke, fire, wind, water, and darkness. At a certain point, the Kingdom of Darkness notices the World of Light and becomes greedy for it and attacks it. The Father of Greatness makes the Great Spirit emanate from himself as the Mother of Life, who sends her son, the First Man, to battle with the attacking powers of Darkness, which include the Demon of Greed. The First Man is armed with five different shields—air, wind, light, water, and fire (reflections of the five Shekhinas)—which he loses to the forces of Darkness in the ensuing battle, described as a kind of "bait" to trick the forces of Darkness, as the forces of Darkness greedily consume as much light as they can. But the First Man regains consciousness, and he prays to the realm of light.

Then the Father of Greatness calls to the Living Spirit, who in turn calls to his five sons and sends a call to the First Man. This call then becomes a Manichean deity (Call). An answer that again becomes a Manichean deity (Answer) returns from the First Man to the World of Light. Call and Answer unite themselves with the Mother of Life and the Living Spirit and pull up the First Man, but the shields of light remain down in darkness. The next task is then their rescue. The mixture of light and darkness must be brought into a state that makes possible the final

---

9. For the following, cf. Alexander Böhlig, "Manichäismus," in TRE, 22:31–34.

separation of the elements of light from darkness. Yet the evil beings continue to swallow up as much of the light as they can to keep the light inside of them. This results eventually in the evil beings swallowing huge quantities of light and giving birth to Adam and Eve. The Father of Greatness then sends the Radiant Jesus to awaken Adam and to enlighten him to the true source of the light that is trapped in his material body. Adam and Eve give birth to more human beings, trapping the light in human bodies throughout the history of humanity. Through procreation, the separation of light from darkness is delayed. The appearance of the prophet Mani is another attempt by the World of Light to reveal to humans the true source of the spiritual light imprisoned within their material bodies and to free them from their material entanglement.

Mani created a church to inform humanity about the destiny of the living soul and the elements of light and to tell the people that the world will be redeemed if they follow Manichaeism. A human being "should be pure and innocent in mouth, in hands, and in breast. [. . .] By the mouth we are to understand all the organs of sense in the head; by the hands, all the bodily actions; by the breast, all the lustful tendencies."[10] Sinful are bad words but also impure food, all actions that cultivate the earth and what grows on it, especially agriculture and menial activity and every sexual activity, including procreation. Humans are tied to sin by their bodily and psychic existence. Since Mani distinguished between the elect who renounced their own work and marriage and the auditors, meaning the catechumens, his church could survive. The elect lived according to Mani's precepts, while the auditors could live a worldly life and had to provide for the elect. Upon death, all people face judgment. The sinners are punished by death, and the elect and especially qualified auditors are sent on the way to life or are put on the path of mixture of light and darkness for those who are not yet perfect. At the end of the world, there is a final judgment. Through a transmigration of the souls, the auditors are transformed to the status of the elect. Whoever is perfect is clothed with the garment of light and enters the new aeon, having first passed the Milky Way and the moon and from there arrives at the sun.

Mani calls himself "an Apostle of Jesus Christ, by the providence of God the Father."[11] But the strict dualism existing from the very beginning between light and darkness shows his affinity to Zoroastrianism. The heavenly world to which the spiritual essence of humans is rescued reminds us of Gnostic ideas or even of Plato. We encounter in Mani's religion an amazing syncretistic amalgamation of ideas that neither explain the existence of evil nor show its final elimination, only the eventual escape from it.

---

10. Augustine, On the Morals of the Manichaeans (10:19), in NPNF FS, 4:74.
11. Augustine, Against the Epistle of Manichaeus Called Fundamental (5:6), in NPNS FS, 4:131.

The Fatalistic Approach

If the godhead or the circumstances are so overpowering that the human destiny is ordained or preordained by powers higher than humanity, the origin of evil seems to lie in these powers. Human life is characterized either by submission or by passivity, since other forces rule supreme. It is wise for humanity not to challenge them. Otherwise, its destiny might be affected even more by negativity from which humanity cannot escape. This fatalistic approach seems to be advocated especially by religions that originated in the East, such as Islam, Hinduism, and even Buddhism.

Islam

From the Arabic root *slm*, meaning "to be in peace, to be an integral whole," comes the term *islam*, meaning "to surrender to God's law and thus to be an integral whole," and *muslim*, "a person who so surrenders."[12] These definitions show us in a nutshell the religious conviction of Islam: if one wants to maintain order and wholeness, one must accept God's law. While nature obeys God's law automatically, humanity ought to obey it by choice. It is therefore no surprise that in the Qur'an (meaning "recital"), the holy book of the Muslims, we encounter God's omnipotence from which no one can escape and at the same time the call to turn toward him, an action that presupposes free will: "To Him belongs everyone in the heavens and the earth. All are submissive to Him. [. . .] But who can guide whom God leaves astray? They will have no helpers. [. . .] Turning towards Him—and be conscious of Him, and perform the prayer, and do not be of the idolaters" (Surah 30.26.29.31).[13] God created humans with a free will so that they are not predestined to a certain destiny but able to perform good or evil actions.

The God portrayed in the Qur'an is a transcendent, all-powerful God who is also merciful. No creature can share in God's divinity. Similarly to Genesis 1, we hear in the Qur'an concerning God's creative power, "His command, when He wills a thing, is to say to it, 'Be,' and it comes to be" (Surah 36.82). Since whatever God creates has an orderly nature, humanity must follow that order or face the consequences at Judgment Day. The Qur'an states that "on that Day, the people will emerge in droves, to be shown their works. Whoever has done an atom's weight of good will see it. And whoever has done an atom's weight of evil will see it" (Surah 99.6–8). The last judgment will focus upon individual performance. There is also a judgment in history that comes upon nations and communities on the basis of their total performance because "the earth will be inherited by My righteous servants" (Surah 21.105).

---

12. Fazlur Rahman, "Islam: An Overview," in *The Encyclopedia of Religion*, ed. Mircea Eliade (New York: Macmillan, 1987), 7:303.
13. Cited according to "Quran in English: Clear and Easy to Read," trans. Talal Itani, accessed January 22, 2018, http://www.clearquran.com/030.html.

Ideally, the whole life of the Muslim is determined by the Shari'a (the way), the body of regulations that make up Islamic religious law. It contains all the prescriptions of Allah that pertain to human actions, and it stands so high in rank that it has been said that "Allah did not reveal himself but he mediated only his law."[14] "Islam makes no distinction between religion and life, nothing being excluded from religion, or outside it and 'secular'. Islamic law covers not only ritual but every aspect of life."[15] Therefore, theology dominates not Islamic scholarship but rather the study and explication of the law. Since all aspects of life fall under the religious sphere, the Shari'a contains prescriptions concerning religious and cultic duties as well as juridical and political rules. Islam therefore does not actually allow for a separation of religion and politics or of the religious and the secular. This implies a potential conflict between the law of a country and the Shari'a, since a devout Muslim owes prime allegiance to the Shari'a. All actions cited in the Shari'a are divided into five categories:[16] obligatory, not obligatory but recommended, neutral or permitted, not forbidden but reprehensible, and forbidden. For instance, it is obligatory to wash oneself before prayer, it is recommended to start with the right side, it is permitted that warm or cold water be used, and it is forbidden that someone touches the water beforehand. Furthermore, the actions are evaluated according to their validity or invalidity. Of course, most of these laws of the Shari'a are already contained in the Qur'an.

There are two main types of texts in the Qur'an: those that are clear and definite and those that could have more than one meaning. The texts that are clear and definite cover basic beliefs, such as belief in Allah and the last day. They also contain information concerning the origin of the law. When it comes to these texts, there is no freedom of interpretation. As to the texts that could have more than one meaning, they "are concerned with subsidiary aspects of Islam, but not its fundamentals, and have given rise to a plurality of Muslim theories and attitudes which are more or less personal points of view and are far from being obligatory."[17] Here clear reasoning is required. Since reasoning can go in different ways, there arose a diversity of religious and civil practice among Muslim believers.[18] Yet the Qur'an remains the inviolable foundation of faith and the code of legislation. Since there are items contained in the Qur'an that can have more than one meaning, we also have to consider the sunna, or custom that declares "the legislation given by the Prophet on matters not specifically detailed in the Qur'an, and traditions based

14. Annemarie Schimmel, "Der Islam," in *Die Religionen der Menschheit in Vergangenheit und Gegenwart*, ed. Friedrich Heiler (Stuttgart, Germany: Reclam, 1959), 819.
15. *The Concise Encyclopedia of Islam*, by Cyril Glassé with an introduction by Huston Smith (San Francisco: HarperSanFrancisco, 1991), s.v. "Shariah," 362.
16. Cf. to the following *Concise Encyclopedia of Islam*, s.v. "Shariah," 361.
17. Cf. to the following Mahmud Shaltout, "Islamic Beliefs and Code of Laws," in *Islam—the Straight Path: Islam Interpreted by Muslims*, ed. Kenneth W. Morgan (New York: Ronald, 1958), 88.
18. Cf. Mohammad Hashim Kamali, "Law and Society: The Interplay of Revelation and Reason in the Shariah," in *The Oxford History of Islam*, ed. John L. Esposito (Oxford: Oxford University Press, 1999), 110, for more information.

on the actions and utterances of Muhammad as a human being."[19] The value of the sunna lies in the fact that it expounds specific aspects of the general principles of the Qur'an, either by example of action or by adding certain ceremonies not expressly described in the Qur'an. For instance, the Qur'an enjoins prayer, but the sunna tells how prayer is to be performed.

Then there is the hadith, the "account" or "report" that relates the deeds and utterances of the prophet as reported by his companions. But not everything contained in the hadith actually goes back to Mohammed; often its various strands were simply developed in order to support the traditions of various groups within Islam. It serves as a basis of law within Islamic jurisprudence. Through critical studies of the hadith, one is able to establish and maintain the historical continuity between the prophet's lifetime and the present by concluding what Mohammed "might have said had he been asked."[20] Finally, there is discretion employed in the communal consultations concerning issues not specifically covered in the Qur'an and the sunna, and there is the private discretion of the individual to decide through independent thinking. Both kinds of discretion are "not binding for anyone" except for the individual(s) who use(s) them.[21]

Though the numerous legal codes contained in the Shari'a are based on the idea that Allah speaks and commands while the believer submits and obeys, obedience is not merely passive or servile. Muslim theologians assert that "Muslims conceive of their religion as a community which says 'Yes' to God and His world, and the joyful performance of the Law, in most areas of the Islamic world, is looked on as a positive religious value."[22] When we consider the creed, the first of the five pillars of Islam (the others being daily prayers, fasting, giving of alms, and the pilgrimage to Mecca), which is always contained in the first section of the law, we find the confession not only of Allah, of the last day, and of the resurrection but also of Allah's predetermining will. This is a clear indication of how the tension between free will and determinism contained in the Qur'an itself has traditionally been resolved.[23] As Abu Hanifa (d. 767) says in his last will, "We confess that the predetermining of good and evil is all from Allah."[24] So we read in Surah 87.2–3 of Allah, "He who creates and regulates. He who measures and guides." We could interpret that this divine guidance does not preclude exerting our own will. But there are

19. Shaltout, "Islamic Beliefs," 134.
20. So John Alden Williams, *Islam* (New York: George Braziller, 1961), 88.
21. Shaltout, "Islamic Beliefs," 140.
22. Williams, *Islam*, 93.
23. For the discussion on free will and determinism, cf. *Concise Encyclopedia of Islam*, s.v. "Maktub (lit. 'written,' 'ordained')," 249.
24. Arthur Jeffrey, ed., *A Reader on Islam: Passages from Standard Arabic Writings Illustrative of the Beliefs and Practices of Muslims* (Gravenhage, Netherlands: Mouton, 1962), 343. Some Muslims, however, object to a deterministic view of God. Syed Ameer Ali, *The Spirit of Islam: A History of the Evolution and Ideals of Islam with a Life of the Prophet* (London: Chatto & Windus, 1964), 403, for instance, asserts that in contradiction to the stern fatalism of the pre-Islamite Arabs, the teachings of Islam advocate the idea of human volitional liberty. Yet in the light of the Qur'an itself, this assertion is difficult to maintain.

other statements in the Qur'an that leave no doubt that God guides our lives in a way that determines it final outcome. We read in Surah 6.125, "Whomever God desires to guide, He spreads open his heart to Islam; and whomever He desires to misguide, He makes his heart narrow, constricted, as though he were climbing up the sky. God thus lays defilement upon those who do not believe." Allah determines whether someone becomes a believer or an unbeliever. Nevertheless, if one does not believe, one gets punished. A similar contradiction is asserted when we read in Surah 4.78–79, "When a good fortune comes their way, they say, 'This is from God.' But when a misfortune befalls them, they say, 'This is from you.' Say, 'All is from God.' [. . .] 'Whatever good happens to you is from God, and whatever bad happens to you is from your own self.'" How can one reconcile the statement, "All is from God," with, "Whatever bad happens to you is from your own self"?

Already in Islam's early theological debates there were those who upheld the notion of the free will against the advocates of predestination. The school of Qadariyyah, for instance, claimed that humans are absolutely free; they are the own creators of their acts and completely responsible for them. The school of Jabariyyah, however, taught that human actions are completely predetermined. Ash`arite theology, dating back to Al-Ash`arī (d. 944) is a viable attempt to combine revelation with reason with a minimum requirement of causality. The Ash`arites deal with the problem of free will and causality by their theory of atoms. To explain how the creature, lacking the positive and absolute qualities of God, could exercise will and action, the Ash`arites said that the action itself was created by God and then "acquired" by the creature. Yet this position is not entirely satisfactory either. "God knows what will happen from eternity; yet we must still be free in order to be responsible for our acts, whose consequences may result in damnation or salvation. Do we then possess free will?"[25] We are absolutely free in our acceptance or rejection of God, which takes place in our consciousness. But in respect to our actions toward the world, we are restrained by the chain of cause and effect. If our actions then ultimately count, we can only resign ourselves to the will of God and follow his path.

One way of breaking out of this almost overbearing dominance of Allah over human life was found in Sufism. Having its roots in the more mystic strands of the Qur'an, this ecstatic movement gained supreme importance from the end of the ninth century onward by molding the attitude toward life in individual Muslims, especially those in rural areas. To some extent, it symbolizes the victory of the common person "over the earthly mighty and the learned professors and scholars," representatives of the all-embracing law.[26] A Sufi is a person whose heart is empty

---

25. *Concise Encyclopedia of Islam*, s.v. "Kalām," 218.
26. Ghorbal, "Ideas and Movements," in *Islam – The Straight Path. Islam Interpreted by Muslims*, Kenneth W. Morgan, ed. (New York: Roland Press, 1958) 66; cf. also Reynold Alleyne Nicholson, *Studies in Islamic Mysticism* (Cambridge: Cambridge University Press, 1967), 78, who rightly claims that the *wali*, or "saint," bridges the chasm that the Qur'an and scholasticism have set between humanity "and an absolutely transcendent God."

of attachment to anything other than Allah. Through submission to Allah comes faith and awareness of Allah.[27] Under Sufism, common people managed to live in a world of ideas and emotions of their own construction. The movement received considerable criticism from orthodox Muslims because of its "need to submit to the authority of charismatic men who claimed a special relationship to Allah through ecstasy."[28]

We have noticed that through the dominance of Allah, evil and its powers do not actually count, and therefore, the following question is not really addressed: How can the tension between the existence of evil and Allah being merciful be resolved? We are only told that those who do evil things and do not follow Allah's precepts will face dire consequences.

Hinduism

Hinduism is an amalgamation of Indian religions with numerous deities and powers that are perceived to influence human destiny and the world. Though moral evil, which humans do, and natural evil, which befalls humans, are logically distinguished in Hinduism, they are seen as aspects of a single phenomenon for which an explanation must be sought.

The oldest layer of Sanskrit literature and the oldest scriptures of Hinduism are the Vedas. For orthodox Hindu theologians, they are considered revelations encountered by ancient sages. The Vedic period, during which these texts were composed, dates from around 1500 to 500 BCE. In the Vedic religion, there is a unitary view of the universe, with "God" perceived as immanent and transcendent in the forms of Ishvara, the supreme soul or king, and Brahman, the highest universal principle. Conformity with the principle of integration rooted in the absolute enables progress, whereas its violation would lead to punishment. The concept of *pāpa* denotes evil-mindedness, while *karoti* means "evil action." Thus we read the prayer, "Wise Deities, who have dominion o'er the world, ye thinkers over all that moves not and that moves, Save us from uncommitted and committed sin, preserve us from all sin to-day for happiness" (*Rig Veda* 10:63.8).[29] Whether committed or uncommitted, both are sin. Yet pāpa is not our mistake but a mistake of nature so that "evil is not primarily what we do; it is what we do not wish to have done to us."[30] In the *Arthava Veda*, we notice a distinction between moral and natural evil and at the same time their inextricability when we read, "Sleep, specially, Sloth, Nirriti [goddess of destruction, calamity, corruption and death], and deities whose name is Sin, Baldness, old age, and hoary hairs within the body found their way. Theft,

27. Cf. the helpful introduction by Sheik Ragip Robert Frager al Jerrahi in *Essential Sufism*, ed. James Fadiman and Robert Frager (San Francisco: HarperSanFrancisco, 1997), esp. 3–10.
28. Ron Greaves, *Aspects of Islam* (Washington, DC: Georgetown University Press, 2005), 133.
29. "Rig Veda—the First Book," HolyBooks, accessed April 25, 2019, https://tinyurl.com/y25m98dl.
30. Wendy Doniger O'Flaherty, *The Origins of Evil in Hindu Mythology* (Berkeley: University of California Press, 1976), 7.

evil-doing, and deceit, truth, sacrifice, exalted fame, Strength, princely power, and energy entered the body as a home" (*Arthava Veda* 11:8.19–20).[31] Moreover we see here that the gods are not just good. They can be evil. Evil committed by us is the result of *moha*, meaning "delusion" or "confusion," or of *māyā*, meaning "illusion." Again, it is god who brings forth moha and māyā.

In the hymns addressed to Varuṇa, the god of cosmic and moral order, evil is a matter of humans not fulfilling his laws or not performing the ritual properly. Often, it has moral significance in that people are evil-minded or commit adultery. So we read, "Those who regard not Varuṇa's commandments and the dear steadfast laws of sapient Mitra. Like youthful women without brothers, straying, like dames who hate their lords, of evil conduct, They who are full of sin, untrue, unfaithful, they have engendered this abysmal station" (*Rig Veda* 4:5). Those who commit evil deeds must repent before Varuṇa. The sinner then cries to Varuṇa: "If we have sinned against the man who loves us, have ever wronged a brother, friend, or comrade, The neighbor ever with us, or a stranger, O Varuṇa, remove from us the trespass. If we, as gamesters cheat at play, have cheated, done wrong unwittingly or sinned of purpose, cast all these sins away like loosened fetters, and, Varuṇa let us be thine own beloved" (*Rig Veda* 5:85). As O'Flaherty, however, contends, these are exceptional examples of a true sense of sin and repentance in Hinduism. "These are outweighed a thousandfold by instances of sin regarded as the fault of nature."[32] In other hymns, as those addressed to Indra, the king of the gods, evil is personified by demons. Thus the fight against evil is a perpetual combat between personalized good and evil forces.

While the Vedic religion seems to ignore the tragic aspects of life, the period of the Upanishads (500 BCE–ca. 500 CE) provides insight into the essentially evil nature of existence. The Upanishads, also known as the Vedānta, are a collection of more than two hundred religious and philosophical texts, presumably written between 800 and 500 BCE at a time when people in India began to question the traditional Vedic order. The concepts of Brahman (ultimate reality) and Ātman (soul, self) are central ideas in all the Upanishads. While Brahman is the final cause of all that exists, Ātman is the soul, the immortal spirit in an individual and in all living beings, including animals and trees. Ātman as the inner self is in some way identical with Brahman, the universal soul. It strives for liberation through unification with Brahman. This means that these texts provide a pantheistic perspective on ultimate reality and introduce karma as the explanation of evil in the world.

The Sanskrit term *karma* means "action," "work," or "deed" and refers to the sacrificial action in the Vedic religion. Gradually it took on the meaning of both action and the effect of action and referred to the spiritual principle of cause and effect by which intent and actions of an individual (cause) influence the future of

---

31. Ralph T. H. Griffith, trans., *Hymns of the Atharva Veda* (1895), accessed April 25, 2019, https://tinyurl.com/y2vszuap.
32. O'Flaherty, *Origins*, 7.

that individual (effect). Presupposed here is the so-called belief in the transmigration of souls. This is made possible by *saṃsāra*, the continuous cycle of becoming and perishing. One's present experience and situation is the direct result of bad or of good karma that accumulated in past lives and affixed to the transmigrating soul. Ignorance launches karma into action, and karma brings suffering. Therefore, suffering in the present life is the natural consequence of past lives' ignorance, and it has to be endured without questioning. Bad karma can be whittled away by good deeds performed in the present life, but it can never be entirely destroyed. "It is the outward visible sign of past invisible deeds. The evil that we experience is thus justified by evils of the past and will be balanced by rewards in future births; it is not God's fault, nor man's fault, nor a devil's fault; it is part of the eternal cycle, and ultimately all is justified and balanced."[33] Yet such thinking violates the notion of theodicy. If God is under the sway of karma, he is not omnipotent, and if God controls karma, then he is to blame for evil. Moreover, this idea of karma generates anxiety over one's future, and it leaves the person with a feeling of helplessness. Even the gods are not always exempt from the power of karma, which is often "cited in justification of their immoralities."[34] "The gods bear not justification for the fate of humanity and need not morally justify themselves."[35]

The gods in Hinduism are, on the one hand, sovereign to the dictates of karma, and on the other—just like humans—they are subject to it. We notice this especially in the epics and in the Puranas. The Puranas, literally "ancient" writings, function as one part of scripture for the Hindu tradition. These texts were written over a long period of time, from about the fourth century BCE to the eleventh century CE. The Puranas offer answers to the big questions of life by detailing how the world was created and who created it. For instance, in the Vishnu Purana, we read that "Viṣṇu as Brahmā created the world. [. . .] This deity created the gods, sages, progenitors, demons, men, animals, trees, and the rest, that abide on earth, in heaven, or in the waters."[36] This means both good and evil beings are created by Brahmā. In the third creation, he also created humans. "They abound with the light of knowledge, but the qualities of darkness and of foulness predominate. Hence they are afflicted by evil, and are repeatedly impelled to action. They have knowledge both externally and internally, and are the instruments (of accomplishing the object of creation, the liberation of soul). These creatures were mankind."[37] While there are good qualities in humans, their evil qualities predominate. The lord Brahmā created fierce humans who are full of passion and in whom unhappiness preponderates. This implies that negativity, which humans exercise, goes back to the creator god Brahmā. But as we have seen, the creator god is also the originator

33. So O'Flaherty, *Origins*, 14.
34. Cf. O'Flaherty, *Origins*, 17.
35. Peter Gerlitz, "Theodizee I, Religionsgeschichtlich," in TRE, 33:212.
36. Vishnu Purana in Horace Hayman Wilson, *The Vishnun Purana* (Delhi: Parimal, 1840), book 1, chap. 5, accessed April 24, 2019, https://tinyurl.com/y4hkr4ua.
37. Wilson, *Vishnun Purana*.

of both good and evil beyond the human sphere. It states in the *Markandeya Purana*, "O brāhman, after having paid adoration to the Forefather Brahmā, the lord of the universe, the origin of the universe, who presided over creation, who in the form of Viṣṇu *presides* over its maintenance, and who in the form of the terrible Śiva destroys it at the dissolution."[38] The gods seem to be interchangeable not only in their goodness and badness but also in the way that they can appear as one specific god or another. We read for instance in the *Linga Purana*, "The great lord is the sole agent for this creation, sustenance and dissolution. [. . .] He is the first creator of all beings, their protector and annihilator. So lord Maheśvara [i.e., the Supreme Spirit] is the overlord of Brahmā. He is also known as Śiva, Sadāśiva, Bhava, Viṣṇu and Brahmā since he is all."[39]

Humans cannot excuse themselves that they were created with a propensity for evil deeds. There is another factor that decidedly shapes human behavior—namely, karma. We read in the Vishnu Purana, "Created beings, although they are destroyed (in their individual forms) at the periods of dissolution, yet, being affected by the good or evil acts of former existence, they are never exempted from their consequences. [. . .] This did the divine Brahmā, the first creator and lord of all: and these things being created, discharged the same functions as they had fulfilled in a previous creation, whether malignant or benign, gentle or cruel, good or evil, true or false; and accordingly as they are actuated by such propensities will be their conduct."[40] This shows that though the creator god created each creature, karma supervenes and determines if one turns out to be good or bad. Karma solves the problem of the origin of evil by showing that there is no origin. There is an eternal cycle that limits the ultimate responsibility of both gods and humans. Therefore, karma is often used as an excuse for a temporary weakness of both humans and gods. Though the claim of "karma made me do it" might be used to explain evil, it does not diminish the obligation to strive for the good. This seemingly paradox situation with regard to evil in Hindu mythology is caused by the fact that the gods cannot be at the same time sovereign and in tune with karma. If the gods are responsible for the existence of evil in the world, they either create evil willingly and therefore are evil themselves or are forced to create it by the law of karma and then are weak. An actual theodicy, which addresses the question of why God allows for evil, is avoided rather than provided.

Buddhism

In Buddhism too the main question is not, Where does evil come from? but rather, How can I escape from *saṃsāra*, the eternal cycle of birth and rebirth? Since this

---

38. Frederick Eden Pargiter, *The Markandeya Purana* (Delhi: Parimal, 1904), book 45, accessed April 24, 2019, https://tinyurl.com/yxg3y4f9.
39. *The Linga Purana*, part I (3:35.37), trans. J. L. Shastri (Delhi: Motilal Banarsidass, 1951), 11.
40. Vishnu Purana in Wilson, *Vishnun Purana*.

eternal cycle determines my destiny in this life and beyond, it is also the cause of suffering here on earth. Once one has discovered the basic facts of life, one is able to overcome an existence characterized by suffering. Since the overpowering might of gods is denied, there is neither beginning nor end of birth, and rebirth and everything is carried over from one form of existence to another.

Buddhism was founded by the Indian prince Siddharta Gautama, who belonged to the tribe of the Sakyas and lived approximately between 560 and 480 BCE in the northeast of India, an area that is today known as Nepal. According to tradition, he left his home at the age of twenty-nine against the will of his parents, cut his hair and beard, and became a monk to search for *nirvāṇa*, the eternal, blissful peace. His sudden decision was caused by the discovery that all life was suffering and that it had to be extinguished by the extinction of existence itself. Mara, the personification of evil, accompanied him on his journey and promised him an empire if he would desist from his plans. But Gautama did not give in. For years he wandered from place to place in search of a teacher who could guide him to attain supreme enlightenment. Since none could satisfy him, he finally decided to struggle alone. Together with other monks, he practiced Yoga and asceticism, and after years of meditation, he came to the conclusion at the age of thirty-five that the right way to achieve nirvāṇa lies midway between the extremes of worldly activity and strict asceticism. The rest of his life he spent preaching his newly discovered doctrine, with often more than five hundred disciples following him.

The center of Prince Gautama's, or Buddha's (i.e., the enlightened one), teachings is the Four Noble Truths, which he exemplified by his own life.[41] The first noble truth is to understand that all life is usually characterized by suffering (*dukkha*), beginning with birth and extending to sickness, senescence, and death. There is no innocent suffering, since even the suffering of a small child is due to its former existence. Who attains the insight that all life is suffering is already an arhat, a perfect saint. The second noble truth is to understand the cause of suffering. The main cause of suffering is in the craving for life. There are three main poisons that further this craving: greed, hatred, and delusion. We must abolish this cause by eliminating the fundamental evils of sensual desire: desire to be, wrong beliefs, and ignorance. The third noble truth lies in the insight of how to attain cessation of suffering. Since one wants to escape the cycle of birth and rebirth, one must diminish karma, in both its good and bad forms, so that saṃsāra is without "nourishment" or content. Saṃsāra—this suffering-laden cycle of life, death, and rebirth, without beginning or end—then ceases suffering, and one has reached nirvāṇa. Finally, the fourth truth is the Eightfold Path, which leads to the cessation of suffering and thereby achieving nirvāṇa. It consists of instructions of how to arrive at the goal outlined in the first three truths. The Eightfold Path consists of

---

41. Cf. Jagadish Kashyap, "Origin and Expansion of Buddhism," in *The Path of the Buddha: Buddhism Interpreted by Buddhists*, ed. Kenneth W. Morgan (New York: Roland, 1956), 27–28.

eight practices: right view, right resolve, right speech, right conduct, right liveli-hood, right effort, right mindfulness, and right *samadhi* (meditative absorption or union). It contains methods of concentration and meditation to subdue the self and to curb the craving for life. Yoga exercises, control of breathing, fast-ing, and mystic concentration are included here. Important are also ethical virtues and a compassion for all forms of life. If one follows these precepts, suffering and incompleteness can be overcome, and through enlightenment, nirvāṇa—that is, highest happiness and liberation from saṃsāra—can be achieved.

At first glance, Buddhism appears pessimistic and world negating. For Buddhists, it is already futile to spend thoughts on the idea of a personal creator of the universe because the purpose of Buddhist doctrine is to release beings from suffering and not to speculate on the origin of the world. Yet Buddhist thought does not result in radical pessimism. While reflecting a complete disillusionment with the world as it is, it shows an extreme sensitivity to pain, suffering, and any kind of turmoil and a total dedication to the alleviation of these evil causes.[42] Buddhists also insist that the object of Buddhist life is not negation but search for freedom from ignorance and reincarnation, since partial knowledge leads to wrong deeds or to evil karma. We wonder, however, whether a Buddhist such as Beatrice Lane Suzuki (1870–1939) was right when asserted that "Buddhist life is an open war on bondage, slavery, and attachment of all kinds."[43] At least the politics of alleged Buddhist countries, such as Myanmar and Thailand, do not bear out this assertion.

But there are progressive Buddhist sects, such as the Japanese sect Soka Gakkai, founded in 1930 by a Tokyo schoolteacher as the Value-Creating Educational Society and rapidly expanding throughout Japan. Makiguchi, the founder, based the society's program on a combination of the teachings of the Buddhist sect Nichiren Shoshu and his own theory of value.[44] Makiguchi proposed a student-centered education with the purpose of ensuring the happiness of the learner. He held that there are three ultimate virtues: beauty, gain, and goodness. The purpose of life is then found in the pursuit of happiness through the attainment of the three supreme virtues. In Nichiren's teachings, Makiguchi found support for his theory of value creation and a worldview consistent with his aims of edu-cational reform and social betterment centered on addressing the subjective

---

42. Cf. H. Saddhatissa, *Buddhist Ethics: Essence of Buddhism* (London: George Allen & Unwin, 1970), especially his chapter on "Sanctions of Moral Conduct: The Precepts," 87–112. One cannot but notice the similarity between the Judeo-Christian tradition and Buddhist ethics as far as basic precepts are concerned.

43. So Beatrice Lane Suzuki, *Mahayana Buddhism: A Brief Outline*, foreword by Ch. Humphreys (New York: Macmillan, 1969), 75. Such aggressive attitude, however, seems to be incoherent with the principles laid out in the Four Noble Truths.

44. Nichiren Shoshu is one of the many sects based on a reinterpretation of Buddhism by the thirteenth-century Japanese religious leader Nichiren. *Shoshu* means "true religion," or as the followers of Soka Gakkai prefer to say, "true Buddhism." Adherents of Nichiren Shoshu hold Nichiren to be the true Buddha, replacing Siddharta Gautama. For a good introduction to Gakkai, especially in its social dimension, cf. James Allen Dator, *Soka Gakkai, Builders of the Third Civilization: American and Japanese Members* (Seattle: University of Washington Press, 1969).

realities of the individual. Therefore, the goal of his followers is to promote this type of Buddhism as the only true kind. The year 1937 was the first general meeting of the Value-Creating Educational Society. The membership eventually came to change from teachers interested in educational reform to people from all walks of life drawn by the belief in Nichiren Buddhism. While it was disbanded by the government during World War II, it expanded after the war from a prewar estimate of three thousand members to a claimed total of 750,000 households in 1958. Through explosive recruitment, it has now according to its own account more than twelve million members in 192 countries and territories worldwide. This has been accompanied by a similar increase in cultural and political activities. For instance, Komeito, a center-right political party closely aligned with Gakkai, joined the ruling government coalition in 1999. However, within Buddhism, such a world-affirming movement is still an exception, and it does not change the overall picture—namely, that for Buddhism, humans are strangers on earth.[45] Their task is to regain the state of perfection that was theirs before they fell into this world. Thus self-denial can be adapted to highly political and capitalistic endeavors, such as the rebirth of Japan after World War II.

Yet what does this mean for the origin of evil and for theodicy? Since there are no gods or a God in Buddhism, transcendent actors have nothing to do with the cause of evil. Though Buddha was convinced that eventually one can escape the fangs of evil by eliminating suffering, true freedom is only to be found in nirvāṇa. Since the cause of evil comes with saṃsāra, the ever-turning wheel of life, even if a person succeeds in escaping to nirvāṇa, the world goes on a usual. A world without a God who rules supreme and who is not a ruthless and heartless trickster does not give an answer to the cause of evil. Evil has always been there and always will be. Only individuals can escape from evil and suffering. But the world as a whole will continue with its injustice and pain.

At least we have here an eschatological vindication of some people who follow the precepts of Buddha. They will be rescued from evil and suffering. This end-time solution of theodicy that the trials of this world will come to an end at least for some people is assured in many religions whether there is a godhead or there is none. Persons who behave well will be rewarded, and those who do not will be

---

45. In our attempt to understand the progressive spirit of Gakkai, we should not forget the special character of Japanese Buddhism as an imported religion. It was amalgamated with native beliefs, and initially, it was primarily used for practical (ethical) ends (cf. E. Dale Saunders, *Buddhism in Japan: With an Outline of Its Origins in India* [Philadelphia: University of Pennsylvania Press, 1964], 261–263). The rise of a number of new syncretistic sects or religions based on ideas drawn indiscriminately from Christianity, Shinto, and Buddhism also indicates a certain dissatisfaction of society with religion as it attempts to adjust itself to the problems of modern (Western) civilization. We might not be wrong to consider Gakkai, with its largely pragmatic and Kantian persuasions (So Dator, *Soka Gakkai*, 9), as an attempt to cope with a foreign civilization while still striving to preserve some of its own cultural and religious heritage. We are surprised to hear Dator (*Soka Gakkai*, 140–141) say that in contrast to the "Americans," the Japanese do not seem to be a "religious people." Should this mean that the renunciation of its religious heritage was the price that Japan had to pay to become the most "Western" of all far eastern countries?

punished. Yet we are left in the dark about whether evil will be totally eliminated or whether at the end, individually conceived, some will just beyond the reach of evil. Furthermore, the vexing question of why a deity or some other higher power has allowed evil to raise its head remains unanswered. This is somewhat different from the pedagogical version, where evil even in the form of innocent suffering is used to teach human compassion for suffering creatures and to increase the appreciation of the good. Still the question of why there is evil is not answered. Is it necessary for us so that we pursue the path of goodness, or are we simply defective beings? If this were true, we are still contemplating moral evil and not evil that we confront in nature. At this point, perhaps it would be helpful to delve into the Judeo-Christian tradition to see how it handled the issue of evil and see whether there we can obtain a satisfactory answer to the question of why there is evil.

2 Evil in the Judeo-Christian Scriptures

Already on the first pages of the Bible we encounter evil in the story of the fall of the first humans. From the fall to the construction of the Tower of Babel, sin and evil spread like a wildfire. Yet it is interesting that the story of the fall is relatively isolated in the Old Testament and only gains renewed and increasing attention in the so-called intertestamental period between the Old and the New Testaments. This might indicate that the Old Testament too showed little interest in the origin of evil. But just like other religious texts, the Old Testament is full of accounts of evil acts usually committed by humans. Yet where is God in this situation?

God and Evil in the Old Testament

When we read the Bible, we notice on the first page the story of the creation of the world and the repeated assertion, "And God saw that it was good" (Gen 1:10, 12, 18, etc.). Just two pages later, we then read of the seduction of Eve by the serpent and of the fall. How does the assertion of "it was good" fit together with the story of seduction and fall?

The Mysterious Cause of Evil

When we consider the cause of evil, we instinctively think of the story of the fall in Genesis 3. Though this story is not picked up by any of the Old Testament writers, it is not an isolated event. The Yahwistic primeval history in Genesis 3 sets into motion an entire series of sin stories: In chapter 4, we read of the fratricide of Cain and Lamech's unrestrained threats of revenge. In Genesis 6, we encounter the marital union of "the sons of God" with "the daughters of humans." These divine beings of the heavenly court "take the initiative and breach the boundary between heaven and earth by taking human wives," since they saw that they were beautiful.[1] The angelic beings are enticed by the beauty of human females and, in sinful manner, leave their place in the heavenly world. Since God's spirit came with this union into humans beyond the initial measure, God issues a decree that such a union will not result in human beings who live forever and limited the human life span to 120 years. Since human sinfulness, however, continued unabated, the flood followed (Gen 6–8). Finally, the primeval history concludes with the story of

---

1. Terence E. Fretheim, *The Book of Genesis*, in NIB, 1:383, in his exegesis of Gen 6:2.

building the Tower of Babel (Gen 11). Each account sheds light in its own unique way on the mysterious breach between God and humanity as well as God's response to this breach. Among these stories, the incident in Genesis 3 is not simply one among many but the very first sinful incident that occurs with the first woman and the first man, whose name, Adam (the Hebrew word for "man" or "humanity"), becomes a proper name in the latter part of Genesis 3. In speaking of Adam as a particular person, the Yahwist shows the archetypical character of this event. The sin committed in Genesis 3 is not just a violation of God's command not to eat from the tree of the knowledge of good and evil. Much more central is here the human mistrust of God. The original basis of life, as sketched in the Yahwistic creation narrative, is characterized by innocence, "as living in a pure childlike relationship to God. This is a life which is also reflected in the relationship of man and woman."[2] Now the harmony between God and humanity is destroyed. The Yahwist's effort to bind creation and fall closely together is not intended to show how the once good creation allegedly became so bad, for even after the fall, the world, including humanity, remains God's good creation. The Yahwist's prime intent is to demonstrate the reason for the present fate of humanity.

It has often been claimed that the disruption of the original harmony was advantageous, since it led to a realization of human possibilities. The philosopher Georg Wilhelm Friedrich Hegel (1770–1831), for example, understood sin as logically necessary for recognizing the good, for if a person "has no knowledge of evil, he has no knowledge of good either."[3] He claimed that "the phase of negation is, indeed, a necessary element in human development." The German playwright and philosopher Friedrich Schiller (1759–1805) thought similarly and wrote concerning the fall, "This instinctive fall of humanity brought, to be sure, moral evil into the creation, but only in order to make the morally good possible. Hence the fall is without a doubt the most fortunate and greatest occurrence in human history. From this moment on humanity realized its freedom; here also was laid the first remote cornerstone of human morality."[4] This idealistic conception of human sinfulness is also affirmed by many psychoanalysts. Thus Erich Fromm, 175 years after Schiller, claimed that "his first act of disobedience is man's first step toward freedom." The human is driven out of paradise and is now able "to make his own history, to develop his human powers, and to attain a new harmony with man and nature as a fully developed individual instead of the former harmony in which he was not yet an individual."[5] Carl Gustav Jung was somewhat more cautious when

2. Theodorus C. Vriezen, *An Outline of Old Testament Theology*, 2nd ed. (Oxford: Blackwell, 1970), 414.
3. Georg Wilhelm Friedrich Hegel, *Lectures on the Philosophy of Religion*, trans. E. B. Spies and J. B. Sanderson (New York: Humanities, 1962), 1:276; *The Philosophy of History*, with a preface by Charles Hegel and an introduction by C.J. Friedrich, trans. J. Sibree (New York: Dover, 1956), 407.
4. Friedrich Schiller, *Etwas über die erste Menschengesellschaft: Übergang des Menschen zur Freiheit und Humanität* (1789), in *Gesammelte Werke*, ed. Reinhold Netolitzky (Gütersloh, Germany: Bertelsmann, 1959), 4:103.
5. Erich Fromm, *The Heart of Man: Its Genius for Good and Evil* (New York: Harper, 1966), 20.

he wrote, "Here is a deep doctrine in the legend of the fall: it is the expression of a dim presentiment that the emancipation of the ego-consciousness was a Luciferian deed."[6] Inasmuch as French Jesuit priest and paleontologist Pierre Teilhard de Chardin (1881–1955) described the same facts, he likewise came close to an idealistic view when he claimed that evil was a necessary by-product of evolution, by means of which nature, through many errors and trials, moves upward in its evolutionary path. He wrote, "The involuting universe [. . .] proceeds step by step by dint of a billion-fold trial and error. It is this process of groping, combined with the two-fold mechanism of reproduction and heredity [. . .], which gives rise to the [. . .] tree of life."[7]

An evolutionary model provides the basis of the idealistic interpretation of the fall in which the later stages are characterized as more highly developed and therefore better. Against this view, however, two objections must be raised. First, it is difficult to prove that an evolutionary development to a higher level is necessarily better. From the perspective of biology, for instance, humans are not "better" than reptiles, although on the evolutionary scale, they are a far more highly developed species. A similar argument can be made with regard to cultural development among humans. A more highly developed culture is not necessarily qualitatively better than a "more primitive" culture, even if it allows a higher living standard.

The story of the fall would also seem incompatible with evolutionary theories, even if this does not hold true for every evolutionary interpretation. This can be shown in two ways. First, the origin of sin as related in Genesis 3 cannot be causally deduced from God's good creation. When Adam was questioned by God concerning his behavior, he sought to make such a deduction and said, "The woman whom you gave to be with me, she gave me fruit from the tree, and I ate" (Gen 3:12). In this way, he attempted to justify himself by ascribing the cause of evil to God. The woman attempted to make a similar causal deduction, although not quite as daring of one, when she responded to God's reproach by saying, "The serpent tricked me, and I ate" (Gen 3:13). In both instances, it is suggested, with apologetic intent, that the cause of evil is to be found outside the human sphere. But before God, neither of these attempts can excuse the seriousness of the situation.

Second, there exists no causal connection between these first sins and the appearance of subsequent sins, as the later theories of inherited sin want to show. To be sure, the Yahwist illustrates in drastic manner the rapid growth of evil, which spreads like a wildfire. But nowhere is the appearance of a new sin tied to the commission of a previous sin so that the burden of guilt of later sins might be reduced and sinning became unavoidable.

6. Carl Gustav Jung, "The Phenomenology of the Spirit in Fairytales" (para. 420), in *Collected Works*, trans. R. F. C. Hull (New York: Pantheon, 1959), 9.1:230.
7. See Pierre Teilhard de Chardin, *The Phenomenon of Man* (New York: Harper, 1959), 301–302. Cf. also 310, where he uses the same terminology and speaks of the "evil of disorder and failure" as a necessity in the evolutionary process.

Evil came in the world through the appearance of the first man and the first woman, and it continues to show itself in conjunction with the appearance of humans. One might remember here what behavioral psychology adduced concerning the phenomenon of aggression. In a variety of forms, aggressive drives are found among animals. These drives normally serve, however, to facilitate the survival of a species and not to jeopardize it. This applies likewise to aggression directed toward other species (as in the case of defense or hunting) and even within species (as in the establishment of hierarchies, defensive behavior, or the selection of mates). As human beings appeared, however, and began to exercise dominion over one another and their environment and to develop increasingly sophisticated tools and weapons, the aggressive drives that they inherited from the animal kingdom became increasingly ambivalent. They increased the potential for good as well as for evil. Thus many animal species were annihilated and others domesticated, and some civilizations throve, while others were destroyed. As psychoanalysis has shown, human activities are highly ambivalent; they comprise the drive for life while at the same time spread fear and death.

The appearance of evil was not a disastrous stroke of fate against which humanity was helpless. We must not overlook the fact that it is not the man or the woman but rather the snake who appears as the tempter in the account of the fall. We would overstep the limits of the interpretation of the temptation story to claim that the woman had a more direct access to the dark side of life than the man, since she was first tempted and then becomes the temptress. The temptation story shows, however, that humanity was not sinful from the very beginning, temptation originated externally. The cause of evil, however, is not some God-opposing principle external to God's creation, even though this view was held within gnosticism. The snake, which becomes the tempter, is described as an animal and thereby as part of God's creation but not as a part of the heavenly court. Moreover, in the temptation story, the emphasis is not on the serpent but on the human response to the possibilities the serpent presents, the choice of which seduces the first human beings away from God and into sin.

Still, the primeval history gives no answer to the fundamental question of where evil comes from. Along with the rest of the Old Testament, not the slightest attempt is made to take refuge in either a dualistic or pluralistic worldview. The question of why a part of God's good creation became the tempter is beyond the interests of the Yahwist, since the answer to this question would not contribute to the description of human sinfulness. Only in the intertestamental period the connection is made between the serpent and the devil: "Through the devil's envy death entered the world" (Wis 2:24)[8] and "That ancient serpent, who is the Devil and Satan" (Rev 20:2). The guilt, in all its severity, is allowed to stand as unexplained guilt. Still,

---

8. All Apocrypha and Pseudepigrapha quotations are from James H. Charlesworth, ed., *The Old Testament Pseudepigrapha*, 2 vols. (Garden City, NY: Doubleday Image, 1983).

there are two additional facts that require further clarification—namely, what provoked humans to sin, and what were the consequences for humans after they had fallen into sin?

The first human pair was tempted to become like God—that is, to know good and evil. Yet is it difficult to accept that God would have created a creature capable of becoming his potential challenger so that the first human being "is potentially God."[9] While for the Yahwist it is absurd that anyone could equal Yahweh, it is not incredible for him to propose that a human would desire to be equal to the divine being Elohim. Yet the stimulus to sin goes beyond the human aspiration to be like God. As humans were tempted to recognize good and evil, they wanted to be aware not only of the difference between good and evil but rather of everything—that is, the totality of all things from good to evil. The human temptation at that time consisted of and continues to consist of the desire to know everything and to know it better than our human or divine "opponent." This arrogant stance threatened God and neighbor and every harmonious relationship with them. Yet this stance must not be confused with the inquisitive human spirit, for the goal of its efforts is not the egoistic "knowing better" but rather the analytical, measuring knowing concerned with the relationship between things. Sinful knowing it all consists of the destructive desire of humanity not to acknowledge a "You" that possesses its own sphere but rather to regard it as an "It" that is not allowed to have any secrets. This human hubris destroys fundamentally the relationship to God as well as to the neighbor and damages the created character of nature inasmuch as it regards nature as a thing to be possessed by humans. At the same time, they now stand alone and have to decide for themselves what is in their own best interests. They now operate totally out of their own resources to decide on good and evil.

Recognizing their inadequacy for living a good life on their own, they hide before God. But God does not react to the sinful pride of humanity as an offended tyrant. God even comes to them subsequent to their sin and engages them into a dialogue. The conversation between God and the first humans shows that the harmonious union with God is severed, and then the first human pair is expelled from the garden. But the threat that Adam and Eve would die on the day in which they ate from the tree of knowledge of good and evil (Gen 2:17) was not realized through their sin. They were only reminded that they would return to dust, from which they were formed (Gen 2:7; 3:19). Indeed, almost as if to hold the original threat in contempt, Adam now ventures to name his wife Eve—that is, the mother of all living. Even the obligation to work cannot be understood as an actual curse resulting from the fall, since Adam was already supposed to tend the garden (Gen 2:15). However, as the harmonious relationship with God was broken, the harmonious relationship between humanity and nature as well as between man and woman

---

9. This view is expressed by Erich Fromm, *You Shall Be as Gods: A Radical Interpretation of the Old Testament and Its Traditions* (New York: Holt, Rinehart and Winston, 1966), 23.

also disappeared. The Yahwist acknowledges that life is difficult, filled with hatred and passion and permeated by a yearning after harmony. But life did not cease, for "the Lord God made garments of skins for the man and for his wife, and clothed them" (Gen 3:21). Instead of lamenting evil, the Yahwist points to signs of grace that were given to the first human pair on their journey through life: garments of skins and God's assistance in dressing. This merciful act of God might be better understood as a foreshadowing of the Gospel than Genesis 3:15, a text that usually is referred to as the *protoevangelium*, or proto-Gospel, that speaks of the lasting enmity that will hold sway between the serpent and humanity.

Nevertheless, this passage of Genesis 3:15 in which God speaks to the serpent ("I will put enmity between you and the woman, and between your offspring and hers; he will strike your head, and you will strike his heel") is surprising! A message of hope is given to humanity. While God punishes the offenders, God speaks of humans having offspring. God's blessing on future generations of humans has not been removed. This is in itself a declaration of mercy. But God also informs the serpent of the enmity between the serpent and the woman. This is reinforced by the second part of the sentence, "between your offspring and hers." God's judgment upon the serpent contains for humanity a promise of ultimate victory through the woman by her offspring. But for this, we have to wait until the book of Revelation, where we read, "The great dragon was thrown down, that ancient serpent, who is called the Devil and Satan, the deceiver of the whole world—he was thrown down to the earth, and his angels were thrown down with him" (Rev 12:9). But up to this last book of the Bible, we hear hardly anything of the serpent and of its defeat.

Evil as Divine Punishment?

When we leave the Genesis account of the fall and seek to determine the cause of evil from other Old Testament sources, our task becomes difficult. On the one hand, the official reading is very clear, as we can gather from the injunction in Deuteronomy:

> See, I have set before you today life and prosperity, death and adversity. If you obey the commandments of the Lord your God that I am commanding you today, by loving the Lord your God, walking in his ways, and observing his commandments, decrees, and ordinances, then you shall live and become numerous, and the Lord your God will bless you in the land that you are entering to possess. But if your heart turns away and you do not hear, but are led astray to bow down to other gods and serve them, I declare to you today that you shall perish. (Deut 30:15–19)

Since God is the God of Israel, the obedient receive blessings from God, and the disobedient receive curses. We read the same in the book of Judges: "The Israelites again did what was evil in the sight of the Lord; and the Lord strengthened King Eglon of Moab against Israel, because they had done what was evil in the sight of the Lord. [. . .] But when the Israelites cried out to the Lord, the Lord raised up for them a deliverer" (Judg 3:12, 15). Evil is seen as the result of divine punishment on account of Israel's misdeeds. This even holds true for the prophets. For instance, we read in Amos, "Thus says the Lord: for three transgressions of Judah, and for four, I will not revoke the punishment; because they have rejected the law of the Lord and have not kept his statutes, but they have been led astray by the same lies after which their ancestors walked. So I will send a fire on Judah, and it shall devour the strongholds of Jerusalem" (Amos 2:4–5). Again, evil is the result of moral wrongdoing. Ultimately, it is God who stands behind both good and evil. Therefore, Yahweh asks his people, "Does disaster [i.e., evil] befall a city, unless the Lord has done it?" (Amos 3:6). When we read the Psalms, however, we hear often the cry of the distressed who prayed to God for deliverance (Cf. Ps 102:1–2). It seems that obedient people receive evil, but disobedient people receive blessings. The connection between keeping the laws of the Lord and being blessed quite often does not bear out in reality. We find the prime example of this in the figure of Job. We read of him, "That man was blameless and upright, one who feared God and turned away from evil" (Job 1:1). But then God allows Satan to test Job with one calamity after another. After Job is seized by misfortune, he is convinced of God's omnipotence and says to his wife, "Shall we receive the good at the hand of God, and not receive the bad?" (Job 2:10). This means that God is the author of these bad occurrences that befell Job. His wife, however, appears to take no comfort in this, for she wants her husband to renounce and even to curse God, since God is the cause of all the evil that has befallen Job.

There is one Psalm that Jesus prayed when he was hanging on the cross: Psalm 22. This prayer for help of an individual in great distress opens with the words, "My God, my God, why have you forsaken me?" (Ps 22:1). Then the psalmist remembers the earlier community of faith who relied on God: "In you our ancestors trusted; they trusted, and you delivered them" (Ps 22:4). Finally, the psalmist receives a response from God and renders praise for God's delivering help, saying, "You have rescued me. I will tell of your name to my brothers and sisters; in the midst of the congregation I will praise you" (Ps 22:21–22). In the midst of such inexplicable suffering, not only is grief voiced but also hope because "God's response to such protest is an attentiveness that provides care, sustenance, and compassion."[10] These Psalms of lament and suffering witness to God, who has been Israel's help in ages past. God will also come to their rescue in the present. Even after all the punishment that according to Amos awaits Israel, God will raise up the fallen "booth of David" (Amos 9:11). Yes, God metes out divine punishment. But Yahve is not a condemning God.

---

10. Walter Brueggemann, s.v. "Theodicy," in *Reverberations of Faith: A Theological Handbook of Old Testament Themes* (Louisville: Westminster John Knox Press, 2002), 214.

God as the Cause of Both Good and Evil

In Deutero-Isaiah, the pressing question of whether God is the cause of evil is likewise answered in the affirmative, for we hear the Lord say, "I form light and create darkness, I make weal and create woe; I the Lord do all these things" (Isa 45:7). In other texts, we discover that the Lord can even incite one person against another (cf. 1 Sam 26:19).

God is the only God, and all the other gods amount to nothing. Therefore, the Psalmist says, "There is none like you among the gods, O Lord, nor are there any works like yours" (Ps 86:8). God knows and executes good and evil, and everything depends on him. We also learn that the Lord sends an evil spirit to Saul once the spirit of the Lord had departed from the king (1 Sam 16:14–23), and this evil spirit tormented Saul. Then David entered the court of Saul "and whenever the evil spirit from God came upon Saul, David took the lyre and played it with his hand, and Saul would be relieved and feel better, and the evil spirit would depart from him." Such a statement does not diminish the understanding that God is the only genuine power, for it is God who sends the evil spirit once the spirit of the Lord had departed from Saul. Now the spirit of the Lord "came mightily upon David" (1 Sam 16:13). It would be tempting to speak here of a demonic god, in light of whose actions no one can be secure. Or we could assume that the Israelites ascribed good and evil to Yahweh in order to preserve a monotheistic faith. However, these attempts are mistaken to solve the mystery of evil. God is not a demon, and God's works are always directed toward the triumph of the kingdom and the advance of God's plan of redemption. Thus the Psalmist is correct when he confesses, "For his anger is but for a moment; his favor is for a lifetime" (Ps 30:5). Israel was nevertheless also convinced that Yahweh ordains for individuals as well as the entire nation tests, afflictions, or even judgment and, in this sense, does "evil." From this perspective, one can understand the story of Job, who was afflicted by God and was led thereby to a deeper understanding of God. God is understood never as a capricious God whose deeds one must fear but rather as a holy God before whom one dare not appear as if one were an equal or approach in a demanding manner. Behind the statements of the incomparable circumspection of a God who creates good and evil stands the recognition of the absolute sovereignty of God over life and death, fortune and misfortune, well-being and calamity.

In the case of God's activity, the opposite of good is not moral evil but rather misfortune or divine judgment, as that which normally results from the evil actions of humanity. "Thus says the Lord of hosts, the God of Israel: You yourselves have seen all the disaster that I have brought on Jerusalem and on all the towns of Judah [. . .] because of the wickedness that they committed" (Jer 44:2–3). When humans abandon their evil actions, God can avert the misfortune that was intended for them. The inhabitants of Nineveh learned this as they pursued a path of moral repentance. "When God saw what they did, how they turned from their evil ways, God changed his mind about the calamity that he had said he would bring upon them; and he did not do it" (Jonah 3:10). Yet the ways of God are not always easy to fathom. One must recognize the incomparable sovereignty of the God who says, "My thoughts are not your thoughts, nor are your ways my ways" (Isa 55:8).

But how should one respond when one reads, for instance, in Judges 9:23, "God sent an evil spirit between Abimelech and the lords of Shechem; and the lords of Shechem dealt treacherously with Abimelech"? Again, in the case of Abimelech, we should remember that he was not an innocent person but became judge after he had murdered all his brothers except one who hid himself (Judg 9:5). After this horrible act did God send the evil and divisive spirit as just retribution for the murder of his father's seventy sons? The issue is somewhat different when we read of the sons of the high priest Eli: "But they would not listen to the voice of their father; for it was the will of the Lord to kill them" (1 Sam 2:25). Do we not encounter here a demonic, sinister, treacherous, and unpredictable God? Not really, since we read how old Eli pleads with his sons to change their ways but to no avail. "God is the power that will bring Eli's sons to the death their sin has made necessary. The description of the sins of Eli's sons makes clear that they have chosen this particular path."[11] As the text explains, if anyone sins against the Lord as they have done, there is no intercession possible. Therefore, the death of Eli's sons seems justified. But what about the command from Yahweh that the prophet Isaiah received to go to his people and harden their hearts so that they hear but do not understand and see but do not recognize (Isa 6:9–10)? Gene M. Tucker in his commentary to this passage gives a very interesting explanation:

> No reason is given for this announcement of disaster, only that the word of the Lord through the prophet is to make repentance impossible and thus to effect judgment. There is a hint of indictment in the prophet's initial reaction to the vision of the Lord: "and I live among the people of unclean lips" (v. 5). The prophet but not the people had been cleansed. It is possible that the judgment announced here is finally to purify the people. There is a kind of symmetry, if not a parallel, between the cleansing of the prophet by means of the coal from the altar and the "cleansing" of the people through the destruction. At the end, even the stump is burned, and then—in the final form if not in the original vision report—there is the seed, the possibility of renewal. The editors of the book, if not Isaiah or the earliest tradents, saw that the national disaster could be a cleansing punishment and that new life could grow out of it.[12]

---

11. So Bruce C. Birch, *The First and Second Book of Samuel*, in NIB, 2:987, in his exegesis of 1 Sam 2:25.
12. Gene M. Tucker, *The Book of Isaiah 1–39*, in NIB, 6:104.

Indeed, God metes out disaster for Israel. But these people are not innocent. Through this disaster, the people may indeed be brought back on the right track. To this end, there is a seed left that allows for renewal and a new beginning. Even Isaiah 6 indicates that the idea of an unpredictable, demonic God who plays dice with his creation and his people is far from the truth. Yet the Old Testament leaves no doubt that God is in control of his creation and that God will also bring judgment if the people leave God's ways.

Up to and including the time of the great writing prophets, such as Isaiah, God is viewed as an absolutely sovereign God from whom comes both good and evil. The question of theodicy, or of how a just God can also cause evil without thereby himself becoming evil, is not posed in this form. The emphasis, in fact, is upon God's sovereignty, since only from a sovereign God one can expect the mighty acts that show God to be the Lord of history. Consequently, all the effects of life—the dark as well as the light ones, the frightening as well as the cheerful, the threatening as well as the saving—are transferred to Yahweh. He is the final ground of all things and the sole causality of life.

The Issue of Divine Justice

In the book of Ecclesiastes (ca. 230 BCE), it is emphasized that "God made human beings straightforward, but they have devised many schemes" (Eccl 7:29). The wickedness of humanity finds its origin not in God but rather in humanity alone. The issue of theodicy is treated in wisdom literature, to which belong Ecclesiastes together with Sirach and the book of Job. Therefore, we will deal more extensively with the latter two. The closest parallels to this so-called wisdom literature occur outside the Bible, particularly in ancient Egyptian and Mesopotamian literature associated with educational contexts. One type of wisdom literature explores existential questions, chiefly the matter of innocent suffering and what this implies for divine justice. The vexing problem of divine justice surfaces prominently in argumentative contexts of Sirach. This book was written probably around 185 BCE. Ben Sira (Sir 50:27) was presumably a professional teacher (Sir 41:16) who encountered a vocal group who denied God's just governance of the world. He stands in a venerable tradition of wisdom teachers. His speech forms resemble those in Proverbs, Job, and Ecclesiastes, which he studied thoroughly (along with the Torah and prophetic literature). He covers a wide range of subjects that deal with daily existence—such as the proper attitude toward money or the right conduct at banquets—and extensively deals with the issue of divine justice.

The origin of sin in a perfect universe placed a special burden on defenders of divine justice, particularly when it was attributed to the creator. The serpent's presence in the garden indirectly indicted the Lord. Later biblical texts compromise divine justice further, insisting that God overrides human freedom, forcing pharaohs and others to persist in obstinacy. Ben Sira stoutly resisted such ideas, for he believed that everyone acts with absolute freedom (Sir 15:11–20). Neverthe-less, he realized that irresistible forces put extraordinary pressure on free will (Sir 33:11–13). "That ambiguity characterizes much biblical thinking about sin, but Ben Sira brings the issue of free will into the arena of public discussion."[13]

In a fictional debate, Ben Sira tries to answer some accusations against God and to counter justification for wicked conduct. "Do not say, 'It was the Lord's doing that I fell away'; for he does not do what he hates. Do not say, 'It was he who led me astray'; for he has no need of the sinful. The Lord hates all abominations; such things are not loved by those who fear him. It was he who created humankind in the beginning, and he left them in the power of their own free choice" (Sir 15:11–14). The fundamental problem that Ben Sira addresses here arose from widespread belief that Israel's God had created a world in which, due to human freedom, sin was a live possibility. "The skeptic asked why such a universe was formed when a deity capable of creation could surely have made one that rendered transgression impossible. Three possibilities for the origin of evil naturally came to mind: (1) God created both good and evil; (2) Satan introduced sin into the world; and (3) human beings brought evil into a perfect world."[14] At this point, Ben Sira strongly attaches blame to men and women who willingly rebel against their maker. In his view, any attempt to shift blame from humans to God ignored one essential fact: God cannot do that which God despises.

Skepticism about divine recompense for sinful deeds seemed to support the claim that Yahweh either approved of evil or simply overlooked it. When a delay in divine visitation coincided with reverse expectation, such as numerous children being born to wicked people, traditional understandings of divine justice became suspect. That situation demanded a thoughtful response from a teacher like Ben Sira. In offering a rebuttal to such skepticism, he put forth at least one bold statement that was at odds with tradition: barrenness coupled with virtue surpasses a large family of wicked children (Sir 16:1–4). To overcome doubt about divine punishment, he lets Scripture demonstrate the reality of God's wrath on sinners of all sorts. Ben Sira's answer to those who considered their sinful actions inconsequential in God's eyes amounts to a teacher's harsh rebuke for sloppy thinking. To be sure, we also read in Sirach that "good things and bad, life and death, poverty and wealth, come from the Lord" (Sir 11:14). This means that God is the source of all human conditions. In God's sovereignty, "it is easy for the Lord on the day of death to reward individuals according to their conduct" (Sir 11:26). Since Ben Sira rejected a meaningful exis-tence after death—one could even call him on this account a proto-Sadducee—he surmised, "at the close of one's life one's deeds are revealed" (Sir 11:27). One's good name will be remembered and will serve as an inspiration for posterity. Therefore, it held true for Ben Sira that "all the works of the Lord are very good" (Sir 39:16). One cannot blame God for evil. Although God in his sovereign way created both

---

13. James L. Crenshaw, *The Book of Sirach*, in NIB, 5:627–628.
14. Crenshaw, *Book of Sirach*, 5:724.

good and evil, all of his works are so good that one cannot, as the first human pair attempted, diffuse or deflect evil as something inflicted upon humans from outside themselves. In addition, Sirach indicates that the works of God "will be done at the appointed time" (Sir 39:16). God has organized everything in accordance with his goal, including that which, at the present time, does not seem recognizable as such. As a result, therefore, one can conclude that "humanity, and not some power external to it, creates evil; and even in those instances in which Yahweh appears as the author of misfortune, humanity is not excused from its own responsibility."[15]

A different approach is presented in the book of Job. This book is much older than Sirach and most likely dates from the early postexilic period—that is, sixth to fifth century BCE. There the main issue is not human freedom but is much more directly the issue of divine justice. In this way as well as in many others, this book is part of the Israelite wisdom tradition. As Carol A. Newsom states in her commentary on Job, "The book of Job, although unique in many respects, is best understood as a part of the intellectual and cultural world of wisdom."[16] The so-called Babylonian Theodicy—written around 1000 BCE and which contains close parallels to the dialogues in the book of Job—shows that the issue of theodicy has been an issue vexing people since time immemorial. This topic seems to have been picked up by wisdom literature in different cultural contexts.

When we begin to read the book of Job, we notice that Satan is depicted as one of "the heavenly beings" who present themselves before the Lord (Job 1:6). Satan is seen not yet as the opponent of God but as a being who is part of God's heavenly court and who brings sinful or corrupt human beings to God's attention. This implies that God is the sovereign ruler from whom everything proceeds. If something bad occurs, then humans question why God allowed it to happen. For the wicked, it is divine judgment, since "the wicked writhe in pain all their days" (Job 15:20). But it can also be an educational discipline, since we read, "How happy is the one whom God reproves; therefore do not despise the discipline of the Almighty. For he wounds, but he binds up; he strikes, but his hands heal" (Job 5:17–18). It can also come as a divine warning, since the Lord "opens their ears, and terrifies them with warnings, that he may turn them aside from their deeds" (Job 33:16–17). For the righteous, bad things are simply something to be borne with the confidence that God will eventually restore their well-being, since "God will not reject a blameless person" (Job 8:20). In every situation, the proper response is to turn to God in humility, trust, and prayer.

Yet after all kinds of calamities strike Job, he no longer agrees with these explanations. He claims that God has no right to cause something bad for a person unless that person deserves punishment. But reality is different because God is

---

15. Herbert Haag, *Vor dem Bösen ratlos?* (Munich: Piper, 1978), 61. Yet when Haag maintains that this holds true for the Old Testament from its earliest to its latest writings, one must disagree, for there developed an increasingly strong impression that an external power must be at least coresponsible for evil.

16. Carol A. Newsom, *The Book of Job*, in NIB, 4:327.

indiscriminate in his actions, and humans must learn what God wants to communicate to them when he metes out bad things. God is a violator of justice, since he "has taken away my right" (Job 27:2). Even worse, God is a capricious God because "your hands fashioned and made me; and now you turn and destroy me" (Job 10:8). And finally, "[God] has torn me in his wrath, and hated me" (Job 16:9). Such a God can no longer be the object of adoration. As we can see from Psalm 73, Job is not alone raising the problem that exists between a just God and the injustice people face in the world. Regardless of the issue of injustice that is so glaringly apparent in the world, Job does not give up the idea that ultimately God will be revealed as a God of justice. He is certain that "the godless shall not come before him [God]," and "I know that I shall be vindicated" (Job 13:16, 18).

The friends of Job argue differently and believe more straightforward in God's goodness and justice. Elihu, for example, says, "God will not do wickedly, and the Almighty will not pervert justice" (Job 34:12). How do Job's friends back up their position? First, they appeal to tradition, asking Job to "inquire now of bygone generations" (Job 8:8), and second, they appeal to reason, saying, "Therefore, hear me, you who have sense, far be it from God that he should do wickedness, and from the Almighty that he should do wrong" (Job 34:10). For them, it is an axiomatic truth that God is good and whatever he does is correct. Job, on the other hand, argues from his own experience and asks them in his dire state, "Teach me, and I will be silent; make me understand how I have gone wrong" (Job 6:24). He even desires to argue his case with God (Job 13:3), showing him that he is an innocent sufferer who has done nothing wrong.

Finally, however, "the Lord answered Job out of the whirlwind" (Job 38:1). Yet the Lord's answer does not explicitly engage the particular arguments Job has made. While Job argues from his own experience in terms of moral and social assumptions, God begins with the great structures of creation and speaks scarcely at all of the places human beings occupy in the cosmos and thereby exposes the limits of Job's anthropocentric categories. God shows him the fundamental order of creation and the restricted but still powerful forces of nature and of the huge, fear-causing animals to make him understand a different aspect of the nature of reality. Confronted with God's power and might, it makes little sense to argue with such a God. Job's response shows that he now has gained a different understanding of God's majesty when he says, "I know that you can do all things, and that no purpose of yours can be thwarted." [. . .] "Therefore I have uttered what I did not understand, things too wonderful for me, which I did not know. 'Hear, and I will speak; I will question you, and you declare to me'" (Job 42:2–4). Citing God's words, Job emphasizes that it is God who does the talking and he who listens. Humility and letting God be God who is in ultimate control seems to be the appropriate response to history wrought by God.

But then we hear that God says to one of Job's friends, "My wrath is kindled against you and against your two friends; for you have not spoken of me what is right, as my servant Job has" (Job 42:7). Was the unwavering conviction of Job's friends that God is good and whatever he does is right not true either? The book of Job does not answer this question. It only states in the end that "the Lord restored the fortunes of Job" and his brothers and sisters, plus other people "showed him sympathy and comforted him for all the evil that the Lord had brought upon him" (Job 42:10–11). We hear here explicitly that the Lord had brought evil upon Job. Does this mean that God is the originator of evil and not just of divine punishment? The book of Job does not give an answer. The prose frame of the beginning of the book (Job 1–2) and the end (Job 42:7–17) provides a narration with a happy ending and a smooth and satisfying conclusion. But if we consider the whole book, including the speeches, then "the ending creates dissonance and disruption."[17] As long as one perceives God as the author of everything, as the book of Job does, and still wants to reason why the good God also metes out the bad, one is perplexed with this God. This is shown in the book of Job. There is, on the one hand, the causal nexus between "good behavior" and "good fortune," but on the other, there is the reality of "good behavior" and "misfortune." The two simply do not go together. This was the experience of individuals as we see in the book of Job as well as in the Israelite nation as a whole.

As the Israelites could no longer look back upon the great acts of God through a presumed direct lineage and as Israel increasingly saw itself within the broadening historical context as a playing ball of world powers, it was no longer so easy to attribute everything to God and continue, nevertheless, to hold fast to his promises of salvation. If God was to remain in the future the one upon whom salvation ultimately depended, then the Israelites could not continue to understand God as the author of both good and evil. Evil was, so to speak, excluded from God without falling into a dualism in the process. We can already notice an inkling of this exclusion in the book of Job when Satan as a subordinate divine agent attacked Job's character (Job 1:6–11). Satan's actions are therefore not directly attributable to God and may even be rejected. In later centuries, the figure of Satan develops into the dualistic opponent of God, as we will see consistently in the New Testament. Thus one could distinguish between evil as an act or thing and its underlying causal forces that are distinct from God.

The Exclusion of Evil

When one views evil as a causal force distinct from God, mythological imagery can be employed in which an unequivocal identification of evil is not important. One can also comprehend evil through a more personally related understanding that recalls, for instance, persons involved in court proceedings. In the mythical imagery of the poetic writings and also of the prophets, Leviathan—a multiheaded,

17. We agree here with Carol A. Newsom in her insightful commentary Book of Job, 4:635.

largely mythical primal creature—becomes the embodiment of evil. According to the view of the Old Testament, Leviathan was either killed by the creator of the cosmos (Ps 74:13–14) or was abidingly subdued (Ps 104:26–27). The most disparate symbols and identifications are to be found in Leviathan. As a creation of Yahweh, Leviathan is roughly comparable with the crocodile as a large, dangerous creature (Job 41:1–3), yet on the other hand, it becomes the embodiment of the power that opposes God (Isa 27:1). The prophet Isaiah expresses the hope that in the last days, God will usher in the new creation, whereby the chaotic force Leviathan, also called the twisting serpent and dragon, will be decisively defeated. A similar and perhaps even identical chaotic force is Rahab, who was likewise defeated by the creator in primordial times (Isa 51:9; Job 26:12–13). Metaphorically, the threatening power *Rahab* can be identified with Egypt (Isa 30:7). The God-opposing power introduced with these various images resists God's plan of redemption. These images point no doubt to Babylonian influences and primeval myths. They were combined with the Israelite conception of the correspondence between end-time and primordial time, for one expected in "the end times a new assault of the chaos dragon against God and a new victory of God over him."[18] Important here is that evil and the God-opposing power in their symbolic form resist both the creation and the final deliverance through Yahweh and desire to bring both to naught but will, however, themselves be defeated.

In an entirely different manner, much less mythological and almost profane, another power is encountered in the Old Testament, the already mentioned figure of Satan. The original meaning of the word *Satan* in its verbal form is "to be at enmity with, to persecute, and more specifically, to demonstrate enmity through accusation."[19] This means that this term belongs initially to the realm of the profane and only gradually took on theological significance. As substantive, the term *Satan* in the Old Testament can also be used to designate an enemy. For example, the leaders of the Philistines feared that David could become their adversary (Satan) in battle (1 Sam 29:4). Often, the adversary (Satan) is an enemy of Israel who accuses Israel in the name of Yahweh and points to the evil that Israel has done (1 Kgs 11:14, 23). The ancient passage concerning Balaam and his ass shows us that Satan can be identified with someone who is part of God's heavenly court, as we have seen in Job. We read there, "And the angel of the Lord took his stand in the road as his [i.e., Balaam's] adversary" (adversary = Satan; Num 22:22). Because Balaam unconsciously does something against God's will, the angel of the Lord

---

18. Haag, *Vor dem Bösen ratlos?*, 96. Cf. also in this regard Gerhard Schmitt, "Rehab," in *Biblisch-historisches Handwörterbuch*, ed. Bo Reicke and Leonhard Rost (Göttingen: Vandenhoeck & Ruprecht, 1966), 3:1547–1548; and Marie-Louise Henry, "Leviathan," in *Biblisch-historisches Handwörterbuch*, ed. Bo Reicke and Leonhard Rost (Göttingen: Vandenhoeck & Ruprecht, 1962), 2:1076–1077.
19. So Kurt Lüthi, *Gott und das Böse: Eine biblisch-theologische und systematische These zur Lehre vom Bösen, entworfen in Auseinandersetzung mit Schelling und Karl Barth* (Zürich: Theologischer Verlag Zürich, 1961), 116.

becomes an adversary, blocks Balaam's way, and hinders him from carrying out his own will (Num 22:32).

In the previously mentioned book of Job, the function of Satan as the accuser is portrayed with particular clarity. As a member of God's heavenly court, Satan questions whether Job is really as blameless and upright as he appears (Job 1:9–11). Since Satan is understood not as a demonic power but as one of the sons of God, he needs God's permission in order to test the integrity of Job. Consequently, it is ultimately God who tests Job. It is, however, difficult to understand Satan as the accuser in analogy to a legal trial. Against such a view, one might mention the fact that there were many other life-threatening powers that worked against Job, such as disease, death, theft, and the devastating forces of nature. The "cause of the evil," however, takes place in conjunction with God and not in opposition to him, whereas the temptation by the serpent in the fall narrative takes place "behind God's back." Nevertheless, Satan functions in the story of Job as a heavenly opponent of a peaceful life and earthly comfort.[20] The result of his activity, however, is not the destruction of Job, as one might fear, for Job achieves a deeper piety and surrenders himself fully to God as a result of the fateful blows dealt him.

In the fourth vision of the prophet Zechariah, the accusing function of Satan is once more made clear. Just like in the book of Job, he is an agent of the heavenly court with the charge of patrolling the earth. Unlike in the New Testament, he is not yet an independent figure who acts against God. He functions as the accuser who stands at the right side of the accused high priest Joshua as both appear before the angel of the Lord (Zech 3:1–3). It is not explicitly clear of what Satan accuses the high priest, perhaps of evil deeds sought during the exile and his lacking fitness as a high priest. But remarkably, it is Yahweh who speaks in Joshua's defense saying, "The Lord rebuke you, O Satan! The Lord who has chosen Jerusalem rebuke you! Is not this man a brand plucked from the fire?" (Zech 3:2). It is no longer clear that Satan acts with the intention of advancing the kingdom of God. God finally intervenes in that case through an angel in order to allow the high priest to receive grace and forgiveness.

In 1 Chronicles 21, Satan's position as independent of God is advanced still further. This is the only text in the Old Testament in which Satan is used as a proper name. In 2 Samuel 24:1, we read, "The anger of the Lord was kindled against Israel, and he incited David against them, saying, 'Go, count the people of Israel and Judah.'" The chronicler, however, reports the same event with the following words: "Satan stood up against Israel, and incited David to count the people of Israel" (1 Chr 21:1). When we compare here the Old with the New Testament, we notice a similar shift. In Hosea 11:10, God is compared to a roaring lion, while in 1 Peter 5:8, it is the devil who is called a "roaring lion." The statement that God could incite David to sin was

---

20. For this and the following, see Gerhard von Rad, "Diabolos (the Old Testament View of Satan)," in TDNT, 2:73.

probably regarded as objectionable at the time of the writing of Chronicles. In both versions, however, that of the Chronicler and that of the book of Samuel, we read that God decrees the punishment for David's sin. Nowhere in the Old Testament does Satan achieve the status of a dualistic opponent of God who restricts God as the principle of the good. Finally, even the satanic temptations must further God's redemptive plan. This can also be seen in the previously cited account concerning David. Because his royal power was diminished through the punishment of God, he became more receptive to the will of God.

In this passage, it is again evident that God was originally understood without exception as the source of both good and evil. Yet the tendency arose to see God's function in reference to the cause of evil only in judging humanity for its sinful behavior. This means that the cause of the activation of evil in humanity must be found outside of God; first, the temptation by someone out of God's good creation, then in the image of the heavenly accuser, and finally, in the increasingly independent figure of a malevolent Satan. But we can hardly agree with the otherwise very instructive work of Rivkah Schärf Kluger when he states that in the case of the "figure of Satan we have to do with the result of a developmental process within God."[21] It is not the divine person that had developed, but rather, the Israelite conception of God had gradually become clearer. This process of clarification is continued with increased vigor in the New Testament. We must, however, recall once more a decisive point: regardless of to whom the cause of evil is attributed in an event, the Old Testament contends that the existence of an evil tempter external to humans does not decrease their responsibility for their own actions. Even when the temptation appears irresistible, the responsibility of humans for their actions endures unchanged. We can read this clearly in the Chronicler's version of the temptation of David, for there he confesses, "Was it not I who gave the command to count the people? It is I who have sinned and done very wickedly" (1 Chr 21:17).

In order to fully understand the figure of Satan, we must look beyond the Old Testament and turn, at least briefly, to the extrabiblical and intertestamental material, which was also influential for the sources of the New Testament. Since the principle references to Satan (Zech 3:1; Job 1–2) appear first in the early postexilic

---

21. Rivkah Schärf Kluger, *Satan in the Old Testament*, trans. H. Nagel (Evanston, IL: Northwestern University Press, 1967), 79. It is also questionable whether Herbert Haag, *Teufelsglaube*, with contributions by Katharina Elliger, Bernhard Lang, and Meinrad Limbeck (Tübingen, Germany: Katzmann, 1974), 217, is correct when he maintains that the coming to prominence of Satan in the Old Testament is the result of an ever-stronger inclination to prevent the clouding of the transcendence and holiness of God by unclean elements. We must agree that there exists without doubt a conspicuous development in the Old Testament understanding of God. This would seem, however, to be accounted for much more by the nature of the (political) reality, which stood in increasing disharmony with the expectations of salvation, as the exile became a part of the past, and nothing decisive was achieved toward the reestablishment of the Jewish kingdom. In the event that one wished to continue to believe in the realization of God's salvation history, one had to assume obstructing factors external to God and humanity. Regarding the problem of the gradual clarification of the concept of God, see Hans Schwarz, "The Lord of History," in *The God Who Is: The Christian God in a Pluralistic World* (Eugene, OR: Cascade Books, 2011), 195–215.

period, Babylonian and Iranian influences could have easily contributed to the Israelite conception of Satan. In fact, there exists a close parallel between the biblical book of Job and the previously mentioned Babylonian Theodicy, or "Poem of the Righteous Sufferer."[22] This poem tells of a persecutor who brings diseases upon a righteous man. While this Babylonian persecutor, or disease demon, has similarities with the tempting function of Satan, this function in the biblical book of Job is only one characteristic of Satan. Additionally, the Babylonian disease demon will be ultimately defeated by a good god, whereas according to the book of Job, Satan does not oppose God but rather acts with his permission. Therefore, the righteous Babylonian man attributes his suffering to the accuser, while Job ascribes his predicament to God. Although definite textual parallels are to be recognized between the Babylonian and the biblical narratives, the theological reasoning at decisive points runs in opposing directions.

There is, however, another aspect in which the Babylonian conception becomes important for the biblical understanding of Satan. When the dealings of Satan are described in the Old Testament, they often show affinity to resemble Babylonian texts. In Babylonian mythology, the relationship between God and humanity resembles that of the court ceremonial. God is the judge, and humans seek justice. In the ceremonial appears an accuser, a royal official, who travels throughout the land and represents the "eyes of the king."[23] The concept of the "eyes of the king" is likewise known in Media, Persia, and Egypt. Since this image is so widespread, we should not be surprised to find traces of it in the accusing function of Satan in Job 1–2 and Zechariah 3:1–3.

Of much greater significance than these Babylonian parallels is the influence of Zoroastrian doctrine upon the Old Testament conception of Satan.[24] The similarity between certain teachings of Zoroaster and the gradual perception of the figure of Satan in Israel cannot be denied. In both cases, the cause of evil is excluded from the conception of God and attributed to a power external to God. Some of the characteristics of Angra Mainyu are again encountered in the New Testament view of Satan. When we remember that in the Old Testament, God is emphasized as the Lord of history and the creator of the world and that the attempt is consistently made to portray Satan in such a way that he belongs ultimately within the sphere of God's rule, then we notice the fundamental difference between the monotheism

22. For the following, cf. Kluger, Satan, 87–89, 133. For a brief description of this text, cf. also Georg Fohrer, Das Buch Hiob, in Kommentar zum Alten Testament (Gütersloh, Germany: Bertelsmann, 1963), 16:44. Fohrer does not, however, mention Satan in this connection. For a translation of the Babylonian Theodicy, see Robert H. Pfeiffer, trans., "I Will Praise the Lord of Wisdom ('Poem of the Righteous Sufferer')," in Ancient near Eastern Texts Relating to the Old Testament, ed. James B. Pritchard (Princeton, NJ: Princeton University Press, 1950), 434–437. Cf. also Newsom, Book of Job, 4:333–334, who concedes only an indirect relationship within the larger context of wisdom literature.

23. Kluger, Satan, 135.

24. Cf. in regard to this paragraph the excellent publication by Geo Widengren, Die Religionen Irans (Stuttgart, Germany: Kohlhammer, 1965), 74–78, where he provides a short summary of the teaching of Zarathustra.

of the Old Testament and the cosmo-ethical dualism of Zarathustra.[25] In contrast to Zoroaster, the Old Testament authors never once ventured to express the thought that Yahweh was the father of Satan. For the Israelites, it was so important that God was the Lord of history that they were not interested in establishing a causal connection between God and Satan. That does not, however, diminish the strong possibility of a catalytic influence of Zoroastrianism upon the Judeo-Christian tradition that served to reinforce and clarify the conception of Satan.

Dramatic Dualism in the Intertestamental Period

In Judaism of the pre-Christian era, which in many respects provides the direct background for the message of the New Testament, Satan was usually understood as the one who sought to destroy the relationship between God and humanity and especially that between God and his people. Moreover, the Old Testament conception of Satan was continued and enlarged during this period. In Enoch, for example, we read that a multitude of satans is led by Satan (1 Enoch 53:3). They have regular access to heaven and can appear before the Lord of spirits (1 Enoch 40:7). Their function is threefold: (1) they accuse human beings before God (69:6), (2) they attempt to incite humans to evil (69:6), and (3) they act as angels of judgment (53:3; 56:1). The satans are responsible for the fall of the sons of God and their marriages to the "daughters of the people" (1 Enoch 69:4). In 1 Enoch 6, it is said that two hundred angels led by Azazel (8:1) took human wives. In the book of Jubilees, we read that these evil spirits "practice all error and sin and all transgression" and that they "destroy, cause to perish and pour out blood upon the earth" (Jub 11:5). Thus Noah asks God to capture the evil spirits and incarcerate them on the site of the destruction (10:5). Sin is here attributed to the fall of the angels and their progeny.

In another passage, we read that humans are responsible for their own sins and that sin can be traced back to the fall of Adam (Apocalypse of Abraham 23 and 26). The fall of the angels or of Adam is not, however, the cause of sin but merely its historical inception. This is expressed clearly in 2 Baruch 54:15, 19: "For, although Adam sinned first and has brought death upon all who were not in his own time, yet each of them who has been born from him and has prepared for himself the coming torment. [. . .] Adam is, therefore, not the cause, except only for himself, but each of us has become our own Adam." It is here asserted that through Adam's fall, physical death came into the world, a thought that is taken up by Paul in the New Testament. The fall, however, is not viewed as the cause of spiritual death. This

---

25. In D. F. A. Bode and P. Nanavutty, trans., *The Songs of Zarathustra: The Gatas* (London: G. Allen & Unwin, 1952), 49 Yasna 30:3–4, we read, "(3) Now in the beginning, these two Mainyu, the twins, revealed themselves in thought, word, and deed as the Better and the Bad; and, from these two, the wise chose aright, but not so the unwise. (4) And thus, when these two Mainyu first came together, they generated life and the absence of life, and so shall human existence continue till the end of time; the worst life for the Followers of the Lie, but the supreme beatific vision for the Followers of Truth."

latter idea is only occasionally found in the Jewish literature of the pre-Christian period—for example, 2 Bar 48:42–43 and 4 Ezra 3:21. Occasionally, Adam is seen as the cause of the corruption of humanity. But at no point is a clear connection drawn between Adam's sin and the sin of his descendants. We read for instance in 4 Ezra, "For the first Adam, burdened with an evil heart, transgressed and was overcome, as were also all who were descended from him. Thus the disease became permanent; the law was in the people's heart along with the evil root, but what was good departed, and the evil remained" (4 Ezra 3:21–22). This means that the free will of humanity was substantially weakened after the fall.

The uninterrupted tenor in the Judaism of the pre-Christian era exhibits itself in the following admonition: "So understand, my children, that two spirits await an opportunity with humanity: the spirit of truth and the spirit of error" (T Jud 20:1). Humanity must choose between light and darkness, between the law of the Lord and the works of Beliar (T Levi 19:1). In the Qumran texts, this demand for personal decision takes on cosmic dimensions. The history of the world is understood as a battle between light and darkness.[26] There exists no neutral ground between the sons of light and the sons of darkness who fight in this world for the final victory. Humanity, however, is not a helpless playing ball in the contest between the two spirits, for humanity receives its destiny from the hands of God. In Judaism of the pre-Christian era, Satan, Beliar, Mastem, or Azazel, as evil was called, was understood as a power that battles against God and brings his honor in dispute. Since the authors of the later Jewish period lived in a time of colossal political and spiritual crises, their perspective is appropriate to the circumstances. Still, they did not simply see the world suspended in an undecided battle that went back and forth. The view still prevailed that God was the ruler of the world. Through the catalytic influence of Zoroastrian Parsism, the Jewish authors could make sense of a hostile world and its history without compromising their Israelite belief in God's ultimate power. They arrived at a dynamic, ethical dualism, the cornerstone of which was already laid in the Old Testament. This "modified dualism," as the American biblical scholar William Foxwell Albright (1891–1971) called it, deeply influenced the Christian faith.[27]

The New Testament

In the New Testament, the central focus is on Jesus of Nazareth; his life, ministry, and destiny; and their implications for humanity. In a dramatic, dualistic manner, his life is depicted in continuous struggle against the anti-Godly powers.

---

26. For the following, see Werner Foerster, "Satanas," in TDNT, 7:156.
27. William Foxwell Albright, *From the Stone Age to Christianity: Monotheism and the Historical Process* (Baltimore, MD: Johns Hopkins University Press, 1957), 362.

Jesus's Struggle against the Destructive Powers

Satan, or the anti-Godly powers (as we prefer to name this destructive force), appears at the decisive events in the life and ministry of Jesus: at the beginning in the story of the temptation of Jesus (Mark 1:12–13) and at the conclusion of his work in the betrayal by Judas Iscariot (Luke 22:3). The story of Beelzebul (Mark 3:22–27) explains that the entire demonic sphere is under the control and supremacy of Satan. "Baal-Zebul" was originally the name of a Syrian god that was mispronounced as Beelzebub, meaning "Lord of the Flies" (cf. 2 Kgs 1:2). At the time of Jesus, Beelzebul was—within Judaism, in many respects—equated with Satan. In Jesus's casting out of demons, the greater act of casting out Satan is made manifest.

But Satan attempts to thwart the ministry of Jesus. The synoptic Gospels show that Satan has made it his goal to further subjugate humanity and especially to hinder Jesus of Nazareth in his effort to bring salvation to humanity. Satan is perceived as the originator of every possible life-degrading disease (Luke 13:16). Thus the work of Jesus, in contrast to the activity of Satan, was directed toward "doing good and healing all who were oppressed by the devil" (Acts 10:38). Satan, the enemy of everything good, sowed his seeds among the "children of the kingdom" (Matt 13:38) and also attempted, through Peter, to destroy the work of Jesus (Matt 16:23). While the destructive power of Satan cannot be overestimated, the New Testament authors reject the popularly held view of the time that every personal misfortune is the result of a person's preceding sins (cf. Luke 13:1–5). Jesus was asked, for instance, whether those eighteen who were killed when the Tower of Siloam fell on them were especially sinful persons. Jesus did not condone the popular notion that every calamity is the result of personal misconduct. Satan certainly causes evil in the world, but Jesus was not interested in establishing an action-consequence connection, a causal linkage between one's sinfulness and the resulting "punishment" through disease or other evils, even if this belief was widespread among the people at that time. Jesus as portrayed by New Testament writers intends much more to show that these evil events can serve the salvific purposes of God.

The New Testament shows not only the destructive powers of Satan, but it also knows that he is defeated through Jesus Christ. Through the story of the expulsion of Beelzebul by Jesus (Mark 3:26–27), it is made clear that Satan has found his conqueror. This fact is confirmed through each of the subsequent actions of Jesus up to and including his sacrificial death (1 Cor 15:57). Satan continues to accuse humans before God, yet Jesus counters these accusations with his intercessions so that their "faith may not fail" (Luke 22:32). Jesus occupies here a position that, in Judaism, was attributed to the angels, especially the archangel Michael. Nevertheless, in Jude 9, we read that the archangel Michael contends and disputes with the devil, and in the book of Revelation, we hear of a "war in heaven" in which Michael and his angels fought against the dragon and his angels. The later "were defeated, and there was no longer any place for them in heaven. The great dragon was thrown down, that ancient serpent, who is called the Devil and Satan, the deceiver of the whole world—he was thrown down to the earth, and his angels were thrown down with him" (Rev 12:8–9).

Though the devil still leads the whole world astray, an important difference existed between the older Judaism and that of the time of Jesus in that Satan had now lost his position of importance and his access to heaven. Jesus saw the creation as it was liberated from Satan and again placed under the reign of God, and he experienced its reality in his works and in those of his disciples. Thus he could claim, "I watched Satan fall from heaven like a flash of lightning" (Luke 10:18). This corresponds with the observation made in the book of Revelation: "For the accuser of our comrades has been thrown down, who accuses them day and night before our God" (Rev 12:10). Since Satan is defeated, it is not surprising that Jesus gives his disciples the authority "to tread on snakes and scorpions, and over all the power of the enemy." They have power over the seductive, anti-Godly forces of evil (Luke 10:19).

As we see from the New Testament Epistles, Satan is once again active, as Jesus is no longer bodily present upon the earth, and seeks to destroy the growing Christian community. Thus Jesus taught his disciples in the Lord's Prayer to pray, "deliver us from evil," so that they do not become subject to the power of evil. But Satan nonetheless sought to bring to naught the work of the apostles (1 Thess 3:5). He persecutes the Christians (1 Pet 5:8–9) and disguises himself as an angel of light in order to lead people astray with false doctrine (2 Cor 11:14). Paul can even say that some of the obstacles encountered in his missionary travels are to be attributed to the influence of Satan (1 Thess 2:18). The God-opposing activity of Satan culminates in the arrival of the antichrist who will proclaim himself to be God (2 Thess 2:3–9). Then the desire of Satan will be fulfilled, as it is expressed in the apocalyptic writing the Life of Adam and Eve "that he will set his throne above the stars of heaven and will be like the Most High" (15:3). Although Christians dare not underestimate Satan, they need not be afraid of him. They are promised, "The God of peace will shortly crush Satan under your feet" (Rom 16:20). Through "the shield of faith," they can "quench all the flaming arrows of the evil one" (Eph 6:16), or they can simply avoid tempting situations (1 Cor 7:5). Christians are not uninformed about the evil one as are the heathen, who do not even realize that they are under the reign of Satan (Acts 26:18).

A dramatically dualistic tendency is especially pronounced in the Johannine writings in which the world is divided into two spheres of influence—one that Christ rules and the other one that stands under the influence of Satan. In the Gospel of John, we read, for example, that the devil was "a murderer from the beginning and does not stand in the truth, because there is no truth in him. When he lies, he speaks according to his own nature, for he is a liar and the father of lies" (John 8:44). In contrast to the divine Logos, he is not "in the beginning" so that an initial dualism is avoided. Instead, he is "from the beginning" and is therefore secondary to the Logos. He is, however, a murderer, the father of lies, and "the ruler of this world" (John 12:31). The human inhabitants of the world are his children. "Everyone who commits sin is a child of the devil," but those who have been born of God do not sin (1 John 3:8–9). Satan or the devil is understood to be the direct cause of sin and evil.

Yet in the dialogue "with the Jews," we hear Jesus say that "everyone who commits sin is a slave to sin" (John 8:34). This means that the children of the devil are at the same time slaves to sin. They cannot break away from sin and their evil deeds. If Jesus makes them free, then they are "free indeed," as Jesus declares (John 8:36). Being enslaved by these evil powers is not an eternal destiny. Although one cannot choose by one's own strength to break the enslavement, Jesus can free one from that bondage. This means that we do not encounter a cosmic dualism in the Johannine writings. There are not two primordial powers, God and the evil forces that fight each other for supremacy. No. God has no equal, and through the coming of Jesus, justice is enforced, and the ruler of this world is expelled (John 12:31). This also shows the difference to gnosticism: the world is not divided between an evil cosmos that is the domain of Satan and a heaven that is a safe haven for all believers in which the heavenly Father reigns. According to John, the world remains the creation of God that is created through the Logos who "came to what was his own," meaning "into the world" (John 1:11). Likewise, humanity is not divided into those who can be saved and those who are already irretrievably lost. Repentance and being born again are still possible (John 3:3), for "God did not send the Son into the world to condemn the world, but in order that the world might be saved through him" (John 3:17). Even if Christians, through faith in Christ, have "conquered the evil one" (1 John 2:13), they are not immediately transported into another sphere. They continue to live in this world, and the caution is hence necessary: "Do not love the world or the things in the world" (1 John 2:15). The German New Testament scholar Rudolf Bultmann (1884–1976) was thus correct when he wrote, "Each man is, or once was, confronted with the deciding for or against God; and he is confronted anew with this decision by the revelation of God in Jesus. The cosmological dualism of Gnosticism has become in John a *dualism of decision*."[28] This dualism, however, will not last forever. "The world and its desire are passing away, but those who do the will of God live forever" (1 John 2:17). This is the hope that the New Testament faith highlights and allows to become a living hope.

If we wish to summarize the biblical insights concerning the correlation between Satan and the cause of evil, we must first emphasize that within the biblical writings is to be found the increasingly clear view that the cause of evil cannot simply be attributed to God. Especially in the political unrest of the postexilic period,

---

28. Rudolf Bultmann, *Theology of the New Testament*, trans. Kendrick Grobel (New York: Charles Scribner's, 1955), 2:21.

trust in God as the provider of all good things could no longer be reconciled with belief in God as the source of both good and evil. In this regard, another significant factor, alongside the catalytic influence of Zoroastrianism, certainly played a role. This factor is simply that in light of the experience of the exile and the postexilic disappointments, God's control of the historical process upon which the salvation of humanity depends could no longer be trusted as long as God contained within himself the potential for evil. Moreover, the Yahwistic narrative of the fall shows that already much earlier the power of evil was understood as something so colossal that one could not imagine that it originated from humanity itself, whether from a single individual or from humanity as a whole. Attributing the cause of evil, however, to a power external to humanity does not lessen the individual and collective responsibility of humans for their actions. However, since it is certain that God is the creator of the entire world, the cause of evil must originate out of God's good creation.

Just how it came to be that something out of God's good creation denied its creator might be interesting for speculative minds but not, however, for the biblical authors. A clear definition of what precisely is meant by "evil" also lies beyond the interests of the Bible. Although evil is often described as something that restricts the life-supporting process, it is for the most part understood at the same time as something that hinders the advance of the kingdom of God. Even biological impairments (such as diseases of physical challenges, like blindness) or natural events (such as earthquakes) can fall under the category of evil. The reason no distinction is made between so-called naturally and spiritually caused evil events appears to be based on the biblical conviction that the whole world is not yet perfected and therefore lies under the spell of imperfection and evil. Yet the biblical witnesses are convinced that both imperfection and the cause of evil must ultimately and occasionally even proleptically glorify God (John 9:3).

The Limits of Human Freedom

While Jesus's ministry was depicted as a continuous battle with God-opposing powers, the situation after Jesus's death and resurrection became even more precarious. When Paul was interrogated by King Agrippa about his mission, he defended himself, saying that he was sent by Jesus Christ to the Gentiles "to open their eyes so that they may turn from darkness to light and from the power of Satan to God, so that they may receive forgiveness of sins" (Acts 26:18). This means that humans are under the power of Satan from which Paul is supposed to free them. In his letter to the Christians in Rome, Paul then tells them that they once had been "slaves of sin," but now they have been set free from sin to become "slaves of righteousness" (Rom 6:17–18). While in their former lives they were unable to obey God and his precepts, now this obedience to God is done willingly, joyfully, and naturally. It is not done by coercion, as with literal slaves, even if Paul uses the term *slaves of righteousness.*

The letter of James makes it clear why bad things happen when he writes, "No one, when tempted, should say, 'I am being tempted by God'; for God cannot be tempted by evil and he himself tempts no one" (Jas 1:13). It is evident here that God is not the source of good and evil and is also above any temptation. God is the source of everything good. Yet one should also not immediately look at the evil one for the bad, since Jesus already cautioned, "Do you not see that whatever goes into a person from outside cannot defile" (Mark 7:18). "It is what comes out of a person that defiles. For it is from within, from the human heart, that evil intentions come" (Mark 7:20–21).

This evil that arises out of humans themselves is not inconsistent with the simultaneous conviction that an evil (one) as the ultimate ground of the negative stands behind humanity. Testimony to this ultimate ground of evil is to be found in the negative things that we receive fatefully in our own lives (Luke 16:25). Finally, the human individual is also confronted with the evil actions of others (Rom 13:3–4). Yet according to Paul, all persons know that they themselves commit the evil that they want to avoid and do not accomplish the good for which they strive (cf. Rom 7:19). From this perspective, evil is understood not only as moral evil but also as a self-contradictory lifestyle. Evil is the godlessness in which human beings continually find themselves.

Humans, to be sure, want to do good and honor and obey God. They have not yet entirely forgotten their inner purpose and their origin in God the creator. But they are not able to get any further than the most modest approaches to a just way of life. They sink repeatedly into sin so that they are no longer their own masters when they do these things but succumb to "sin that dwells within" them (Rom 7:20). Sin is thus the activity of humans who have lost their anchorage in God. This alienation from God expresses itself in evil deeds. Nevertheless, Paul appeals, "Do not be overcome by evil, but overcome evil with good" (Rom 12:21). This takes place, on the one hand, by putting to death evil desires (Col 3:5) and, on the other, through the love that does no evil (Rom 13:10)—a possibility facilitated through the love that comes from Jesus Christ.

In the New Testament, evil is described by the Greek words *kakos* and *poneros*. The first occurs less frequently and is limited to the human realm, "for God cannot be tempted by evil and he himself tempts no one" (Jas 1:13). The second term, *poneros*, is used to indicate evil; it confronts us first of all in the sense of the Old Testament term *raah*, as that which is not useful or unsuitable—that is, as that which is as such negative. Thus we read that an evil or bad tree produces bad fruit (Matt 7:18) and that one can be an evil or wicked servant (Matt 18:32). *Poneros* can also, however, mean "bad," "dangerous," or "disastrous" so that we read of the "evil day" as a critical day that brings with it great distress (Eph 6:13) or metaphorically of a "foul [evil] and painful sore" (Rev 16:2) that afflicts humanity. Much more frequently, however, we read of evil people (Matt 7:11) who stand in contrast to God who alone is good. Thus Jesus can speak of an "evil and adulterous generation" (Matt 12:39) that because it contains evil can only bring forth evil things (Matt 12:35). Those who are evil appear to have decided against Jesus and are therefore threatened with eschatological judgment.

When people are evil in their basic orientation, they will be fatefully drawn ever further into the web of evil. Thus Paul speaks of those who are "wicked people and impostors," for they slide ever further into the evil for which they themselves are the agents (2 Tim 3:13). From the heart come "evil intentions," in which context "evil" can be the translation of *poneros* as well as of *kakos* (Matt 15:19; Mark 7:21). In addition to individual stirrings of the senses, the entire person can be called evil (Heb 3:12). The wickedness spoken of here consists in "apostasy from faith, in self-will and turning from God." If the human conscience is separated from God, it can be called "an evil conscience" (Heb 10:22). The deeds committed by believers in their pre-Christian lives are also characterized as evil (Col 1:21), since they occurred under the sign of enmity with God. Paul can thus speak of "every evil attack" from which the Lord will rescue him, whereby he perhaps makes concrete reference to an evil plot against him or to imprisonment or persecution (2 Tim 4:18). Also interesting is a passage in Matthew, which recurs in a similar form in Luke, in which an "unclean spirit" that brings still other spirits "more evil than itself" is spoken of (Matt 12:43, 45; Luke 11:24, 26). It appears that reference to a hierarchy of evil spirits is made here, a view that one also finds in late Judaism.

Finally, John speaks of evil actions that are carried out by people in darkness rather than in the light (John 3:19). The actions of the world that occur in antithesis to the light and to the revelation of God are fundamentally evil (John 7:7), for they do not originate from God. Whatever is contrary to the Gospel is evil, for it is the word of God that decides what is good and evil. Here we encounter once more a dramatic dualism that John introduces through his use of contrasts, such as good and evil or light and darkness.

Alongside the adjectival use of *poneros*, through which certain forms of behavior or things are more precisely labeled, we encounter frequently in the New Testament the substantival use of *poneros* through which evil is spoken of in the singular or plural. Thus we hear in a parable of Jesus that at the end of the world, those who are evil will be separated from the righteous (Matt 13:49) or in the Sermon on the Mount that God makes the sun "rise on the evil and on the good" (Matt 5:45). Both passages show that Jesus rejects a strict application of the action-consequence connection. The just and the unjust live together upon the earth, and only at the end of time are they separated, and the evil ones receive the punishment that they have earned. At the same time, Jesus indicates that it is through God's generosity that good and evil persons still live together. This means not that God is indifferent toward humanity but rather that God's generosity rises above our understanding of justice and that he genuinely intends what is good for both good and evil persons, for the just and the unjust.

Not only a person or persons can be denoted by the term *poneros*, but in the singular form, this substantive can also represent the devil as the evil one who stands in absolute contrast to God. This is the meaning of the word, for instance, in the parable of the sower in Matthew: "When anyone hears the word of the kingdom and does not understand it, the evil one comes and snatches away what is sown in the heart" (Matt 13:19). In the parallel passage in Mark, however, we read, "Satan immediately comes and takes away the word that is sown in them" (Mark 4:15). In the version of this parable found in Luke's Gospel, we read that "the devil comes and takes away the word from their hearts" (Luke 8:12), in which "devil" is a translation of the Greek word *diabolos*. Thus we see that Satan, or the devil, can also be denoted as "the evil one." We find this also outside of the Gospels—as, for instance, in Ephesians 6:16, where "the flaming arrows of the evil one" are spoken of. The term *poneros* is employed on several occasions to indicate Satan. In 1 John, we read of the evil one who is defeated by Christians (1 John 2:13–14). The human individual is the battlefield in the conflict between Christ and Satan. Those who are in Christ, however, have already been victorious and have fought on the side of Christ.

Often, "evil" appears to be used in a neuter sense. We see this, for instance, in the explanation of the parable of the tares, in which Jesus speaks of the children of the kingdom (of God) and the children of the evil one (Matt 13:38). A similar usage of *poneros* in neuter form is to be found in Jesus's high priestly prayer in which Jesus, making reference to his disciples, prays that God will "protect them from the evil one" (John 17:15). And finally, in the Lord's Prayer, Jesus asks that God deliver us "from the evil one" (Matt 6:13). When in regard to this last passage reference is made to the distress of the last days—that is, to eschatological evil, a conception with parallels in the Pauline tradition (as, for instance, in the promise to the Christians in Thessalonica that God would guard them "from the evil one" [2 Thess 3:3])—one may not simply remain with this neuter usage of the phenomenon of "evil." Evil is no simple neuter. Especially in its eschatological orientation, it cannot be attributed to sinful human efforts with any less difficulty than it can be derived from God. The term *evil*, therefore, must remain open to include the concept of an "evil one." This metaphysical connection gives evil the weight and the threatening force that is repeatedly demonstrated in the New Testament. In the final analysis, this means that humans do not simply have the power to do or not to do evil, but rather, they stand under the power of sin—that is to say, they are overshadowed by the power of evil.

God as the Lord of History and Human Entanglement in Evil

We have seen so far that the life and destiny of Jesus was a continuous battle with the forces of evil. Humans are victims of these forces and are unable to extricate themselves from the evil that they willingly pursue. Jesus as the human face of God appeared on this earth not as the doomsday prophet to proclaim God's punishment for a sinful world but to bring back humanity and the whole of creation from their alienation to these destructive forces. At the same time, he was deeply aware of the reality of sin and human alienation from God. Yet he understood himself in his words and actions as the conqueror of sin. Therefore, he announced, "I have come to call not the righteous but sinners" (Matt 9:13), and "there will be more joy in heaven over one sinner who repents than over ninety-nine righteous persons who need no repentance" (Luke 15:7). He discloses himself to those to whom he is sent and who live in alienation from God. He desires to bring them back to God. The extent of God's rejoicing over the repentance of humans is illustrated, for example, in the parable of the prodigal son (Luke 15:11–32). In this parable, it is also clear that sin signifies the forsaking of the parental home for godlessness and alienation from God.

Jesus desires to lead individuals back to God and shows them that God will once more accept them and rejoice over their return. Sin, however, is no trifling matter but rather something that requires remorse and repentance (Luke 15:21) as well as the recognition that one has wronged God through the alienation from him. As the one who proclaims the reign of God, Jesus eats with sinners, removes the barrier between the sinner and God, and establishes a new community with God. He does not erect barriers between himself and those who live in alienation from God. This is demonstrated in the symbolic act of the sinful woman (Luke 7:37–39), in the instance of the tax collector Zacchaeus (Luke 19:1–3), and in the parable of the prodigal son (Luke 15:11–13), as well as by many additional words and deeds of Jesus.

Jesus's relationship to sin is expressed most clearly in his sacrificial death. This becomes evident in the explanatory words of the Lord's Supper. At the institution of the eucharistic meal, Jesus gives the disciples the chalice with wine and pronounces, "This is my blood of the covenant, which is poured out for many for the forgiveness of sins" (Matt 26:28). Jesus describes his death as an eschatological Passover offering. His substitutionary death (for many) puts into effect the final redemption, "the new covenant of God."[29] Jesus understands himself as the eschatological Passover lamb through whose death the realization of salvation is made possible. As promised in Jeremiah 31:31–34 and explained by Jesus at the institution of the Lord's Supper, a new covenant is being established that through the death of Jesus will be set in force. Analogous to the blood of the Passover lamb, the blood of Jesus is the blood of the covenant. Thus the words of Deutero-Isaiah concerning the servant of the Lord are fulfilled: "He bore the sin of many, and made intercession for the transgressors" (Isa 53:12). As the New Testament writers show, Jesus is the servant of the Lord who through his suffering and death bears the sins of humanity and overcomes the gulf between God and sinful humanity.

The words and actions of Jesus indicate that God seeks communion with sinners and that God's new world is dawning. Through his death and resurrection, a

---

29. See in this regard Joachim Jeremias, *The Eucharistic Words of Jesus*, trans. Norman Perrin (New York: Charles Scribner's, 1966), 226.

new reality has emerged: sin is defeated, and the foundation for God's new world is laid. For this reason, Jesus is described by John the Baptist in the Gospel of John as the lamb of God "who takes away the sin of the world" (John 1:29). Jesus is the one who builds a bridge over the chasm of sin separating God and the world and who sacrifices himself for the many. Through Jesus, however, a division in the world is also brought about. The judgment announced in the kingdom parables of Matthew 13 becomes a present reality. Those who do not believe that Jesus is the self-disclosure of God will die in their sins (John 8:24). If Jesus, therefore, had not come and confronted humanity with the self-disclosure of God, they would have still been without sin—that is, without the knowledge of their sins (John 15:22). Only in confrontation with Jesus as God's self-disclosure people realize that they live in sinful alienation from God. Now they have no longer an excuse for their sins, for they could have recognized who Jesus was and what God required of them. It is precisely for this reason that they see but do not perceive and that they are burdened with sin (John 9:41). Christ has come into the world and confronted his audience with the decision between life and death. Whoever accepts him receives the word of forgiveness; whoever rejects him remains in his or her own sins. The "helper" or "comforter" that Jesus will send furthers the work of Christ, for he will convict the world of "sin and righteousness and judgment" (John 16:8).

One can also, however, sin out of ignorance in regard to the Son of Man. Such sin carries with it no eternal consequences. It is forgivable. When one rebels, however, in the face of Jesus's message and curses it, even though one recognizes it through the Holy Spirit, then in full awareness of the actual situation one has pronounced judgment upon one's own self. Such sin against the Holy Spirit is unforgivable.[30] Those who in full awareness set themselves against God and his revelation are separated from God, and this separation cannot be removed.

Jesus has given us the possibility to once more draw close to God from our state of sinful alienation from him. This occurrence is reflected in the Gospels. Paul goes one step further and reflects on the consequences of Christ's death and resurrection. First, however, he demonstrates that humans have always fallen short of their own being, for their aspirations are from the very beginning perverted and evil. In the opening chapters of his Letter to the Romans, he points out that humans have no excuse for their evil inclinations. They know the will of God, but in their actions, they do exactly the opposite (Rom 1:32). The reason for this is clear, for through Adam, sin and death have entered the world as ruling powers (Rom 5:12). This cannot, however, serve as an excuse for human misbehavior, for humans do willingly the opposite of that which they have recognized to be good. Those who

---

30. So Walther Grundmann, "Hamartia," in TDNT, 1:307. Otto Procksch, "Hagios," in TDNT, 1:104, claims that this saying has a "Pentecostal content." Important, however, is the intention of the sin, that it takes place with full knowledge and awareness and thereby excludes itself from the possibility of forgiveness. Whether one can conclude, however, that the sin against the Son of Man is forgivable, since God's presence in him is still hidden, is questionable because the decision against him has eternal consequences.

have fallen into sin no longer possess their own will, which could lead them to do what is right. Thus Paul can say, "For I do not do the good I want, but the evil I do not want is what I do. Now if I do what I do not want, it is no longer I that do it, but sin that dwells within me" (Rom 7:19–20). Humans still have, therefore, the ability to want to do what is right, but they lack the strength to carry it out. Humans are the subject not of their sinful actions that they do against their own wills but rather of the sin that possesses them. Sin and its power, therefore, can take on directly personal characteristics.

The term *law* plays an important role in the Pauline understanding of sin and is used by him in very different ways. For example, Paul speaks of the law in the sense of a compulsive necessity in that evil is present in humans even though they want to do good. Then Paul confesses that he rejoices within over the law of God, whereby he means the Law of Moses, the Torah. Finally, he speaks of another law that exists within his members that is in conflict with the law of his reason and holds him captive to the law of sin by which his members—that is, his carnal impulses—are ruled. With this testimony, we encounter the contrast between the good commandment or law of God and that law that prevails through sin—that is, that which through longings awakened by sin desires that which the law forbids. A means of death and sin, therefore, has developed out of God's good gift of the law. This is to be seen in the example of Adam, who would have never known sin had not the law prescribed that he should not desire, thus awakening desire within him. Paul will not, however, simply set aside the law, for he knows that the law is good. But the law was and is too weak to fend off sin. Thus it brings sin to our awareness but does not help us become free from sin. Rather, it is precisely through the holy law (Rom 7:12) that we are entangled ever more in sin, since we are overpowered by desire, violate the law, and bring about our death and our own eschatological judgment.

This fall into sin and death, which Paul emphasizes very strongly, leads necessarily to the question of whether humans still bear responsibility for their actions on the basis of which they could be held accountable. Two things are to be noted here: First, by their own nature, as Paul emphatically states, humans have no chance to escape from sinfulness. Rather, their own efforts lead them ever deeper into sin. We may think here of Martin Luther when he had entered the monastery. He tried everything to please God. But the more he tried the more he became aware that his actions were still deficient. This is precisely what sinful persons notice when they recognize that they do what they do not want to do. Therefore, they sin not blindly but rather knowingly and, one could say, also willingly. Second, regarding the question of individual responsibility, however, a second point is even more important, which Paul addresses in the following manner: "For the law of the Spirit of life in Christ Jesus has set you free from the law of sin and of death" (Rom 8:2). Hence humans have a way out and can live freely and responsibly. This way is only open, however, through the redemptive work of Christ and not through our will.

Therefore, Paul can joyfully announce, "But thanks be to God, who gives us the victory through our Lord Jesus Christ" (1 Cor 15:57). The one who rejects this possibility that Christ opens has willingly rejected the freedom from the compulsion of sinning and is fully responsible for his or her own actions.

Paul, therefore, says nothing about the genetic or psychological constitution of humanity. He views humanity, rather, from one of two possible viewpoints: either from the perspective of not having the possibility that Christ has made available or from the perspective of this new possibility. What Paul says about sin, therefore, is "oriented to the revelation of God in Christ. Hence it is not an empirical doctrine of sin based on pessimism. It is the judgment of God on man without God as it is ascertained from the revelation of Christ and revealed in full seriousness in the cross of Christ."[31] In contrast to Jesus, Paul lived already in a Christian age. From this vantage point, he could look back upon what had been made possible through Christ. Paul himself had sought to use the law as a means of salvation and had, for this reason, persecuted the early Christian community. Sin, therefore, not only is an offense against the divine majesty but constitutes also an active enmity against God and a striving against God's will.

In agreement with Judaism, Paul answered the question of the origin of sin by affirming that sin came into the world through Adam. The first human being set himself against God, and thus sin was born. With sin, death also came into the world, for it is, so to speak, the consequence of sin, since there is no life in alienation from God. As N. T. Wright alerted, "The entry of death into the world through the first human sin is to see 'death' here as more than simply the natural decay and corruption of all the created order."[32] Through the reign of death, the universality of sin is to be seen, for all people are marked by death. Death, however, is not a fatalistic power, as it was thought to be in Hellenism and Greek culture, but rather the human individual's own power that pursues sin and through which death gains its mastery. Sin is thus the author of everything evil.

For Paul, sin is not only a single deed but a universal context within which all persons find themselves. Human individuals are from the very beginning of their lives placed within a condition of collective sinfulness so that they no longer have the freedom to choose whether to do good or evil. We could say that sin is contagious. An inseparable connection therefore exists between Adam's action and our own condition. It must, however, be emphasized that Paul did not develop a doctrine of original sin in which sin is passed from one person to the next. Rather, he has seen the entirety of humanity in its alienation from God, which made it impossible for humanity, of its own accord, to return to God. That there is an escape from this context of sin is made apparent to Paul in pointing to Christ's death and resurrection. The powers of darkness, the evil action of humans at Calvary, did

---

31. So Grundmann, "Hamartia," 308.
32. N. T. Wright, *The Letter to the Romans*, in NIB, 10:526, in his exegesis of Rom 5:12.

not win the day. Through the power of the Holy Spirit, God resurrected Christ to a new and imperishable life-form. This demonstrated that negativity, death, and sinful behavior had lost. Therefore, Paul could claim with the hymn in Philippians 2 "that at the name of Jesus every knee should bend, in heaven and on earth and under the earth, and every tongue should confess that Jesus Christ is Lord" (Phil 2:10–11). With the Easter event, it has become clear who rules the world, not the powers of darkness, but God in Christ Jesus.

The death and resurrection of Jesus, as the overcoming of our own entanglement in sin, are bound closely by Paul with baptism. "For if we have been united with him in a death like his, we will certainly be united with him in a resurrection like his. We know that our old self was crucified with him so that the body of sin might be destroyed, and we might no longer be enslaved to sin" (Rom 6:5–6). Through baptism, we receive by transferal what Christ has done for us through his death and resurrection—namely, substitutionary atonement for our sins and the overcoming of the barrier of death. In baptism, our old humanity dies, and we are born again as new persons. Paul qualifies this, however, by pointing out that as Christians, we continue to live upon this earth and thus are not yet released from our sinful context, even if we must no longer sin unavoidably. Paul can therefore admonish Christians to live a Christ-conforming life. Sin shall no longer reign over Christians, for we are no longer under the law but are under grace (Rom 6:14).

While humans under the law are in the grip of the demonic power of sin that rules them and "rewards" their actions with death, sin has been overcome through the Christ event. The One who knew no sin was made sin for us so that in him, we might experience the righteousness of God (2 Cor 5:21). Through Christ and his overcoming of sin, we have become new creatures. The cross is the symbol of victory over sin and the demonic reign of death. The preaching of the cross is thus the power and wisdom of God through which human pursuits of salvation are declared insufficient and irrelevant. Through baptism, we are dead to sin and liberated to new life. This great change must continually be brought to the awareness of humans so that they can fend off the lordship claims of sin and not submit once again to a new servitude. Christians stand, therefore, in a suspenseful dilemma: on the one hand, they are liberated from sin, but on the other, they are so menaced by sin and its power that they must be called to daily renewal. Only through the return of Christ will sin and its final effect—death—be fully destroyed, and the reign of life that began in Christ will be carried out universally and visibly. Thus the Christian in active anticipation of the universal reign of God awaits the future glory of God's kingdom that shall be made manifest (Rom 8:18).

When we summarize how the rule of God in the world is depicted according to the perspective of the New Testament, we notice, in continuation to the Old Testament hopes and expectations, that salvation from the powers of darkness and evil has drawn nearer. In Christ, God has claimed victory over these powers in a preliminary way. Humanity is still in a world characterized by its entanglement in evil. The hope shines through, however, as in the Old Testament, that this state of affairs that is characterized by the reign of evil and sin will be replaced by the universal reign of God. Moreover, an improvement is recognized, for in the Christ event, the foundation for a new world order has already been laid that is experienced for the individual as a present reality through baptism and participation in the Lord's Supper. Humans, therefore, no longer simply fall into evil. They no longer stand under the disastrous compulsion of alienation from God and rebellion against God. On the contrary, they can already participate in the new communion with God. Humanity has been given a new covenant. This cosmic turning point is made possible through the Christ event, for in Jesus of Nazareth, evil has met its vanquisher. Through his self-sacrifice on the cross, he has essentially disarmed evil and given us the possibility of new life. Yet why the new world promised in the Old Testament and proleptically anticipated in the Christ event has not yet been inaugurated is not thematized in the New Testament writings. This is part of the enigma of world history and of the history of each individual human being who eventually faces death and therefore makes theodicy an ever-new topic of theological reflection.

3 The Early Church

Since the first Christians expected that the end of the world would come soon, there was not much initial interest in the existence of evil as a historical or cosmological phenomenon. All the evils of the world would soon be overcome, and to that effect, Christians also strove for moral perfection. Yet how could they achieve this?

Irenaeus: Humans Are Created in the Image of God

Irenaeus originally came from Asia Minor, but then after the death of Bishop Pothinus of Lyons in 177 CE, Irenaeus became bishop in that city and died around 200 CE.[1] He wrote a massive tome, *Against Heresies*, in which he battled especially against dualistic gnosticism. His starting point was that a human person "was made in the likeness of God."[2] Through the fall, however, humans lost the similitude.[3] But not everything is lost of the original likeness of God. As Irenaeus asserts, a human being "left carnal, shall be an imperfect being, possessing indeed the image [of God] in his formation (*in plasmate*), but not receiving the similitude through the Spirit; and thus is this being imperfect."[4] Imperfection does not mean that a human being cannot do the good. Irenaeus insists, "There is no coercion with God, but a good will [toward us] is present with Him continually. And therefore does He give good counsel to all. And in man, as though as in angels, He has placed the power of choice."[5] Humans have a free will to do the good or to do the wicked both with corresponding consequences.

Irenaeus himself raises the question of why God has not made human beings perfect from the very beginning.[6] His answer was that everything that is created has to be somewhat inferior to the one who created them. While God could have created humans perfect from the very beginning, humans could not receive this perfection, since they were newly created. Perfection and immortality are therefore attained only in the eschaton. The free human being is supposed to be obedient to God to become immortal. "Because man is possessed of free will from the beginning, and God is possessed of free will, in whose likeness man was created, advice is always given to him to keep fast the good, which thing is done by means of obedience to God. And not merely in works, but also in faith, God

---

1. Cf. Paul L. Maier, *Eusebius: The Church History; A New Translation with Commentary* (Grand Rapids, MI: Kregel, 1999), 181.
2. Irenaeus, *Against Heresies* (5.6.1), in ANF, 1:531.
3. Irenaeus (5.16.2), 544.
4. Irenaeus (5.6.1), 532.
5. Irenaeus (4.37.1), 518.
6. Cf. Irenaeus (4.38.1), 521.

has preserved the will of man free and under his own control."[7] This means that humans have a free will not just to do good works but also to be faithful to God. On account of this freedom, God exhorts us to submit ourselves to God's precepts, but in no way are we coerced to be faithful to God. Irenaeus also rhetorically asks how Jesus and the apostles could have given us commandments if we were not able to follow them.

Yet why would people sin? The answer for Irenaeus is simple: in a state of confusion, Adam transgressed God's command and thereby "lost his natural disposition and child-like mind."[8] God then drove Adam out of Paradise, and since God pitied him, he removed him far from the tree of life that he should not continue to sin forever, "nor that the sin which surrounded him should be immortal, and evil interminable and irremediable."[9] On the one hand, sin was all around, but on the other, there was to be an end to sin, since sin should not be present forever. Almost like a remedy, Adam had to die eventually so that he would cease to live with sin and might begin to live with God. Nevertheless, all of humanity was disobedient in Adam and was "cursed by God,"[10] which meant, as a consequence, that "in Adam we do all die, as being of an animal nature."[11] Evil then has become something natural in human beings, since they are likened to animals.

It is clear for Irenaeus that God cannot be blamed for evil. It is the free choice of the humans, albeit being seduced by the serpent, who then received severe punishment from God. For humans, however, free choice is important, as Irenaeus declares, "But if some had been made by nature bad, and others good, these latter would not be deserving of praise for being good, for such were they created; nor with the former be reprehensible, for thus they were made [originally]. But since all men are of the same nature, able both to hold fast and to do what is good; and, on the other hand, having also the power to cast it from them and not to do it,— some do justly receive praise."[12]

There is a logical necessity, according to Irenaeus, for humans to have free choice for good and bad, and there is also a logical necessity for the bad, since otherwise the good deed did not deem a reward, since it would be a necessity on account of the missing choice. There is a logical necessity of the bad to exist. The good needs the contrast to the bad. Otherwise, it could not be perceived as good. There is indeed this bad, the intent of which is to destroy the good and which creates havoc in God's good creation. But this destructive character of the bad seems to be outside of Irenaeus's reflections. Augustine, who lived two centuries later, is more discerning in this matter.

7. Irenaeus (4.37.4), 519.
8. Irenaeus (3.23.5), 457.
9. Irenaeus (3.23.6), 457.
10. Irenaeus (3.23.3), 456.
11. Irenaeus (5.12.3), 538.
12. Irenaeus (4.37.2), 519.

Augustine: God's Providence and the Existence of Evil

Augustine (354–430 CE), later bishop of the North African city Hippo Regius, present-day Annaba in Algeria, joined the Manicheans at age nineteen, although he was already a catechumen—that is, a candidate for baptism—in the Christian church. The young Augustine found the rational understanding of evil by the Manicheans especially attractive. Their dualistic proposal to understand the world as a battlefield between the principles of good and evil and to ascribe the origin of the immoral to the later appeared to free him of personal responsibility for evil. Yet after about ten years, he no longer found the Manichean doctrine satisfying, and he came under the influence of Bishop Ambrose of Milan, whose understanding of the Old Testament greatly impressed him. He also engrossed himself in the study of neo-Platonic philosophy, especially in the works of Plotinus (204–70 CE). In 385 CE, he had broken free of Manichaeism and the next year decided to once again become a catechumen in the Christian church. In this year, late in 386 CE, he wrote a dialogue in two books with the title *De ordine* (On order), which on the basis of its content, one might better translate as "Divine providence and the problem of evil."[13]

In this writing, Augustine tackles the problem of evil. He is confronted immediately with the dilemma that if evil is real, then God is either not almighty or he himself wills evil. In the face of this alternative, he admits that he would rather portray God as limited in his sphere of activity than label him as the author of evil and thereby as cruel. Augustine next distinguishes natural evil, as it is manifest—for example, in natural catastrophes—from moral evil, which is seen in the human will.[14] Evil within nature can, according to Augustine, have either a goal or be completely senseless. Though many natural occurrences surpass the limits of human understanding, one cannot simply attribute them to chance. They must fulfill some purpose that transcends human understanding. Nevertheless, Augustine admits that many natural occurrences appear to make no sense. Augustine suggests, however, that we probably have too anthropocentric a starting point to easily perceive a divine purpose within such events. Rather than occupy ourselves with detailed questions that could be painful for us, we should seek to view our own misfortune in light of a universal plan.

The perfection of the universe postulated by Augustine is not easily reconciled with his unmerciful openness to the reality of evil. Another problem is his assumption that God is always just. In light of the fact that there is also injustice in the world, it is a short step to the conclusion that evil exists eternally alongside God. Neo-Platonism appears to offer a solution to this dilemma, which Augustine

---

13. For the dating of this work, see the edition in J.-P. Migne, *Patrologiae Cursus Completus, Series Latinae*, in MPG, 32:977–1022.
14. For a summary of this dialogue, see David E. Roberts, "The Earliest Writings," in *A Companion to the Study of St. Augustine*, ed. Roy W. Battenhouse (New York: Oxford University Press, 1969), 100–103.

follows in locating the origin of evil in nonbeing. God did not, therefore, cause evil, since no positive reality exists outside of divine providence. Yet the examples given by Augustine are unconvincing. He mentions, for instance, the example of cockfighting and believes that beauty is to be found even in this brutal sport, since it occurs in accordance with the laws of nature. In another place, he introduces the example of the gruesome office of executioner, which is indeed something negative yet contributes to the order of a well-functioning state. He similarly describes prostitution as evil yet suggests that its elimination could lead to even greater evils. Everything evil, according to Augustine, contributes to perfection, since its nonoccurrence would destroy perfection. At this point, one is tempted to ask why evil should be resisted at all when it contributes to good.

Although not completely satisfying, this dialogue is Augustine's first attempt to free himself from a Manichean type of dualism. Evil is allowed no place of its own but must rather always contribute to the good. Augustine does not remain, however, with the enigmatic character of evil, probably out of fear that this could once again be interpreted dualistically.

In another dialogue, begun two years later and completed in Africa, Augustine went a decisive step further. As he wrote in his *Retractations* at the end of his life, the work was written in order to refute the Manichean claim that Christians ultimately attribute evil to God. The work *De libero arbitrio* (On free will) was highly rated by Augustine as well as by his contemporaries. He commented in a letter to Jerome, "A few years ago I wrote some books on free will—which have gone out into many hands and are possessed by many more. [. . .] [I opposed] with all my might those who were trying to prove that nature was endowed with its own principle of evil in conflict with God. These were the Manichaeans."[15] This relatively short writing, in the form of a dialogue between Augustine and Evodius, a youth from his hometown of Tagaste, begins with the fundamental question, "Is not God the cause of evil?"[16]

Augustine distinguishes between committing evil and suffering from evil. Since God is good, he cannot commit evil. Yet because God punishes evil and this punishment is itself experienced as something evil, God is the cause of suffering from evil in the sense of a divine punishment. The evil that we do is done by us freely, otherwise it could not be justly punished. Augustine goes a step further and maintains that the evil deeds of humans are not learned, since learning and teaching are good. To this, Evodius asks from whence evil comes if it is not learned (1.2.4). Augustine replies that this question had driven him into heresy, since he wanted to find an answer to it. Finally, he arrived at the following explanation: "We believe that everything which exists is created by one God, and yet that God is not the cause of sin. The difficulty is: if sin goes back to souls created by God, and souls go back to

15. Augustine, *Retractations* (1.8.2), in FaCh, 60:32.
16. For this and the following, see Augustine, *The Problem of Free Choice: De libero arbitrio*, in ACW, 22, here (1.1.1):35.

God, how can we avoid before long tracing sin back to God?" (1.2.4). In order to avoid this conclusion, we must, according to Augustine, assume that God is almighty and completely immutable. He is the creator of all good things, although he transcends these, and he is the perfectly just ruler over everything that he has created. He is self-sufficient and unassisted by any other being in the act of creation.

After clarifying his understanding of God, Augustine sought to establish his conception of evil. When something evil takes place, its dominant motive is to be located in the *libido* or the *cupiditas*, meaning "in human passion" (1.4.9). Evil deeds such as murder, blasphemy, and adultery arise out of human passion. Even when one commits evil deeds out of fear, the motive is still to be found in covetous desires—namely, in the desire for a life without fear. Of course, human law can permit something that we perceive as evil so that passion is excluded from an evil deed. But such a law would be contrary to the eternal law that consists of principles that, in contrast to human laws, never change. That which is correct in temporal laws is derived from the eternal law that alone should be our point of orientation. Augustine speaks next of the distinction between humans and animals and explains that humans possess a spirit that determines and directs all other elements within them so that they are directed according to the divine order (1.8.18). Human wisdom, then, consists in giving such place to the human spirit that passion cannot reign over humans, for apart from God, there is nothing better than a sensible and wise spirit. The spirit is therefore rightly punished when it enslaves passion and sins.

At the beginning of the second book, Evodius asks why God has given humans a free will, to which Augustine replies that without a free will, humans could not live as humans. Evodius then asks why this decision of God was correct if we are able to misuse our free will. Augustine attempts to explain that the free will is good. According to Augustine, we possess three types of good things: virtues, which we cannot misuse; bodily things, which Augustine does not regard as being of particular importance; and the power of the soul as a good of secondary status. This later can be either rightly or wrongly used. It is used correctly when we place our trust in God, for he is unchanging good, truth, and wisdom, and humans can obtain a happy life through him. Evil consists in turning away from the unchanging good. Since we do this freely, the consequent punishment is just.

In the third book, Augustine takes up the subject of God's foreknowledge and declares that no predestination is implied here. Yet what Augustine says concerning natural evil is hardly convincing. He dismisses, for example, the problem of suffering among children by saying that there is no need to suffer any longer once suffering (along with this life) has come to an end. Additionally, one does not know what compensation God has in store for such children who suffer. Also, the question concerning the suffering of animals only shows that we understand nothing of the nature of the excellence of the supreme good, for animals are by nature mortal. We see also by the suffering of animals that the souls of all creatures "strive for unity in governing and animating their bodies." They resist division and corruption, and through their struggle against suffering, they point to the fact that they were created for unity (3.23.69). Finally, Augustine reflects on the possibilities possessed by the first human pair and claims that they had the means by which, if they had used them well, they could have risen to what they did not possess—that is, wisdom (3.24.72). There is a distinction between whether humans are wise or merely blessed with reason. Humans, however, have forsaken the heights of wisdom. For Augustine, Satan also comes into the picture here. He writes, "And that is 'pride, the beginning of all sin; and the beginning of the pride of man is to fall off from God' (Sir 10:13). The devil added malevolent envy to his pride when he persuaded man to share his pride, through which he knew he was damned. So it was that man suffered punishment designed to correct him rather than to destroy him" (3.25.76).

Finally, Augustine comes to the subject of *superbia* (pride), the beginning of all sin. This writing, therefore, does not pursue the issue of free will, although this topic is repeatedly touched upon, but rather aims to demonstrate, as the opening sentence announced, that God is not the cause of evil. The problem of free will, however, cannot thus be passed over, for it is closely bound up with the problem of evil. When at the end of this writing Augustine addresses once again the question of why there is not only good but also evil, he cannot, in contrast to his earlier work *De ordine*, simply answer that evil belongs to the good. Rather, he must maintain that evil stems from *libido*, *cupiditas*, and *superbia*, whereby God, however, cannot be made in any way either directly or indirectly responsible for evil, since he is immutable and essentially good. Yet Augustine has not yet understood evil dynamically enough as an actual opponent of God. Owing to his own Manichean past, he did not have the courage to do this, since he feared that he might lapse into "heresy." He viewed evil as something that contradicted ratio and was essentially connected with the will. It is still largely a deficiency of the good. It is the power that continually opposes, which is separated from God and which sinks into corruption and base actions.

Only one side of reality is thus addressed—namely, that there is just one primal principle: God. This God is just and good. Everything that is evil has no causal relationship with God but exists on the basis of its own self and in opposition to God. As Augustine correctly admitted in his *Retractations*, there is yet another side: "For it is one thing to inquire into the source of evil and another to inquire how one can return to his original good or reach one that is greater. Hence the new Pelagian heretics who treat free choice of the will in such a way as not to leave a place for the grace of God, for they assert that it is given according to our merits, should not boast as though I have pleaded their cause."[17] Because Augustine said very little here about the necessity of grace for the attainment of salvation, the Pelagians sought, albeit unjustly, to cite him as a supporter of their own position. In this publication, Augustine dealt almost exclusively with

17. Augustine, *Retractations* (1.8.2–3), 33.

the question of the origin of evil. This in turn raises the question of how evil can be overcome or avoided.

We have seen that Augustine argued for the unity of God over against the dualistic worldview of Manichaeism. According to Augustine, there are neither two separate principles, one good and one evil, nor is there a graduated order of reality in which, so to speak, good is stronger than evil so that it will ultimately prevail. Rather, there is only one God and one creation. When evil exists, and Augustine never entertained the slightest doubt as to its reality, then it exists only to the extent that a part of God's good creation has risen up against its creator and entered into conflict with him. Many questions, however, remain unanswered, such as issues concerning the origin and function of that within nature that is objectively bad. Likewise, despite Augustine's assertion that humans themselves are responsible for their sinfulness, this was not thought through so thoroughly as to overcome all contradictions in relation to human freedom and responsibility. Not surprisingly, there has been much conflict over the question of the relationship between freedom and accountability in the early church, at the start of the Reformation, and at many other periods in the history of the church.

Before we leave Augustine, we should consider one more point: the issue of "just war." Augustine is convinced "that there is no such thing as a human heart that does not crave for joy and peace."[18] Even a robber, he claims, maintains some kind of peace, however shadowy, with those he cannot kill, and certainly in his own home he wants to be at peace with his wife and children. Humans are peace loving. Yet there is one war after another. Augustine explains, "A good man would be under compulsion to wage no wars at all, if there were not such things as just wars. A just war, moreover, is justified only by the injustice of an aggressor; and that injustice ought to be a source of grief to any good man, because it is human injustice."[19] For the sake of peace and to ward off the injustice of an aggressor, one can wage a just war. Augustine does not consider that such a war again inflicts misery on both good and bad people. Since Augustine is convinced that "there can be no nature completely devoid of good," there is no radical evil that stands over against God. And since God cannot be the source of evil either, evil actions are the result of human actions.[20] From these evils and all others, we are freed only by death. To demarcate himself from Manichean dualism, he did not dare to go any further. Furthermore, the notion that this world, though good, is not yet perfect was not developed further by Augustine either.

18. Augustine, *City of God* (19.12), abridged ed. (New York: Doubleday Image, 1958), 451–452.
19. Augustine (19.7), 447.
20. Augustine (19.13), 457.

4 Middle Ages and the Reformation Period

When we come to the Middle Ages, we naturally focus on Thomas Aquinas, since even today he is the most prominent representative of that period. During the Reformation, however, his indebtedness to Aristotle brought him under great suspicion by the reformers, especially by Martin Luther. Yet in 1567, he was elevated to teacher of the church by the Roman Catholic Church.

Thomas Aquinas: The Goodness of God and the Deficiency of Evil

Thomas Aquinas (1225–74) was born in the castle Roccasecca near the town of Aquino. As a five-year-old, he was sent to the Benedictine monastery Monte Cassino, where a brother of his father was abbot. He first studied at the University of Naples, and in 1244, he entered the Dominican order against the will of his relatives who wanted to see him as successor of his uncle at Monte Cassino. Then he studied the arts with Albert the Great (ca. 1200–80) and followed him to Cologne. He taught in Paris and Rome, where he wrote his *Summa Theologica* and many of his commentaries on the works of Aristotle. His *Summa*, a massive multivolume work, is a masterpiece of Scholastic theology and expounds the Christian faith in every detail through a question and answer method. It is by far the most influential theological product of the Middle Ages.

In considering generally the issue of goodness in his *Summa*, Thomas asserts that every creature of God is good. "Therefore no being can be spoken of as evil, formally as being, but only so far as it lacks being. Thus a man is said to be evil, because he lacks some virtue; and then an eye is said to be evil, because it lacks the power to see well" (ST 1q5a3o2). Evil therefore is a deficiency and not the result of some active evil force. Thomas marshals the support of Socrates and Aristotle to arrive at the conclusion that everything is called "good" by reason of the similitude of the divine goodness belonging to it, which is formally its own goodness. Thereby, it is denominated good.

In question 22 of the *Summa*, Thomas deals with divine providence. At the outset, he asserts that "it is necessary to attribute providence to God," for all the good that is in created things has been created by God (ST 1q22a1o3). This is true not only in regard to their substance but also with regard to the order toward an end. And the good order existing in things created is itself created by God. The next question then is whether everything is subject to the providence of God. He concedes that it looks like not everything is governed by providence. For instance, providence would exclude necessity, since things done by necessity would not need any providence, and it would also exclude chance and, of course, anything evil. Yet Thomas counters these objections, saying, "The providence of God is nothing less than the type of order towards an end, [. . .] it necessarily follows that all things, inasmuch as they participate in existence, must likewise be subject to divine providence" (ST 1q22a2o5r). Providence is then primarily the ordering toward an end in an ultimate and penultimate sense. It is the providential activity not in each minute detail but rather in the overarching ultimate goal. This, of course, immediately raises the question of whether God also executes intermediate providence over everything. Thomas now distinguishes between the prime cause that is God and secondary causes that are the executors of his orders. While we cannot understand many things simultaneously, this is different from God "who sees everything simultaneously at one glance, and who still cannot turn in the direction of evil" (ST 1q22a3r3). But with the assertion that God oversees everything and that God cannot turn toward evil, Thomas has not really answered the question of providence with regard to detail. His reference to the human limitation seems to imply also that our perception with regard to providence in detail is limited. This means God's ways are not always within our possibility of comprehension.

The next question that Thomas tackles is whether divine providence imposes necessity on every occurrence. Here he observes that some events occur by necessity, while others are contingent. Since the latter are not actually part of the causal nexus but occur, so to speak, spontaneously, Thomas can assert that "the mode both of necessity and of contingency falls under the foresight of God, who provides universally for all being; not under the foresight of courses that provide only for some particular order of things" (ST 1q22a4r3). Providence assures that there is some order of things that will ensue in a preordained goal. History then moves forward to that goal either through the chain of cause and effects or through contingent occurrences. But in both instances, it is divine providence that makes it happen.

When Thomas addresses the issue of evil, he states at the outset that what evil is must be known from the nature of good, whereby evil is "the absence of good" (ST 1q48a1o5r). We heard this already from Augustine: that good is the overarching status, and evil is its deficiency. Since evil is a privation of the good, it does not affect anything by itself. This would mean that evil is not a serious matter. But Thomas goes on and asks whether evil can corrupt the whole good, since good and evil are contraries. He concedes that this is possible when the good is opposed to evil (ST 1q48a4o3r). Then the good is totally destroyed, such as light through darkness. In other cases, the good remains unaffected or is only diminished.

But why is there evil when God created everything good? Since evil is the absence of good, there must be some cause that draws the good out of its proper disposition. The good does not cause evil that would be contrary to itself. Yet evil is a reality, and for Thomas, God as the principle of good has created the world in which evil shows itself. Good is then perceived as the cause of evil, albeit as an "accidental cause" and not as a direct one. Since through divine providence everything is good, this would immediately lead to the question of whether God as the supreme good is then not the cause of evil. This is exactly the issue that Thomas addresses next.

As to be expected, God cannot be the cause of evil. Thomas explains, "The evil which consists in the defect of action is always caused by the defect of the agent. But in God there is no defect, but the highest perfection, as was shown above (I:4:1). Hence, the evil which consists in defect of action, or which is caused by defect of the agent, is not reduced to God as to its cause" (ST 1q49a2o3r). While God is not the cause of evil, if evil is considered a fault, God is the cause of evil as far as it is a penalty when justice requires it for the sinner. Whether death meted out by God against the sinner can be considered evil in the true sense of the word, as Thomas describes it, is debatable.

Thomas also clearly denies any dualism between good and evil when he declares "that there is no one first principle of evil, as there is one first principle of good" (ST 1q49a3o6r). The admission of two first principles makes one forget the universal cause of all being, and one considers only the particular causes of particular effects. Thomas states, "In the causes of evil we do not proceed to infinity, but reduce all evils to some good cause, whence evil follows accidentally." Indeed, there is no primordial dualism. Yet with the interference of evil from some good cause, not only the evil one is denied but also those anti-Godly powers that threatened to undo God's salvific plan and moreover who will create havoc on earth. Thomas then considers the status of angels and concedes that just like any other created beings, angels can sin. The demons, meaning the fallen angels, exhibit envy and pride. The devil, a fallen angel, desired to be as God, "to have dominion over others" (ST 1q63a3r).

While Thomas does not clearly distinguish between fallen angels, demons, the devil, and so on, it is very clear for him that God did not create anybody fallen or sinful. God's creation was good from the very beginning. Yet once they were created, by their own volition, they moved away and became the devil and the demons. Therefore, Thomas writes, "The agent which brought the angels into existence, namely, God, cannot be the cause of sin. Consequently it cannot be said that the devil was wicked in the first instant of his creation. [. . .] All were created in grace, all merited in their first instant. But some of them at once placed an impediment to their beatitude, thereby destroying their preceding merit; and consequently they were deprived of the beatitude which they had merited" (ST 1q63a6r). Though the demons cannot change the human will, they still tempt humans to sin. But not all sins are committed at the devil's instigation. Some are due to the free will of humans. This means that humans commit sin either by their own choice or by the instigation of the devil. Regardless, they become children of the devil, since they imitate the one who was the first to sin. Therefore, Thomas can claim that the devil is the cause of all our sins because he instigated the first human being to sin, "from whose sin there resulted a proneness to sin in the whole human race" (ST 1q114a3r). While the sins of humanity are ultimately the result of human decisions, they fall back to the first sin committed by the first human being and from there to the devil who instigated the first human being to sin. By sinning, humans become children of the devil.

For Thomas, it is clear that God cannot be blamed for anything in the world that goes wrong, whether on the human level or beyond. God is the creator of the good world and of beings who initially at least were good. Nevertheless, one might ask why God has allowed so much evil to exist in the world when he is the originator of everything that is and created it to be good. Even if things or beings deviated from the original goodness, why has God allowed this to happen, and why has he not brought them back on the track of goodness? Thomas did not address these vexing issues.

John Calvin: The World Is Governed in All of Its Parts by Divine Providence

John Calvin (1509–64), in his massive work titled *Institutes of the Christian Religion*, endeavors to show that God rules the world in every detail. The providence of God as taught in Scripture is opposed to the notions of fortune or luck. All the events whatsoever are governed by the secret counsel of God. Whether the sun rises in the morning or spring follows winter, this is all due to God's providence. This providence follows from God's omnipotence and is ever active. God "overrules all things that nothing happens without his counsel."[1] This means that God's providence is executed through God's actions. In God's incomprehensible wisdom, everything is directed toward God's aims. This means that God not just maintains the order that he has imposed on nature but cares for each of the individual works. Even humans cannot achieve anything without God's power. Calvin sums up, "Everything done in the world is according to his decree" (*Inst* 1.16.6).

Even natural phenomena, such as storms, floods, and fires, are not coming forth without God's special command. There is neither fate, as the Stoics asserted, nor any necessity but only God's blessing, which provides for success, and God's curse, which ensues in calamities and adversities. Calvin refers here to Augustine, who claims, "For nothing is done visibly or sensibly, unless either by command or permission from the interior palace, invisible and intelligible, of the supreme Governor, according to the unspeakable justice of rewards and punishments, of favor and retribution."[2] Though God's counsel, according to Calvin, follows a certain

---

1. John Calvin, *The Institutes of the Christian Religion*, trans. Henry Beveridge (Grand Rapids, MI: Eerdmans, 1957), 1.16.3, accessed April 15, 2019, https://tinyurl.com/4juv7.
2. Cf. Calvin (1.16.8); and see Augustine, *On the Trinity* (3.4), in NPNF FS, 3:59.

arrangement. For us, the accidental meaning is for the most part hidden in God's counsel and therefore cannot be discerned according to the order, cause, purpose, or necessity. Though we do not always understand why something happens, "we ought undoubtedly to hold that all the changes which take place in the world are produced by the secret agency of the hand of God" (*Inst* 1.16.9).

God's providence extends to both past and future because God wants to show with it that he takes care of the whole human race. Again, with reference to Augustine, Calvin claims that God has assumed the right of "governing the whole world, a right unknown to us, let it be our law of modesty and soberness to acquiesce in his supreme authority regarding his will as our only rule of justice, and the most perfect cause of all things."[3] While Calvin is convinced that God governs the whole world with no exception, at the same time, he claims that God's counsel is sometimes withdrawn from our understanding. The only support for Calvin's claim of God's governance is therefore inferred from the biblical witness.

The overarching activity of God does not condone human frivolity. "A provident man, while he consults for his safety, disentangles himself from impending evils; while a foolish man, through unadvised temerity, perishes" (*Inst* 1.17.4). God wants us to use our own good judgment so that we neither tempt God to rescue us because of our missing precaution nor run into calamity. While in this case any human misery is self-induced, the issue becomes more complicated when Calvin writes, "We cannot say that he who is carried away by a wicked mind performs service on the order of God, when he is only following his own malignant desires" (*Inst* 1.17.5). While we cannot but agree with that statement, it sounds inconsequential coming from Calvin. Just before, he asserted that everything done in the world is according to God's decrees. Are the wicked mind and the malignant desires ensuing from God's decrees? Is God then ultimately responsible for good and for bad? If the world is God's theater, then no other conclusion is possible. When Calvin concludes, "He obeys God, who, being instructed in his will, hastens in the direction in which God calls him," he is again contradicting his own presupposition (*Inst* 1.17.5). How can one hasten in the direction in which God calls one, disentangling oneself from evil, if everything is done according to God's providence? Are we then just puppets, and God pulls the strings so that we act according to God's precepts? Again, the all-inclusive providence seems to preclude any true human responsibility.

According to Calvin, even Satan is under God's power, and therefore, Calvin argues that "even the devil himself who, we see, durst not attempt anything against Job without his [God's] permission and command" (*Inst* 1.17.7). This is certainly true in the case of Job, as we have noted previously, since in that story, Satan is considered to be part of the heavenly court. But this does not make undone the later recognition in the biblical documents that Satan is also the adversary of God. Yet

---

3. Calvin, *Institutes* (1.17.2); Augustine, "27. On Providence," in *Eighty-Three Different Questions*, vol. 70, FaCh, 70.

for Calvin, world history and the history of each individual are acted out in God's theater, where "God arms the devil, as well as all the wicked, for conflict, and sits as umpire, that he may exercise our patience" (*Inst* 1.17.8).

Calvin explains, "The devil, and the whole train of the ungodly, are, in all directions, held in by the hand of God as with a bridle, so that they can neither conceive any mischief, nor plan what they have conceived, nor how much soever they may have planned, move a single finger to perpetrate, unless in so far as he permits, nay, unless in so far as he commands; that they are not only bound by his fetters, but are even forced to do him service" (*Inst* 1.17.11). We can rest assured that God is in absolute control, and the evil powers can do nothing to undo God's plans. Calvin comforts us with the conviction that if misery and disaster afflict us, we should remember that all prosperity has its source in the blessing of God and all adversity in God's curse. We are referred back here to Job, who too concluded that both good and bad come from the Lord.

Calvin realizes the difficulty in which he has moved himself. Therefore, he muses, "From other passages, in which God is said to draw or bend Satan himself, and all the reprobate, to his will, a more difficult question arises. For the carnal mind can scarcely comprehend how, when acting by their means, he contracts no taint from their impurity, nay, how, in a common operation, he is exempt from all guilt, and can justly condemn his own ministers" (*Inst* 1.18.1).

Frequently, one has distinguished between God's doing and God's permission. Yet Calvin feels that this distinction does not hold true, since humans cannot affect anything unless God would permit it. Referring again to the book of Job, Calvin shows that in effect, the temptations for Job have God as their originator. The same is true in the situation of Ahab. Through God's judgment, the perfidious Ahab was deceived and the devil offered his agency for that purpose (cf. 1 Kgs 22:20–22). God not just permitted the downfall of Ahab but decreed that it should happen. As it is with the devil, so it is with humans. God also directs our minds insofar as "whatever we conceive in our minds is directed to its end by the secret inspiration of God" (*Inst* 1.18.2). Calvin leaves the impression that there is no free will for anybody except God. Concerning the role of Satan, Calvin contends again, "God often acts in the reprobate by interposing the agency of Satan; but in such a manner, that Satan himself performs his part, just as he is impelled, and succeeds only in so far as he is permitted" (*Inst* 1.18.2). There is no anti-Godly power, since Satan becomes, for Calvin, an agent of God. He does, so to speak, God's dirty work. In wondrous and ineffable ways, things are done not without God's will but contrary to that will. When Calvin talks here about God's "secret providence," one wonders how he has received that information (*Inst* 1.18.4). The same problem arises when Calvin sums up how God works evil in evil persons. He writes, "While by means of the wicked God performs what he had secretly decreed, they are not excusable as if they were obeying his precept, which of set purpose they violate according to their lust" (*Inst* 1.18.4). When Paul talks about humans being in bondage to sin, then it is clear that they are directed not by God but by another power. Yet for Calvin, there is only one efficacious power—namely, God. All others are derived from that one power. In order not to implicate God with evil deeds, Calvin has to resort to God's "secret decrees." Again, the question must be posed, How do we know? By his adamant insistence on God's sole activity, Calvin exceeds the limits of human knowledge. As Israel herself realized in the long run, God cannot be the cause of good and evil without becoming a trickster.

Martin Luther: Though There Is Turmoil God Rules Supreme

Martin Luther (1483–1546) believed, very similar to Calvin, God is in absolute control of all affairs. If that were not the case, salvation would be in jeopardy and so would be grace. This conviction is shown most prominently in *The Bondage of the Will* (1525), directed against the eminent Dutch humanist Erasmus of Rotterdam (1466–1536).

The Hidden and the Revealed Will of God

In *The Bondage of the Will*, Luther distinguishes between the preached and compassionate will of God on the one side and the hidden and terrible will of God on the other. Concerning the latter, he claims, "This will is not to be inquired into, but reverently adored, as by far the most inspiring secret of the Divine Majesty, reserved for himself alone and forbidden to us" (LW 33:139). Luther continues, "To the extent, therefore, that God hides himself and wills to be unknown to us, it is no business of ours. For here the saying truly applies, 'Things above us are no business of ours'" (LW 33:139). Insofar as God remains in his majesty and in God's self, we have nothing to do with him because God does not want that to be sought there.

Luther distinguishes God's hidden aspect from the God who offers himself to us through his word and, clothed in human form, makes himself known. He chides Erasmus for not distinguishing between the hidden and the revealed God. Luther contends, on the one hand, that we cannot uncover the secrets of the majesty of God, since God dwells in an inaccessible light (cf. 1 Tim 6:16). On the other hand, he insists, "Let it [i.e., humanity] occupy itself instead with God incarnate, or as Paul puts it, with Jesus crucified, in whom are all the treasures of wisdom and knowledge, though in a hidden manner [Col 2:3]; for through him it is furnished abundantly with what it ought to know and ought not to know" (LW 33:145–46). The preached God is therefore God incarnate in Jesus Christ.

But there is this other dimension of God: God who does many things without explaining it through his word and intends many things without expressly mentioning through his word that he intends them. "Thus he does not will the death of a sinner, according to his word; but he wills it according to that inscrutable will of his" (LW 33:140). Luther is convinced that nothing can occur without God at least permitting it to happen. When Luther occasionally juxtaposed God and the devil, he did not abandon his conviction that God still ruled God's creation and the devil was God's devil. But why then do so many bad things happen in this world? Searching for an answer in the hidden God, Luther warns, would push us even more deeply into despair. It is rather the preached and revealed God who enables us to make sense of all the cruelty in this world. Even when we cling to God's word of grace, however, we still remember that God is ultimately behind everything and that in his inscrutable will, God wants the death of the sinner. This means that turning to the revealed God and recognizing that God does not want the death of the sinner does not completely solve our anxiety. Coming from the revealed God, we must acknowledge, however, that it is due to our will that we perish. Nevertheless, there remains the awareness of the inscrutable will of the hidden God that reminds us that death is God's own doing. As Luther explains, there is an alien work of God that works indiscriminately everything in everything, as we see with the hardening of Pharaoh's heart (Exod 7:3). But Luther insists we must flee from this mysterious and hidden God to the revealed God, to his graciousness in Jesus Christ.

Yet there remains this other, mysterious dimension of God. Distinguishing between the hidden and the revealed God, Luther did not solve the issue of evil and suffering. With fear and trembling, he remembered that even God incarnate experienced this hiddenness on Golgotha. Therefore, Luther concedes, "This belongs to the secrets of his majesty, where his judgments are incomprehensible [Rom 11:33]. It is not our business to ask this question, but to adore these mysteries" (LW 33:180).

Luther confronts a mystery in God that he cannot explore but that he adores, since it is part of the divine majesty. But adoration is not the reason for Luther to talk about the hidden God. He introduces the notion of a hidden God to avoid seeking God in the wrong place. He rightly distinguishes between that which is knowable of God because he has allowed himself to be known and that which is and remains inscrutable. Any speculation would rather hinder than further our work as theologians, as Luther explained in the *Heidelberg Disputation* (1518). There he introduced the distinction between a theology of glory and a theology of the cross. The cross of Christ became for him an important interpretative tool to discern how God does work—namely, under the appearance of the opposite of what we would expect.

Emphasizing the hiddenness of God's work under the appearance of the opposite, Luther intends thereby not just to say that God does not wish to be sought where God has not revealed his own self; it is also decisive for Luther that God alone, in the revelatory event, is the one who works. God chose the way of the cross that he might remain the sovereign Lord of all saving work and of the entire revelatory event. No one expected salvation to occur as it actually did. This has been true from the very beginning. We see this with the so-called astrologers who inquired first in the city of Jerusalem about the newborn king of the Jews, not in the unimportant village of Bethlehem (Matt 2:2). God does not allow his salvific work or the divine self-disclosure to be grasped by any rational principle. We are always dependent on God's self-disclosure to discern God's ways.

Since God is God, his eternal plan and providence stand behind all things. The divine power is sovereign and cannot be restricted. Salvation lies beyond our power and depends wholly upon God. Luther concludes from this that when God is not present and at work in everything that we do, the result will be evil, and we will necessarily do that which is of no avail for our salvation. Luther does not mean, thereby, that without the spirit of God, humans do evil against their will as if they were physically forced to do so; rather, he means that they do evil out of their own obliging will. One is quite naturally reminded here of Luther's hymn "A Mighty Fortress Is Our God" (in *ELW*, 228), where he writes, "No strength of ours can match his might! We would be lost, rejected."

Luther speaks of a necessity of unchangeableness—that is, that the human will is not only unable to change itself and go in the right direction but also inclined to continue in its original evil direction. When God works graciously within us, the will is changed and acts likewise out of its own inclination and its own willing and not out of coercion so that it cannot be changed toward the wrong direction through an opposing will. Just as the will previously willed and found satisfaction in evil, it now wills and rejoices in that which is good. Luther thus comes to the point that is most discussed and that he explains as follows:

If we are under the god of this world, away from the work and Spirit of the true God, we are held captive to his will, as Paul says to Timothy [2 Tim. 2:26], so that we cannot will anything but what he wills. For he is that strong man armed, who guards his own palace in such a way that those whom he possesses are in peace [Luke 11:21], so as to prevent them from stirring up any thought or feeling against him; otherwise, the kingdom of Satan being divided against itself would not stand. And this we do readily and willingly, according to the nature of the will, which would not be a will if it were compelled; for compulsion is rather (so to say) "unwill." But if a Stronger One comes who overcomes him and takes us as His spoil, then through his Spirit we are again slaves and captives—though this is royal freedom—so that we readily will and do what he wills. Thus the human will is placed between the two like a beast of burden. If God rides it, it wills and goes where God wills, as the Psalm says: "I am become as a beast [before thee] and I am always with thee" [Ps 73:22–23]. If Satan rides it, it wills and goes where Satan wills; nor can it choose to run to either of the two riders or to seek him out, but the riders themselves contend for the possession and control of it. (LW 33:65–66)[4]

The first impression of Luther's argument is that he introduces a dualism that divides the world into two spheres of influence. The focus here is not the two powers (God and Satan), however, but rather humanity. Humans, according to Luther, live not in a neutral vacuum but always in a particular context that decisively influences them and from which they orient their lives and in which they live. If this context is formed by God, then they desire and do that which is of God. If, however, it is determined by the anti-Godly powers, humans desire and do what the interests of these powers demand. Even when one takes both powers into consideration, Luther leaves no doubt that God wins as the stronger of the two. As we will see later, Satan is not equal in power to God but is a creature, even if he has anti-Godly rank, and is ultimately dependent on God for his being. Humans only have freedom within a context that is determined either by God or by the anti-Godly powers. As creatures, humans do not have the freedom to choose their context but rather live within a context or sphere of influence that they can only leave if they are transferred into the other context. The questions of freedom of the will and freedom of choice are not thereby touched upon, but rather, the question of whether humans can choose by their own power the sinful context, a possibility that Augustine always emphasized, is discussed. Luther, however, appears to reject this possibility, since he seems to advocate a twofold predestination toward good and toward evil.

Luther next distinguishes between the preached and offered grace of God, on the one hand, and the hidden and frightening will of God, on the other. In the latter, God determines through his own counsel that persons shall be the recipients of his preached and offered grace. One can only worship the divine will in reverence but cannot penetrate it. This awesome aspect of the divine majesty is reserved for God alone.

> God must therefore be left to himself in his own majesty, for in this regard we have nothing to do with him, nor has he willed that we should have anything to do with him. But we have something to do with him insofar as he is clothed and set forth in his Word, through which he offers himself to us and which is the beauty and glory with which the psalmist celebrates him as being clothed. In this regard we say, the good God does not deplore the death of his people which he works in them, but he deplores

4. As noted there, the simile of the beast and its riders are not Luther's own invention. As a student of Augustine, he gleaned it from a pseudo-Augustinian writing. See the detailed study by Harry J. McSorley, *Luther: Right or Wrong? An Ecumenical Theological Study of Luther's Major Work, "The Bondage of the Will"* (Minneapolis: Augsburg, 1969), 129–215, who provides here a helpful historical-theological overview.

the death which he finds in his people and desires to remove from them. (LW 33:139–40)

We must distinguish "between God preached and God hidden, that is, between the Word of God and God himself" (LW 33:140). Since God is all-working and there is no other power equal to him, Luther must necessarily distinguish between two wills in God: the revealed will, out of which good comes to us, and the hidden will, which we ultimately cannot ground and which contains, so to speak, that which is cruel and evil. The later also predestines certain persons to evil. It is through God's will, as it were, that it is decided whether certain persons come to stand in the sphere of influence of God the Redeemer or whether they spend their lives under the reign of evil in alienation from God. Why someone would be excluded from salvation is not answered by Luther, who instead points to the hidden will of God that we can ultimately only worship and honor but not fathom.

Luther sought to shed light upon the evil that God works in still another way and gives the hardening of Pharaoh as an example. The starting point here is the assumption that God does not cause sin. Luther begins with the efficacy of God and reminds Erasmus that he himself admitted that God works all in all (1 Cor 12:6).

Now, Satan and man, having fallen from God and been deserted by God, cannot will good, that is, things which please God or which God wills; but instead they are continually turned in the direction of their own desires, so that they are unable not to seek the things of self. This will and nature of theirs, therefore, which is thus averse from God, is not something nonexistent. For Satan and ungodly man are not nonexistent or possessed of no nature or will, although their nature is corrupt and averse from God. [. . .] Since, then, God moves and actuates all in all, he necessarily moves and acts also in Satan and ungodly man. But he acts in them as they are and as he finds them; [. . .] When God works in and through evil men, evil things are done, and yet God cannot act evilly although he does evil through evil men, because one who is himself good cannot act evilly; yet he uses evil instruments that cannot escape the sway and motion of his omnipotence. (LW 33:175–76)

Because of the omnipotence with which God moves all things, Satan is able to hold on to his followers. Yet God does not work in such a way that he himself brings about evil, a fact that Luther continually emphasized, but he rather moves further along and hardens that evil that he finds already before him. Evil occurs not through a mistake of God but rather through our false behavior, since we are evil through our fallen nature. In accordance with God's omnipotence, evil persons are driven further along in their own evil activity, although God, in accordance with his wisdom and for God's glory and our salvation, can also use this evil for good.

Two points are here noteworthy: first, Luther's statement that "he [God] cannot help but do evil with an evil instrument" (aliter facere non possit) and second, that Satan became evil "through God's deserting it and Satan's sinning" (LW 33:178; deserente Deo et peccante Satana malam factam). The fact that God made Pharaoh's will unrepentant can be derived from God's omnipotence. That he could not have changed Pharaoh's will, however, appears at the very least unusual and would seem to contradict God's omnipotence. Also, the fact that Satan became evil because God forsook him and he sinned seems to trace evil back to God, a consequence that Luther does not want. He wishes rather to show that it is an aspect of God's omnipotence to move everything further along, whether good or evil, according to its own character. In this way, he begs the question of why God does not transform evil into good but instead actually strengthens evil in its wickedness. Luther advises that this belongs to the mystery of God's majesty, which we can only worship but cannot explain. God is simply God, and for God's will, there is no cause or rule of reason that we could use as a measure, since nothing is equal or superior to his will, but his will is itself the ruler of all things. Hence God himself is the final rule and measure of his action and his judgment.

At the conclusion of The Bondage of the Will, Luther summarizes his argument once more in three points: First, God foreknows and predetermines all things. He can neither make mistakes in his foreknowledge nor be hindered in his predetermining. Nothing happens that God does not will to happen. Second, Satan is the ruler of this world who constantly battles against the kingdom of Christ with all his might. He would allow no one to escape the sphere of his power if he were not forced to do this through the divine power of the Spirit. Third, original sin has so damaged us that it causes many problems in the fight against evil even in those who are led by the spirit of God. Without the help of the spirit of God, therefore, there is nothing in humans that is able to turn toward the good but rather only toward evil.

For Luther, humans have an inclination toward evil placed upon them by original sin and turning away from God and seeking to please themselves. Erasmus interprets Luther's view as determinism. He desires, therefore, despite the recognition that humans are sinful, to hold fast to the idea that humans can contribute at least something to their salvation. But Luther does not embrace determinism. This becomes clear when he concedes that there is a kingdom to the left in which humans can do what they will through their own choice and counsel, while in the other kingdom (to the right), things are directed by the choice and counsel of God. Erasmus makes no distinction between the two kingdoms. Worldly respectability leads, for him, simultaneously to heavenly acceptance. It is not surprising, then, that the key thoughts of On the Bondage of the Will, even if they appear to be extreme, are necessary for Luther's dispute "with a theology that is largely semi-Pelagian or has even become Pelagian."[5] Luther emphasizes God's omnipotence so much so that in an implicit way, God also becomes the author of evil even if Luther vehemently rejects this idea. Yet this overwhelming insistence on God's omnipotence is mitigated by a conflict motif that was also advanced by Luther.

Two Kingdoms in Conflict

While in his massive work *The City of God* Augustine describes the conflict between two cities—the city of this world and the city of God that are ruled by opposite standards—Luther, as a former Augustinian, employed the metaphor of two kingdoms.[6] Yet for Luther, these two kingdoms are not just side by side or even mixed together, as Augustine suggests. They are in continuous conflict. Luther writes,

> There are two kingdoms. The first is a kingdom of the devil. In the Gospel the Lord calls the devil a prince or king of this world [John 16:11], that is, of a kingdom of sin and disobedience. To the godly, however, that kingdom is nothing but misery and a vast prison. [. . .] Thus he who submissively serves the devil in sin must suffer much, especially in his conscience, and yet, in the end, he will thereby earn nothing but everlasting death. Now all of us dwell in the devil's kingdom until the coming of the kingdom of God. However, there is a difference. To be sure, the godly are also in the devil's kingdom, but they daily and steadfastly contend against sins and resist the lusts of the flesh, the allurements of the world, the whisperings of the devil. After all, no matter how godly we may be, the evil lust always wants to share the reign in us and would like to rule us completely and overcome us. In that way God's kingdom unceasingly engages in combat with the devil's kingdom. [. . .] The others dwell in this kingdom, enjoy it, and freely do the bidding of the flesh, the world, and the devil. If they could, they would always stay there. [. . .] The other kingdom is that of God, namely, a kingdom of truth and righteousness. [. . .] It is the state when we are free from sin, when all our members, talents, and powers are subject to God and are employed in his service. [. . .] That comes to pass when we are ruled not by sin, but only by Christ and his grace.[7]

The kingdom of the devil is the world in which everyone lives, whether Christian or non-Christian. Luther takes up here, along with Augustine, the testimony of John 16:11 that tells us that Satan is the prince of this world. In his familiar, realistic

---

5. Bernhard Lohse, "Dogma und Bekenntnis in der Reformation: Von Luther bis zum Konkordienbuch," in HDT, 2:39.
6. On the distinction between the two kingdoms, cf. Cargill Thompson, *Studies in the Reformation: Luther to Hooker*, ed. C. W. Dugmore and Philip Broadhead (London: Athlone, 1980), 45, who traces the distinction of the two kingdoms back to Augustine.
7. Martin Luther, *An Exposition of the Lord's Prayer for Simple Laymen*, in LW, 42:38–40.

manner, Luther does not glorify the world as the already in-breaking kingdom of God, but he rather characterizes it as a place plagued by many problems and evils. In this kingdom of the devil, we must persevere and defend ourselves, for we are constantly in conflict with the devil. Luther indicates much the same thing in his *Small Catechism* when he writes "that the old person in us with all sin and evil desires to be drowned and die through daily sorrow for sin and through repentance, and on the other hand that daily a new person is to come for and rise up." The kingdom of God struggles with the kingdom of the devil, although the former is, in a strict sense, an eschatological phenomenon that only fully breaks into the world when the latter passes away. Luther also points out that the kingdom of God does not come with outward signs but is already present in humans and that we should pray that it will be established and increase within us and grow strong. God's grace and his kingdom together with all virtues shall come to us just as "Christ came to us from heaven to earth; [for] we did not ascend from earth into heaven to him."[8] While the kingdom of the devil manifests itself outwardly, the kingdom of Christ is an inner power active in Christians.

Christians and non-Christians differ from one another in that the latter follow the will of the devil. They seek to advance his kingdom and to destroy the kingdom of God. Therefore, they do not come out of the kingdom of the devil into the kingdom of Christ but, according to their own desire, remain eternally in the kingdom of the devil. Humanity is then divided into two kinds of persons: the one belongs to the kingdom of God but must live in the kingdom of the devil, while the other not only lives within the kingdom of the devil but belongs to it as well.

One cannot simultaneously belong to both kingdoms. Luther expressed this clearly in *The Bondage of the Will* when he wrote,

> For Christians know there are two kingdoms in the world, which are bitterly opposed to each other. In one of them Satan reigns, who is therefore called by Christ "the ruler of this world" [John 12:31] and by Paul "the god of this world" [2 Cor 4:4]. He holds captive to his will all who are not snatched away from him by the Spirit of Christ, as the same Paul testifies, nor does he allow them to be snatched away by any powers other than the Spirit of God, as Christ testifies in the parable of the strong man guarding his palace in peace [Luke 11:21]. In the other kingdom, Christ reigns, and his Kingdom ceaselessly resists and makes war on the kingdom of Satan. Into this Kingdom we are transferred, not by our own power but by the grace of God, by which we are set free from the present evil age and delivered from the dominion of darkness. [. . .] We are bound to serve in the kingdom of Satan unless we are delivered by the power of God. (LW 33:287–88)

8. Luther, 42:41.

If the kingdom of God or the kingdom of Christ did not exist, all humans would be delivered over to the kingdom of Satan. There is no escape from this kingdom unless Christ liberates us so that we are freed from its sphere of influence and transferred into that of the other kingdom. We remember that in *The Bondage of the Will* Luther compared the individual to a beast of burden that is ridden either by God or by Satan. The members of the kingdom of God follow Christ and are one with Christ and he with them, whereas the members of the kingdom of the devil follow the devil and are one with him. In contrast to Augustine, an individual and existential perspective is clearly to be seen in Luther. He does not stress so much the opposing structure of the two kingdoms as he does the opposing manner in which Christians and non-Christians conduct themselves.

If Satan is indeed the prince of this world, as Luther continually emphasizes in agreement with John 12:31, should one then not simply write off this world as evil? It would be a distortion of Luther's position if the world were simply given over to the devil. It is rather the other way around because the devil's power in this world is limited. He is a created being, for he was originally a part of God's good creation. As such, he cannot be equal to God. Although Luther sometimes dramatizes God and the devil dualistically, for him, the devil stands not primarily beside God and over humanity but rather between God and humanity. The devil, so to speak, obstructs our view of God so that humans mistake the devil for God and in presumed obedience to God serve the devil.

In Luther's view, angels are the soldiers, keepers, guides, and governors of God's creation.[9] It is their task to watch over and lead us and the creatures of this creation, whereby they do battle not only for the pious but for all people. Of course, Satan, in Luther's view, since he is the god of this world, has under him many other devils—that is to say, evil angels. These evil angels govern everywhere, from the pope and the emperor to the princes and even in private homes. Through them, the works of the devil are produced, which we see and experience but which the world does not recognize for what they are. As experience shows, the good angels contend with the evil angels. Yet we should not let ourselves be too intimidated. Even if Christ calls Satan the prince of this world, it is God who is the creator and ruler of all. Satan cannot even harm a hair on our head "except by God's will and permission" (LW 6:90). Luther consoles us with these words:

> The power of the devil is not as great as it appears to be outwardly; for if he had full power to rage as he pleased, you would not live for one hour or retain safe and intact a single sheep, a crop in the field, corn in the barn, and, in short, any of those things which pertain to this life. [. . .] You will find more good than bad things and you will also see that a very small part is subjected to the power of the devil. For he is compelled to leave the fish

9. For this and the following, see Martin Luther, *Lectures on Genesis* in LW, 6:87–88.

in the rivers, the birds in the air, the men and animals in the villages and cities, which he would not do if it were not for the protection of the angels. At times, however, he causes great disturbances, brings kingdoms and monarchies into conflict with each other, and throws provinces, states, and households into confusion. To be sure, he causes disturbance, and yet he is not able to carry out what he most desires, to overthrow all things and to mingle heaven with earth. So strong are the walls, fortifications, and hedges of the angels round about us and all things. (LW 6:90–91)

If we disallow in our consideration of evil that which occurs through God when he leads us, for example, into temptation or punishes or chastises us because we have fallen away from him, then, according to Luther, considerably more good than evil occurs. The kingdom of evil upon this earth is sharply curtailed through God's all-encompassing activity. It is not able to destroy the foundational orders of God that belong to his creation and its preservation. These orders can be impaired and even brought into question, but the kingdom of evil and the devil are not able to throw this world into chaos.

But why does God, if he is ultimately the creator and preserver of all things, tolerate at all the kingdom of evil that seeks to transform the good creation into a sea of blood and tears and injustice? Why does God, we could ask today, allow the COVID-19 pandemic that has brought so much misery and disruption into today's world? Luther's answer is, as we noted above, that there should be no discussion about the wisdom of the counsels of God. One should simply let God govern as he does and praise him for his great mercy that even with evil persons, more good than evil occurs. If God and his angels would cease only for a single day to rule the world, the devil would bring everything to an end in a terrible chaos. Luther therefore avoids theodicy—that is, the question of God's righteousness—and points instead to God's unfathomableness and to the fact that, seen as a whole, God is merciful and good. Luther realistically recognizes that there is evil in the world. He does not explain this evil individualistically inasmuch as he would trace it back to humans. Yet he also does not view evil as simply an outgrowth of human society. For Luther, there is a metaphysical power that stands in the background and battles against God's creation, seeking to destroy it.

For the preservation of temporal order, God has established the worldly regiment or kingdom. According to Luther's categorization, humans belong either to the kingdom of God or to the kingdom of the world. "Those who belong to the kingdom of God are all the true believers who are in Christ and under Christ, for Christ is the King and Lord in the kingdom of God."[10] These persons do not, in principle, need the temporal law or sword—that is to say, the worldly force that is exercised against persons who do not observe the law. Since the Holy Spirit works in their hearts and teaches them that they should do no one injustice and love all

10. Martin Luther, *Temporal Authority: To What Extent It Should Be Obeyed*, in LW, 45:88.

people, they do of their own accord what one would require of them. But there are also those persons in this world who belong to the kingdom of the world. "The unrighteous do nothing that the law demands; therefore, they need the law to instruct, constrain, and compel them to do good" (LW 45:89). For non-Christians, who actually belong to the kingdom of the world and do not just live within it as do Christians, temporal law is necessary for the preservation of law and order. Luther, exhibiting his typical realism, said that if it were not for temporal authority, "men would devour one another, seeing that the whole world is evil and that among thousands there is scarcely a single true Christian. No one could support wife and child, feed himself, and serve God. The whole world would be reduced to chaos. For this reason God has ordained two governments: the spiritual, by which the Holy Spirit produces Christians and righteous people under Christ; and the temporal, which restrains the un-Christian and wicked so that—no thanks to them—they are obliged to keep still and to maintain an outward peace" (LW 45:91).

The temporal regiment of God, through which God keeps the world from self-destruction, is a divine order of preservation that is implemented, as it were, through the law—that is, through temporal law and corresponding punishment. All persons are subject to this regiment of God whether Christian or non-Christian: the Christian willingly, however, while the non-Christian often unwillingly. From this regiment is to be distinguished God's government through the Gospel—that is, through grace and consolation—through which humans find entry into the kingdom of God. Law and force have no place here, for faith cannot be forced upon anyone but is rather God's own work. Hence there is a necessary connection between Luther's *two kingdoms doctrine*—that is, Luther's conviction that there is a kingdom of God and a kingdom of the devil—and the *two regiments doctrine*, his view that God governs differently in the temporal sphere than he does in his very own kingdom of the Gospel.[11]

Luther thus goes a decisive step beyond Augustine. With Augustine, it was difficult to understand how the ordinances of the city of the world could be affirmed, since its purpose and its citizens were earthly and estranged from God. Luther, however, through his distinction between the temporal kingdom of the devil and God's kingdom of the left, has made it unmistakably clear that although the kingdom of evil exists and reigns in the world, it is not identical with the good ordinances of God that also exist in the world. On the contrary, the kingdom of evil always has the goal of destroying God's regiment and holding all persons bound within the kingdom of the devil. The result is that Luther not only sees a dynamic power struggle between the sphere of influence of God and that of the anti-Godly powers, but he

---

11. Thompson (*Studies in the Reformation*, 47–48) has convincingly demonstrated a necessary connection between the two kingdoms and the two regiments. He writes, "Luther's concept of the two divine orders or regiments is profoundly influenced by his doctrine of the eschatological conflict between the kingdom of God and the kingdom of the Devil." Yet he concedes that Luther does not always strictly distinguish between "kingdom" and "regiment."

is also able to affirm God's creation as an unqualified good that cannot be usurped even by the greatest efforts of the anti-Godly powers. Additionally, the kingdom of God, in contrast to Augustine's the city of God, is not a *corpus permixtum*, a mixture of good and evil, but is rather a community of those sanctified by Christ. The kingdom of God, therefore, cannot be confused with the church. Yet neither Augustine nor Luther provides a satisfactory answer to the question of when and why there is evil if there is a good God.

5 The Enlightenment

Once the Thirty Years' War (1618–48) had ended, not only most cities and landscapes in central Europe had been devastated but also the old political system of order and of the medieval understanding of the world including the relationship between God, humanity, and the cosmos had become questionable. With so much misery, was there still a God who directed the world to the promised new heaven and new earth? Therefore, the issue of whether God is ultimately in control of the affairs of this world was discussed with renewed vigor. It was especially during the Enlightenment that the pros and cons were debated both in literary circles and in the educated public. Gottfried Wilhelm Leibniz (1646–1716), for instance, relates that he often discussed with Sophia Charlotte of Hanover (1668–1705; the later queen of Prussia) and others the works of Pierre Bayle (1647–1706) and indicated that Bayle's arguments are not as convincing as some people believed. Bayle was a devout Calvinist for whom faith and reason had nothing to do with each other. Therefore, he emphasized that reason finds in the Christian dogmas only absurdities. Truth is not accessible to reason but can only be grasped through faith. As a result of this attack on reason, Leibniz, who was brought up in Lutheran Saxony, wrote his *Theodicy*, which was published in 1710.

Gottfried Wilhelm Leibniz: The Necessity of Evil

Gottfried Wilhelm Leibniz was a prominent German polymath in the history of mathematics and in the history of philosophy. In philosophy, he was most noted for his optimism and his idea that our world is the best possible one. This idea was vehemently attacked by skeptics such as Voltaire. Yet together with Descartes and Spinoza, Leibniz was one of the leading figures of seventeenth-century rationalism. His more than fifteen thousand letters with learned persons throughout Europe attest to his prominence. Immense influence was exerted by his *Theodicy*,[1] which was published first in French, the learned lingua franca of that time. In English, the title is *Theodicy: Essays on the Goodness of God, the Freedom of Man and the Origin of Evil*.

The problem of evil bothered Leibniz throughout his philosophical career. This is evident in the fact that the first and the last book-length works that he authored, *The Philosopher's Confession* (1672) and the *Theodicy* (1709), were both devoted to this problem. The first book is a dialogue between a philosopher, a catechumen, and a theologian in which the philosopher explains to the theologian on rational

---

1. Cf. Hans Poser, "Leibniz, Gottfried Wilhelm (1646–1716)," in TRE, 20:664.

terms that God takes no delight in the existence of evil and hence is not properly thought to will it. As the theologian admits, "It should be said that God does not will sins in themselves which are understood not to exist; if they exist because the harmony of things requires them thus, it should be said that he permits them; i.e. he neither wills them nor does not will them."[2] To this, the philosopher adds, "Although the harmony is pleasing, nevertheless it does not immediately follow that everything about the harmony is pleasing. If the whole is pleasing it does not follow that the parts are also pleasing. Although the entire harmony is pleasing, nevertheless the dissonances themselves are not pleasing, however much they are mixed in according to the rules of art." For Leibniz, the beauty and goodness of the whole justifies the *apparent* ugliness and evil of some parts. In the end, the world is better because of apparent disorder. Already at this early stage what counts for Leibniz is the whole, the world as the best possible world. Aberrant entities within the whole do not mar the overall picture. Leibniz even asserts with the voice of the theologian: "Evidently sins happen and bring forth the universal harmony of things, distinguishing light by shadows."[3] Perfection requires imperfection to be discerned in the same way as the universal harmony requires disharmony or sin.

His *Theodicy* initially was to be a conversation with Bayle, but Bayle died before this project was published. In it, Leibniz wanted to do away with "old errors" about God and gather up his thoughts and impart them to the public "on the Goodness of God, the Freedom of Man, and the Origin of Evil."[4] In contrast to Bayle, Leibniz wanted to demonstrate that the proper way of vindicating the justice and goodness of God in the face of evil was through reason, not faith. Most people, so Leibniz, employed "lazy reason" and argued,

> If the future is necessary, that which must happen will happen, whatever I may do. Now the future (so they said) is necessary, whether because the Divinity foresees everything, and even pre-establishes it by the control of all things in the universe; or because everything happens of necessity, through the concatenation of causes; or finally, through the very nature of truth, which is determinate in the assertions that can be made on future events, as it is in all assertions, since the assertion must always be true or false in itself, even though we know not always which it is.[5]

This means the future is predetermined and preestablished by God. One simply cannot resist divine providence. Leibniz likens this Christian attitude to Islamic fatalism.

2. Leibniz, "Leibniz: The Philosopher's Confession" (A VI, 3, 130), Leibniz Translations, accessed April 15, 2019, https://tinyurl.com/y6g9chlv, for this and the following quote.
3. Leibniz, "Philosopher's Confession" (A VI, 3, 122).
4. Leibniz, *Theodicy: Essays on the Goodness of God, the Freedom of Man and the Origin of Evil*, trans. E. M Huggard (La Salle, IL: Open Court, 2005), 53 (preface).
5. Leibniz, *Theodicy*, 54 (preface).

Leibniz now lines out his intention, saying, "I will point out that absolute necessity, which is called also logical and metaphysical and sometimes geometrical, and which would alone be formidable in this connexion, does not exist in free actions, and that thus freedom is exempt not only from constraint but also from real necessity. I will show that God himself, although he always chooses the best, does not act by an absolute necessity, and that the laws of nature laid down by God, founded upon the fitness of things, keep the mean between geometrical truths, absolutely necessary, and arbitrary decrees."[6] There is no determinism that would obstruct human freedom. With regard to the goodness of God and the origin of evil, Leibniz then states,

> Concerning the origin of evil in its relation to God, I offer a vindication of his perfections that shall extol not less his holiness, his justice and his goodness than his greatness, his power and his independence. I show how it is possible for everything to depend upon God, for him to co-operate in all the actions of creatures, even, if you will, to create these creatures continually, and nevertheless not to be the author of sin. Here also it is demonstrated how the privative nature of evil should be understood. Much more than that, I explain how evil has a source other than the will of God, and that one is right therefore to say of moral evil that God wills it not, but simply permits it. Most important of all, however, I show that it has been possible for God to permit sin and misery, and even to co-operate therein and promote it, without detriment to his holiness and his supreme goodness: although, generally speaking, he could have avoided all these evils.

Leibniz tackles here the apparent inconsistency of a morally perfect and omnipotent God and the existence of evil. If God were morally perfect, it seems that God would want to eliminate all evil, and if God were omnipotent, then it would be within God's power to eliminate evil. Thus it seems that evil could not exist if God does. However, since evil obviously does exist, it appears that God either does not exist or is not morally perfect and omnipotent. Since, according to Leibniz, God is a morally perfect and omnipotent being, he needed to explain why God allows evil. Leibniz begins by distinguishing three types of evil: metaphysical evil (the evil involved in the existence of finite and imperfect things), physical evil (pain and suffering), and moral evil (sin resulting from human free will).[7] Metaphysical evil is a problem for theism because a perfect God should create a perfect world, and the fact that this world is not perfect shows that such a perfect being might not exist. Leibniz's response is that while God can do anything that is logically possible, it is not logically possible for God to create a perfect world because such a world

---

6. Leibniz, *Theodicy*, 61 (preface), for this and the following quote.
7. Cf. Leibniz, *Theodicy* (1:21), 136.

would be indistinguishable from God. Thus the world must be less than perfect, and evil has its proper place in it.

> God wills *antecedently* the good and *consequently* the best. And as for evil, God wills moral evil not at all, and physical evil or suffering he does not will absolutely. Thus it is that there is no absolute predestination to damnation; and one may say of physical evil, that God wills it often as a penalty owing to guilt, and often also as a means to an end, that is, to prevent greater evils or to obtain greater good. The penalty serves also for amendment and example. Evil often serves to make us savour good the more; sometimes too it contributes to a greater perfection in him who suffers it.[8]

Altogether, Leibniz is optimistic when he concurs with Descartes "that natural reason teaches us that we have more goods than evils in this life."[9] Moreover, evil can be attributed not to God but to humans who misuse their freedom of choice that was given for the good. Evil is not an active force, as we have seen it in Luther's *The Bondage of the Will*. In line with Augustine, Leibniz regards it as "a consequence of privation."[10] Of course, it would have been possible for God to make a world without evil. Yet Leibniz contends, "The best course is not always that one which tends towards avoiding evil, since it is possible that the evil may be accompanied by the greater good."[11] The good in this world by far exceeds the evil. Since Leibniz maintains a teleology of history, he can be optimistic that evil will be overcome. After all, this world is the best possible one. God is in control, and "neither the foreknowledge nor the providence of God can impair either his justice or his goodness, or our freedom."[12]

We encounter in Leibniz a prominent representative of Enlightenment optimism who is convinced that reason alone suffices to demonstrate the truthfulness of the tenets of the Christian religion. Evil is a necessary by-product of the good and can in no way be attributed to God. Evil in nature—namely, that life can only be maintained by destroying other life or the life-threatening evils of floods, earthquakes, and fires—is not considered by Leibniz. One could even surmise that for Leibniz, evil is a human phenomenon arising out of the limits of human existence.

Voltaire: Where Is God?

For Leibniz as well as for Bayle, against whom much of Leibniz' theodicy is directed, it was a matter of fact that God was in control of the affairs of this world. Yet this

---

8. Leibniz, *Theodicy* (1:23), 137.
9. Leibniz, *Theodicy* (3:251), 281.
10. Leibniz, *Theodicy* (3:378), 352.
11. Leibniz, *Theodicy* (objection 1, answer 2), 377–378.
12. Leibniz, *Theodicy* (3:377), 351–352.

sentiment should soon change. At 9:30 in the morning on November 1, 1755, on All Saints' Day, this optimistic view held by Enlightenment philosophers was exposed to a major crisis. Within minutes, a massive earthquake destroyed Lisbon, the capital city of Portugal. Portugal had been a maritime superpower with colonies in Africa, Asia, and Latin America. This earthquake with a magnitude of 8.5–9.0 on the Richter scale took a death toll in Lisbon alone between ten and one hundred thousand people, making it one of the deadliest earthquakes in history. Shocks of the earthquake were felt throughout Europe as far as Finland, and tsunamis as tall as 20 m swept the coast of North Africa and even reached the Caribbean. Western society was shocked that one of the most beautiful and prosperous cities in Europe could suffer such a fate. Where was there the best of all possible worlds? And where did the good by far exceed all evil? This catastrophe caused many Enlightenment thinkers to reevaluate the notion of theodicy.

François-Marie Arouet (1694–1778), the French Enlightenment writer—better known under his adopted name Voltaire—wrote a poem on the Lisbon disaster in November of 1755 and published it the following year. He set the tone right at the beginning:

Come, ye philosophers, who cry, "All's well,"
And contemplate this ruin of a world.
Behold these shreds and cinders of your race,
This child and mother heaped in common wreck,
These scattered limbs beneath the marble shafts–
A hundred thousand whom the earth devours.[13]

After elaborating on the human misery caused by this earthquake, Voltaire then asks,

Will ye reply: "You do but illustrate
The iron laws that chain the will of God?"
Say ye, o'er that yet quivering mass of flesh:
"God is avenged: the wage of sin is death"?

This means that either God is not in control or God has executed this disaster as punishment for human sinfulness. Why Lisbon? Voltaire asks, and not some other city, and what have these young ones done who were condemned to death? The answer that all is well and all is necessary makes the misery only worse. Then he suggests that God could have created a different world without these disasters saying,

---

13. Voltaire, "Poem on the Lisbon Disaster," in *Toleration and Other Essays*, trans. Joseph McCabe (New York: G. P. Putnam's Sons, 1912), accessed April 16, 2019, https://tinyurl.com/y2ccprq8, for this and the following quotes.

Are ye so sure the great eternal cause,
That knows all things, and for its self creates
Could not have placed us in this dreary clime,
Without volcanoes seething 'neath our feet?

Yet Voltaire goes beyond the disaster at Lisbon and considers all life that is maintained on earth. There is endless strife that, according to him, mitigates against the idea of a benevolent creator. Thus he writes,

All death and living things are locked in strife.
Confess it freely—evil stalks the land,
Its secret principle unknown to us.
Can it be from the author of all good?

The Enlightenment optimism has vanished, and Voltaire concedes that we do not know why there is so much evil in this world. Even as God came down to us in Jesus Christ, things have not changed. Then Voltaire explicitly mentions Leibniz and refutes his ideas concerning theodicy, saying,

From Leibnitz learn we not by what unseen
Bonds, in this best of all imagined worlds,
Endless disorder, chaos of distress,
Must mix our little pleasures thus with pain;
Nor why the guiltless suffer all this woe
In common with the most abhorrent guilt.
'T is mockery to tell me all is well.

Yet Voltaire himself has no answer either. While rejecting Enlightenment optimism, his view is tinged by resignation, and then he says toward the end of his poem,

Man is a stranger to his own research;
He knows not whence he comes, nor whither goes.
Tormented atoms in an bed of mud,
Devoured by death, a mockery of fate.

In 1759, Voltaire wrote his satire *Candide* in which he ridiculed again the idea that this world is the best possible one. This book, which was written in three days, relates the story of Candide—a young man who is indoctrinated by his mentor, Professor Pangloss—with Leibnizian optimism. Leaving with his mentor from the parental castle in Westphalia, Germany, he witnesses and experiences the great hardships in this world, which causes in him a slow and painful disillusionment, while Professor Pangloss maintains his optimism to the end and says to Candide,

"There is a concatenation of events in this best of all possible worlds: for if you had not been kicked out of a magnificent castle for love of Miss Cunegonde: if you had not been put into the Inquisition: if you had not walked over America: if you had not stabbed the Baron: if you had not lost all your sheep from the fine country of El Dorado: you would not be here eating preserved citrons and pistachio-nuts."[14] Yet Candide is more practically minded and responds, "All that is very well but let us cultivate our garden." While this satire concludes with lip service to the overall goodness of the world, all important is to be active in it. Therefore, the metaphysical assertions of the best of all possible worlds have lost their significance.

Kant: A Theodicy Eludes Human Reason

Immanuel Kant (1724–1894) published in 1756 three short texts on the Lisbon earthquake. As a young man, he was fascinated with the earthquake and collected all the information available to him and formulated a theory of the causes of earthquakes. Kant's theory was one of the first systematic modern attempts to explain earthquakes by positing natural rather than supernatural causes. Kant added a short note about earthquakes in relation to God's government of the world. In this, his precritical and Leibnizian period, he pointed out that we are not the victims of a dangerous natural order that may irresponsibly destroy us at any time because the course of our lives in prosperity and adversity has been determined by God.

Most important, however, is his brief essay of 1791 "On the Miscarriage of All Philosophical Trials in Theodicy." Having defined what he understands by theodicy, Kant declares, "We call this 'the defending of God's cause,' even though the cause might be at bottom no more than that of our presumptuous reason failing to recognize its limitations."[15] To vindicate God of all wrongdoing, we must prove either "that whatever in the world we judge counterpurposive is not so; *or*, if there is any such thing, that it must be judged not at all as an intended *effect* but as the unavoidable consequence of the nature of things; *or*, finally, that it must at least be considered not as an intended effect of the creator of all things but, rather, merely of those beings in the world to whom something can be imputed, i.e. of human beings (higher spiritual beings as well, good or evil, as the case may be)." This vindication must be done by reason alone. Having played through all the cases that mitigate against that which is the highest purpose in nature or morals, Kant concludes, "Every previous theodicy has not performed what it promised, namely the vindication of the moral wisdom of the world-government against the doubts raised against it on the basis of what the experience of this

14. Voltaire, *Candide*, with an introduction by Philip Littell (New York: Boni and Liveright, 1918), 169, accessed April 15, 2019, https://tinyurl.com/lczqpzu, for this and the following quote.
15. Immanuel Kant, "On the Miscarriage of All Philosophical Trials in Theodicy" (A 196), in *Religion and Rational Theology*, trans. Allen W. Wood and George Di Giovanni (Cambridge: Cambridge University Press, 1996), 255, accessed April 15, 2019, https://tinyurl.com/y2ql5kqc, for this and the following quote.

world teaches."[16] But he also concedes that these do not prove the contrary either. Furthermore, it might be possible that eventually a vindication of the goodness of God could be found.

The reason every theodicy will always fail lies in the fact that "all theodicy should truly be an *interpretation* of nature insofar as God announces his will through it."[17] Yet here we must penetrate to the intelligible world in which the sensible world is grounded. Yet no mortal being can penetrate that far. We can have the idea of the supersensible, intelligible world, but we cannot arrive at its cognition. Kant admits that we could view the world as God's world in which God shows us the intentions of his will. But even in this respect, the world is often a closed book for us, as Kant concedes. Since reason always comes to its limits, Kant finally refers to the book of Job in which he finds an "authentic interpretation," albeit in allegoric manner "as the unmediated definition and voice of God through which he gives meaning to the letter of his creation."[18] When Job finally as a fragile creature resigns himself to the unconditional divine decision, "God deigned to lay before Job's eyes the wisdom of his creation, especially its inscrutability."[19] God shows him the beautiful side of creation as well as the horrible side, which seems incompatible with a universal plan established with goodness and wisdom. Just like Job, Kant asserts, people should honestly and openly admit their doubts and also concede their own ignorance. Speculative reason and pious humility are here out of place. Kant then sums up the issue: "Theodicy, as has been shown here, does not have as much to do with a task in the interest of science as, rather, with a matter of faith. From the authentic theodicy we saw that in these matters, less depends on subtle reasoning than on sincerity in taking notice of the impotence of our reason, and on honesty in not distorting our thoughts in what we say, however pious our intention."[20]

In his *Critique of Pure Reason*, Kant shows that the traditional proofs of the existence of God, which include that God is omnipotent and benevolent at the same time, are beyond the reach of reason. God can be neither proven nor disproven. Yet Kant wanted to show the limits of reason so that there is room for faith, as he claimed in the introduction to his first critique. But already in *Critique of Practical Reason* Kant establishes God and human immortality as morally necessary hypotheses and matters of "rational faith." Then he writes toward the end of his second Critique, "Two things fill the mind with ever new and increasing admiration and awe, the oftener and the more steadily we reflect on them: the starry heavens above and the moral law within."[21] Both the moral law and the awesome teleological order of the universe point to God. The architect, the creator, and the lawgiver

16. Kant, *Theodicy* (A 210), 8:263.
17. Kant, *Theodicy* (A 211), 8:264.
18. Kant, *Theodicy* (A 213), 8:264.
19. Kant, *Theodicy* (A 216), 8:266.
20. Kant, *Theodicy* (A 218), 8:267.
21. Kant, conclusion to *Critique of Practical Reason* (V, 161), trans. Thomas Kingsmill Abbott, Wikisource, accessed April 15, 2019, https://tinyurl.com/y29ueesf.

witness to the order that God has designed. This is not an explicit but an implicit theodicy that Kant advocates. But where does this leave evil?

In his book *Religion within the Limits of Reason Alone* (1793), Kant treats in detail the problem of human sinfulness. He begins by asking how evil expresses itself in humans and from whence it comes. According to Kant, persons are not called evil because they carry out activities that are contrary to the law and are accordingly perceived as evil. Rather, these activities appear to be of such a nature that we can conclude that evil maxims or precepts exist in humans.[22] This means that one can sometimes see how it is that activities will end in opposition to the law, and one is fully aware that they are illegal. Nevertheless, the maxims themselves are not always observable. According to Kant, humans are by nature neither morally good nor evil, but they are only in certain respects good and in others evil.[23]

The human capacity for evil can be shown in three ways: First, it is part of the weakness of the human heart to not consistently observe accepted precepts. A frailty of human nature manifests itself here.[24] Second, there is a tendency in humans to mix morally and nonmorally motivated causes, hence a so-called impurity of motivation. Third, there is an inclination in humans to take up evil whereby they demonstrate a wickedness of human nature or of the human heart. This latter phenomenon is present in all persons, even the best, so that one can say that a general tendency toward evil exists in humans. Humans are understood to be evil to the extent that they are aware of moral laws but nevertheless incorporate occasional deviations from these laws into their maxims.[25] Kant speaks of a radical, inborn evil in human nature that originates, however, through our own selves.

According to Kant, the cause of evil could be seen in the nature of human thinking and in the natural inclinations that arise out of it. But this would restrict evil too much, since humans would thereby be degraded to the level of animals. If one would locate this depravity in the moral, lawgiving reason so as to imply that reason could destroy the authority of the law out of which it comes, this would be to attribute too much to evil. We would then have to do with a reason that is wicked, and humans would be turned directly into demons. If there is an inclination to evil in human nature, then it must be sought in human free will, which is capable of becoming morally evil. Evil is then radical, for it perverts the foundation of all maxims through the human will.[26] Hence Kant guards human free will and neither degrades humans into subhumans nor elevates them into superhumans. Nevertheless, it is difficult for him to adhere to a traditional doctrine of original sin: a deficiency that he seeks to compensate with his notion of the kingdom of evil.

---

22. Immanuel Kant, *Religion within the Limits of Reason Alone* (BA 5, 6), trans. with introduction and notes by Theodore M. Greene and Hoyt H. Hudson and with a new essay by John R. Silber (New York: Harper, 1960), 16. References that follow are to this edition.
23. Kant, *Religion* (BA 8, 9), 17–18.
24. For this and the following, cf. Kant, *Religion* (B21 A19), 24–25.
25. Kant, *Religion* (B27–28 A25), 27.
26. Kant, *Religion* (B36, 37 A33), 32.

Kant relates the biblical story of the fall—including the appearance of two opposing principles—with the prince of this world as the leader of the kingdom of evil.[27] The evil principle is not overcome through Christ, for his kingdom remains standing. Before it can be defeated, a new epoch must begin. Yet the power of the kingdom of evil is broken so that it can no longer hold people against their will, as it had previously done. Another kingdom, one that is moral, is offered as asylum to humans as a place where they can find support for their morality if they desire to leave the sphere of influence to which they previously belonged. Humans must stand under one lordship or another. According to Kant, there is no salvation for humans when they do not thoroughly adopt genuine moral principles in their character. Yet Kant entertained doubt about whether humans could conduct themselves correctly, not because of their sensual nature, but because of a certain self-afflicted perversity, or how one wishes to describe this wickedness that humans have brought upon themselves and through which evil came into the world.

Kant summarizes,

> Now man is in this perilous state through his own fault. [. . .] When he looks around for the causes and circumstances which expose him to this danger and keep him in it, he can easily convince himself that he is subject to these not because of his own gross nature, so far as he is here a separate individual, but because of mankind to whom he is related. [. . .] Envy, the lust for power, greed, and the malignant inclinations bound up with these, besiege his nature, connected within itself, as soon as he is among men. And it is not even necessary to assume that these are men sunk in evil and examples to lead him astray; it suffices that they are at hand, that they surround him, and that they are men, for them mutually to corrupt each other's predisposition and make one another evil.[28]

In order to counter this situation, one must build an alliance against evil and promote the good in the human. Of course, humans are continually at risk of falling back under the sway of evil.

In order to unite individual humans, who by themselves are unable to resist evil, in the pursuit of this common goal, the concept of a higher moral being is necessary. Through this concept, the insufficient powers of individuals are united. In this way, one can resist the evil that is to be found within oneself and within all others.[29] Kant sets the kingdom of sin, therefore, against the kingdom of God, which is exemplified in the church. Sin is not an individual offense but rather manifests itself in the community through which it is continually strengthened and set anew into motion. As an individual, one cannot resist this sin but needs the

---

27. For this and the following, see Kant, *Religion* (B106–115 A99–106), 73–78.
28. Kant, *Religion* (B128–129 A120–121), 85.
29. Kant, *Religion* (B137–142 A129–134), 90–92.

community and the goal toward which this community is directed. Kant understands evil neither atomistically nor as a mystery that plagues human nature. He rejects every natural understanding of sin and maintains a deliberate, intentional deviation of the human will.

Whence does come evil according to Kant? Is the human inclination toward evil self-imposed, or are humans subjected to it from outside forces? We do not receive a straight answer from Kant. He certainly is not a dualist, claiming that two opposing camps, though his distinction between the kingdom of God and the kingdom of evil might point in that direction. Yet God is, for him, the supreme warrant of eschatological fulfillment.

Hume: Between Skepticism and Faith

David Hume (1711–76) is the most important representative of Enlightenment in Scotland. With his skepticism, he incited Kant to write his *Critique of Pure Reason*, in which Kant demonstrated that reason too has its limits. In 1757, Hume wrote *Natural History of Religion*, which was generally rejected in academic circles, and together with all his other writings, it was put on the index of prohibited books by the Vatican.

After his death, *Dialogues concerning Natural Religion* was published. In the dialogues making up the book, three persons converse: Demea, who represents religious orthodoxy; Philo, a philosophical skeptic; and Cleanthes, who argues the position of empirical theism. Philo, who most closely represents the position of Hume, delivers his objections to the argument from design, showing that this argument is faulty. The argument from design attempts to show from the arrangement of the world that it owes its existence to a benevolent creator. Finally, Demea and Philo paint a bleak picture of the universe, showing that the world is actually a miserable place filled with evil. Yet after Philo has shown that the argument from design is manifestly invalid, he reverses his position in the last chapter of the dialogues. Now we suddenly hear from him: as there are also considerable differences between the works of nature and human products, "we have reason to suppose a proportional difference in the causes; and in particular ought to attribute a much higher degree of power and energy to the supreme cause than any we have ever observed in mankind. Here then the existence of a Deity is plainly ascertained by reason."[30] The intricacies of nature require a design and a supreme designer. Forgotten here is the injunction of Cleanthes that it is never "*within the reach of human capacity to explain ultimate causes, or show the last connections of any objects.*"[31] As Charles Hendel writes in his introduction to the selections of Hume's works, "By scientific method, it is admitted, then, we cannot know God, but it is entirely

---

30. David Hume, *Dialogues concerning Natural Religion* (XII), in *Selections*, ed. Charles W. Hendel (New York: Charles Scribner's, 1927), 387–388.
31. Hume, *Dialogues concerning Natural Religion* (VII), 344.

reasonable to assert that our thought when inspired by the living interests of hope and fear may disclose a meaning and a reality which pass the understanding of the methodical reasoner who is accustomed to the processes of science."[32] Therefore, in the end, Hume turns to revelation. Yet it is not the revelation of organized religion whether Christian or pre-Christian, since there he detects too much imperfection. It resembles more a human construct of the nineteenth-century philosopher Ludwig Feuerbach.

While the moral qualities of humans are more defective than their nonmoral qualities, "the Supreme Being is allowed to be absolutely and entirely perfect, whatever differs most from him departs the farthest from the supreme standard of moral rectitude and perfection."[33] Evil is located in humans and not in God. After rejecting organized religion as morally and psychologically harmful, Cleanthes comes out in favor of genuine theism, "which represents us as the workmanship of a Being perfectly good, wise, and powerful; who created us for happiness and who, having implanted in us immeasurable desires for good, will prolong our existence to all eternity, and will transfer us into an infinite variety of scenes, in order to satisfy those desires, and render our felicity complete and durable."[34] Forgotten are the miseries in the world. There is only a supreme and wise God who makes our happiness everlasting. Yet Philo goes even one step further, saying, "To be a philosophical Sceptic is, in a man of letters, the first and most essential step towards being a sound, believing Christian."[35] One must undermine faith in reason and turn toward revelation. If this is indeed Hume's conviction—who, however, was a notorious skeptic—then even for him, there is room for faith, something that Kant attempted to show. While Hume demonstrated that God or a supreme mind governs the universe, the issue of evil and its origin remained unanswered.

---

32. Charles Hendel in *Selections*, xxi.
33. Hume, *Dialogues concerning Natural Religion* (XII), 390.
34. Hume, *Dialogues concerning Natural Religion* (XII), 397.
35. Hume, *Dialogues concerning Natural Religion* (XII), 401.

6 The Nineteenth and Twentieth Centuries

When we come to the nineteenth century, the most prominent representative who extensively dealt with the issue of theodicy was Georg Wilhelm Friedrich Hegel (1770–1831). In the twentieth century, the issue became critical due to the Holocaust, since some theologians, such as Richard Rubenstein (*b. 1924) and Dorothee Sölle (1929–2003), questioned whether after that genocide one could still talk about God and divine justice.

Hegel: History as a Justification of the Ways of God

Hegel's lectures on the philosophical history of the world are geared toward a general audience. He distinguishes between three methods of treating history: original history as historians relate it; philosophical history, which is the true kind; and reflective history, in which the writers are not confined to past history but connect it with the present. One variety of this he calls universal history, since it traverses long periods of time. A second variety he calls pragmatic history, since all occurrences are virtually taken out of the past and made present. The third variety is called critical history. It involves "a criticism of historical narratives and an investigation of their truth and credibility."[1] Hegel calls the philosophical kind of history simply *"the thoughtful consideration"* of history (22). According to Hegel, reason is the sovereign of the world, and "the history of the world, therefore, presents us with a rational process" (22). While in the domain of history as such this conviction and intuition is a hypothesis, in philosophy, it is not a hypothesis but is proved by speculative cognition.

For Hegel, reason is the substance of the universe, that by which and in which all reality has its being and subsistence, and it is also the infinite energy of the universe, capable of producing everything. "While it is exclusively its own basis of existence, and absolute final aim, it is also the energizing power realizing this aim; developing it not only in the phenomena of the Natural, but also of the Spiritual Universe—the History of the World" (23). Reason is therefore the supreme cause and the supreme agent that moves history forward. Hegel then asks the audience of his lectures to have faith in reason. We must have the firm and unconquerable faith that reason does exist in universal history and that the world of intelligence and

---

1. Georg Wilhelm Friedrich Hegel, *The Philosophy of History*, with a preface by Charles Hegel and trans. J. Sibree (Kitchener, Canada: Batoche, 2001), 20. Numbers in parentheses refer to the respective pages of this book.

conscious motivation is not abandoned to chance. According to Hegel, everything develops reasonably and not according to chance, as Darwin would later claim. At the outset, Hegel asserts, "It is only an inference from the history of the World, that its development has been a rational process; that the history in question has constituted the rational necessary course of the World-Spirit" (24). Hegel wants to apply the idea that "reason directs the World" to the religious truth—namely, "that the world is not abandoned to chance and external contingent causes, but that a *Providence* controls it" (26). Hegel then continues to affirm, "The truth, then, that a Providence (that of God) presides over the events of the World—consorts with the proposition in question; for *Divine* Providence is Wisdom, endowed with an infinite Power, which realizes its aim, viz., the absolute rational design of the World" (26). By the providence of God, the world is rationally designed, and God oversees the execution of its historical development. Hegel wants to discern the ways of providence, the means it uses and the historical phenomena in which it manifests itself. He reminds his audience that physico-theology has demonstrated the wisdom of God as displayed in animals, plants, and isolated occurrences, such as thunderstorms. Why, he asks, should the same demonstration not also be accorded to history? Then he comes out to state that his philosophy of history is actually a theodicy of sorts, thereby mentioning Leibniz, saying, "Our mode of treating the subject is, in this aspect, a Theodicaea—a justification of the ways of God—which Leibnitz attempted metaphysically, in his method, i.e., in indefinite abstract categories—so that the ill that is found in the World may be comprehended, and the thinking Spirit reconciled with the fact of the existence of evil" (29). Then he lays out his agenda: to perceive first the ultimate design of the world, then the fact that this design has been realized in it, and that evil has not been able to permanently assert a competing position.

Universal history belongs to the realm of the Spirit, and the term *world* includes both physical and psychical nature. For Hegel, the Spirit, and its course of development, is his most substantial object. The Spirit is endowed with freedom, since it exists in and with itself and is self-contained existence, while matter has a gravity toward a central point and has its essence out of itself. Hegel now wants to investigate the consciousness of freedom that started with the Greeks and was continued with the Christian principle of self-consciousness. He asserts, "The History of the world is none other than the progress of the consciousness of Freedom; a progress whose development according to the necessity of its nature, it is our business to investigate" (33).

For Hegel, the spiritual world is what matters. It is the substantial world, while the physical remains subordinate to it. The destiny of the spiritual world and the final cause of the world at large is the consciousness of its own freedom on part of the Spirit and thereby the reality of that freedom. The essential nature of freedom is displayed as the coming to a consciousness of itself, which means self-consciousness in which its existence is realized. This, Hegel declares, is then the final aim of God's purpose with the world, since as an absolutely perfect being, God can will nothing other than himself, God's own will. The nature of God's will, however, is the idea of freedom. Hegel then asks how freedom is accomplished. When we look at history, we perceive human actions. Only rarely the ideal of reason is actualized, but most of the time, "passions, private aims, and the satisfaction of selfish desires, are on the other hand, most effective springs of action" (34). Even good designs and righteous aims, so Hegel concedes, are associated with unreason. The true result of world history looks grim. Having painted this picture of sin and suffering that history unfolds, Hegel now attempts an answer.

Hegel contends that nothing great in this world has been accomplished without passion. Passion is, for him, however, nothing negative, but it is the impelling and accentuating force for accomplishing deeds. It is the subjective side of energy, will and activity, leaving the object or aim still undetermined. It is then always of essential importance, what is the object of my passion, and whether it is of true and substantial nature. In order to bundle the individual desires and passions, Hegel now focuses on the state. Bringing together the private interests of the citizens with the common interest of the state involves long struggles of understanding before it can be discovered what really is appropriate. It also involves a tedious discipline of the state to bring about the desired harmony. Yet Hegel is aware that "the history of mankind does not begin with a *conscious* aim of any kind, as it is the case with the particular circles into which men form themselves of set purpose" (39). But in the beginning, there is primarily a conscious purpose for security of life and property. Only gradually the purpose becomes more comprehensive. The general history of the world begins only implicitly with its general aim.

The whole process of history is directed to render this implicit aim to become an explicit one. Eventually, the "vast congeries of volitions, interests and activities, constitute the instruments and means of the World-Spirit for attaining its object; bringing it to consciousness, and realizing it. And this aim is none other than finding itself—coming to itself—and contemplating itself in concrete actuality" (39). Individuals and nations seek to satisfy their own purposes. Yet unknowingly, they are instruments of the higher purpose of which they are unaware and which they realize unknowingly. As Hegel stated at the outset, it is "our belief that Reason governs the world, and has consequently governed its history. In relation to this independently universal and substantial existence—all else is subordinate, subservient to it, and the means for its development" (40).

The whole process of world history progresses according to a dialectic. World-historical individuals are devoted to one aim only. These individuals are great because they willed and accomplished something great. Yet on account of their passions and cravings, they had not been moral persons. Nevertheless, these opposites lead forward and enable new syntheses. The forces that are employed here are the spirits of individual nations. The world spirit moves from one nation to another, and therefore, one nation advances and another goes into oblivion.

This is the process that the world spirit uses to advance its aim of self-conscious freedom. This way world history becomes the judgment of the world. Yet it occurs by necessity. "The principles of the successive phases of Spirit that animate the Nations in a necessitated gradation, are themselves only steps in the development of the one universal Spirit, which through them elevates and completes itself to a self-comprehending *totality*" (95–96). What has ultimate significance is neither the individual nor the nation but only the universal spirit who brings everything to its preconceived goal. As Hegel states, "Nothing in the past is lost for it, for the Idea is ever present; Spirit is immortal; with it there is no past, no future, but an essential *now*" (96).

Hegel then concludes his lectures with the statement "that the History of the World, with all the changing scenes which its annals present, is this process of development and the realization of Spirit—this is the true *Theodicaea*, the justification of God in History" (447). What is happening every day is on the surface without God, but essentially, it is God's work. This way the spirit and the history of the world are joined together. Yet it is difficult to see what this has to do with theodicy. It resembles more the notion of a preestablished harmony that once was advanced by Leibniz. By a Hegelian dialectic, the negativity that we encounter in history and nature is too facilely overcome.

Paley and Darwin: Goodness or Cruelty?

William Paley (1743–1805), archdeacon of Carlisle and a contemporary of Kant, pursued to prove God's existence from nature.[2] Just like Leibniz, he compared nature to a preestablished harmony that like a clock ran its course in predesigned order. His *Natural Theology: Or, Evidences of the Existence and Attributes of the Deity, Collected from the Appearances of Nature* (1802) enjoyed in 1820 its twentieth edition. His *Evidences of Christianity* (1794) appeared in 1811 already in its fifteenth edition. As can be gathered from the success of these books, many saw it necessary to combat empiricism on its own field. Paley claimed that "the contrivances of nature surpass the contrivances of art, in the complexity, subtlety, and curiosity of the mechanism."[3] But Paley did not just want to prove that a designer must have created the world. He also wanted to prove the goodness of this creator.

The poof of divine goodness rests upon two propositions: (1) "in a vast plurality of instances in which contrivance is perceived, the design of the contrivance is *beneficial*" (252) and (2) "the Deity has superadded *pleasure* to animal sensations, beyond what was necessary for any other purpose, or when the purpose, so far as it

2. For Paley, cf. D. L. LeMahieu, *The Mind of William Paley: A Philosopher and His Age* (Lincoln: University of Nebraska Press, 1976).
3. William Paley, *Natural Theology: Or, Evidences of the Existence and Attributes of the Deity, Collected from the Appearances of Nature*, illustrated by James Paxton and with additional notes and vocabulary by John Ware (Boston: Gould und Lincoln, 1860), 13. The page numbers in parentheses in the following text refer to this publication.

was necessary, might have been effected by the operation of pain" (252). Paley then sets out to prove these propositions. When we look at the parts of an animal, with very few exceptions, all these parts are subservient to the use of the animal. The complexity of the structure, the success in so many cases, and the felicity of the result show the benevolence of creation. The world therefore was made with benevolent design. Paley then refers to the insects that greedily suck juices, other species that run around, and even young shrimp that bound into the air from the shallow margin of water. These are all signs of happiness. He elaborates, "In every given moment of time, how many myriads of animals are eating their food, gratifying their appetites, ruminating in their holes, accomplishing their wishes, pursuing their pleasures, taking their pastimes!" (256). Paley then continues looking at humans: "In our own species, in which perhaps the assertion may be more questionable than in any other, the prepollency of good over evil, of health, for example, and ease, over pain and distress, is evidenced by the very notion which calamities excite" (256). This means, for him, that happiness is the rule and misery the exception.

Nevertheless, we are insensible to the goodness of the creator. The general benefits of our nature usually escape us. Yet these make up our well-being and happiness. Paley admits that evil does exist. Yet for instance, teeth are made to eat and not to ache. Therefore, their aching is incidental, and their use to chew is providential and provides pleasure. There is no contrivance in nature that will bring about an evil purpose. He concedes, however, that there are venomous animals and animals preying upon one another. The venom and the preying are intended to the effect of killing. Yet Paley asks whether this is ultimately evil. With respect to venomous bites and stings, for the animal itself, this faculty is good, since it is used for defense or for subduing and killing the prey. Usually venomous animals and even animals of prey are not a danger for humans unless "we invade the territories of wild beasts and venomous reptiles, and then complain that we are infested by their bites and stings" (261). This means that everything is well arranged, and the problem only starts if we disturb this preestablished harmony.

Yet how do we understand that animals devour each other and therefore cause each other harm? Paley first asserts that immortality on this earth is out of the question, since without death, there could be no generation and no animal happiness. Life then usually ends through disease, decay, or violence. If an animal is simply left to perish by decay, there is suffering and misery involved. Here the present system of pursuit and prey comes in to alleviate the slowly wasting away of life. Furthermore, the pursuit of its prey constitutes pleasure for a considerable part of the animal creation. Since often animals multiply profoundly, their destruction then almost instantly becomes the parent of life. "All superabundance supposes destruction, or must destroy itself. Perhaps there is no species of terrestrial animals whatever, which will not overrun the earth, if it were permitted to multiply in perfect safety" (264). So even devouring one another shows the goodness of the creator, who makes sure that not one species takes over completely but that there is an equilibrium maintained in the animal world. This, for Paley, shows what he initially contended, "that, in a vast plurality of instances, in which *contrivance* is perceived, the design of the contrivance is beneficial" (265).

Now he comes to his second proposition—namely, the issue of pleasure. Paley asserts that the deity has added pleasure to animal sensations beyond what was necessary for any other purpose. While these properties may not prove the goodness of God in the strict sense, "there is a class of properties, which may be said to be superadded for an intention expressly directed to happiness" (266). These provisions are not necessary for life but are only there for our pleasure. Paley now explains that, for example, eating is necessary, but the pleasure connected with it—for instance, when we eat a juicy peach—is not necessary. It seems to go back to the benevolence of the creator. There is a capacity in our senses to receive pleasure, and there is a supply of external objects that excite the senses. This is similar to animals who call for one kind of food while rejecting another kind. Again, pleasure may be the stimulus for their selection. Since Paley has proven his propositions, he can now ascribe to the deity the character of benevolence.

Paley again returns to the origin of evil and admits that no universal solution has been discovered. Yet he lists four points out of which evil may arise: "First, that important advantages may accrue to the universe from the order of nature proceeding according to general laws: secondly, the general laws, however well set and constituted, often thwart and cross one another: thirdly, that from these thwartings and crossings, frequent particular inconveniences though arise: and, fourthly, that it agrees with our observation to suppose that some degree of these inconveniences take place in the works of nature" (270–71). It becomes very evident in which direction Paley's argument moves: the inconveniences or ills must be seen in a larger context in which they contribute to the good. Even pain can be salutary, since it teaches us vigilance and caution. Concerning death, we hear from Paley, "Of *mortal diseases*, the great use is to reconcile us to death. The horror of death proves the value of life" (274).

When he talks about the cruelties and injustices that one person inflicts on another, Paley reminds us that we are free agents, a fact that always contains the liability to abuse. Yet to deprive us from being free agents would also deprive us of all moral character, of virtue and accountability. Then Paley adds, "Even the bad qualities of mankind have an origin in the good ones. The case is this: human passions are either necessary to human welfare, or capable of being made, and, in a great majority of instances, in fact made, conducive to its happiness" (280). We encounter here the same kind of argumentation that Paley used beforehand: something bad ultimately contributes toward the good. Paley is so convinced of the ultimate goodness of the creator that he gives no consideration to the deviousness of evil and to that which we call the anti-Godly powers. Beyond the human sphere, there is no agent of evil, and therefore, those things that we consider evil will eventually result in something good.

Charles Darwin (1809–82) had grown up with Paley's notion of design. The *Encyclopedia Britannica* even states that Paley's *natural theology* "strongly influenced Darwin."[4] Yet when we check Darwin's own works, we find less than a handful of references to Paley. The two most enlightening ones are from his *Autobiography of Charles Darwin*, which shows that even during Darwin's schooldays, Paley's *Natural Theology* was universally accepted, and the young Darwin was no exception. Darwin writes,

> In order to pass the B.A. examination, it was, also, necessary to get up Paley's *Evidences of Christianity*, and his *Moral Philosophy*. This was done in a thorough manner, and I am convinced that I could have written out the whole *Evidences* with perfect correctness, but not of course, in the clear language of Paley. The logic of this book and as I may add of his *Natural Theology* gave me as much delight as did Euclid. The careful study of these works [. . .] was the only part of the academic course which, as I then felt and as I still believe, was the least use to me in the education of my mind. I did not at any time trouble myself about Paley's premises; and taking these on trust I was charmed and convinced of the long line of argumentation.[5]

Like every undergraduate student, Darwin had been thoroughly acquainted with Paley's writings. And even later in life, he had still high praise at least for the logic of the argument. Yet when he started his career as a naturalist, he arrived at quite different conclusions. It was not evolution that was the problem but suffering. Natural selection emphasized the apparent necessity of suffering in the world, and for someone who had been brought up on Paley's benevolent creator, this was a serious issue. In South America, Darwin saw the devastating effects of an earthquake; he observed how in nature, animals mercilessly killed each other; he registered the immense numbers of species that had become extinct; and he witnessed the terrible struggle for existence faced by the natives of the Tierra del Fuego.[6] Such experiences eventually made it difficult for him to discern in nature the workings of a beneficent deity proposed by Paley.

In *Origin of Species*, Darwin explains, "We need not marvel at the sting of the bee, when used against an enemy, causing the bee's own death; at drones being produced in such great numbers for one single act, and being then slaughtered by their sterile sisters; at the astonishing waste of pollen by our fir-trees; at the instinctive hatred of the queen bee for her own fertile daughters; at

---

4. *Encyclopedia Britannica* (2002), s.v. "Paley, William."
5. Charles Darwin, *The Autobiography of Charles Darwin* (58/9), in *The Works of Charles Darwin* (London: Pickering, 1989), 29:101.
6. Charles Darwin wrote about the Fuegian Indians, saying, "I never saw more miserable creatures." *Diary of the Voyages of H. M. S. Beagle* (February 22, 1834), in *The Works of Charles Darwin* ed. Nora Barlow (London: Pickering, 1986), 1:193.

ichneumonidae feeding within the live bodies of caterpillars; or at other such cases."[7] Then he relates, "The extinction of species and of whole groups of species, which has played so conspicuous a part in the history of the organic world, almost inevitably follows from the principle of Natural Selection."[8] Immense cruelty and the survival of the fittest at the expense of the less fit ones do not fit with the image of a creator who is concerned with goodness. Either the creator permits cruelty—that is, evil—as a ruling principle or the creator even chose this principle to advance evolution. Since Darwin rejected the idea of a special creation of individual species, he accords the process of evolution to secondary causes, saying, "To my mind it accords better with what we know of the laws impressed on matter by the Creator, that the production and extinction of the past and present inhabitants of the world should have been due to secondary causes, like those determining the birth and death of the individual."[9] Yet the pain and cruelty connected with this process ultimately go back to the creator and the laws he impressed on creation.

At the same time, Darwin has not completely abandoned the optimism advanced by Paley concerning the benevolence and goodness of the creator when he writes, "From the war of nature, from famine and death, the most exalted object which we are capable of conceiving, namely, the production of the higher animals, directly follows."[10] Yes, there is evil in this world, but it is a precondition for something good. And the good will ultimately prevail, as Darwin postulates, saying, "As Natural Selection works solely by and for the good of each being, all corporeal and mental endowments will tend to progress towards perfection."[11] Who could blame the creator for "war in nature," for "famine and death," if the end result is "perfection"? Darwin himself seems to eschew the issue, saying that secondary causes cannot be directly blamed on the creator. For example, in a letter to Mrs. M. E. Boole, he wrote, "It has always appeared to me more satisfactory to look at the immense amount of pain & suffering in this world, as the inevitable result of the natural sequence of events, i.e. general laws, rather than from the direct intervention of God though I am aware this is not logical with reference to an omniscient Deity."[12] This answer seems to imply that he does not want to blame God for the evil in this world. Yet his reference to "general laws," as he admits, is not really a solution to the question either: whence evil.

Yet there have been attempts to read Darwin very differently. If the blind forces of nature gave rise to life, then one should not expect a perfect world. This would

7. Charles Darwin, *On the Origin of Species* (1876; 415), in *The Works of Charles Darwin* (London: Pickering, 1988), 16:432.
8. Darwin (417), 16:434.
9. Darwin (428), 16:445–446.
10. Darwin (429), 16:446.
11. Darwin (428), 16:446.
12. Charles Darwin, "Letter to M.E. Boole" (December 14, 1866), in *The Correspondence of Charles Darwin*, eds. Frederick H. Burkhardt et al., vol. 14, 1866 (Cambridge: Cambridge University Press, 2004), 426.

then make sense of the evil side of nature.[13] While in rational theism benevolent God is manifested in an idyllic world, Darwin saw God only as the initial creator. Then the laws of nature took over, being blind and impartial, which would account for evil without directly blaming evil on God.[14] Biophysicist Cornelius G. Hunter (*b. 1957) therefore claims that Darwin "presented what we might call the evolution theodicy, which distanced the Creator from natural evil."[15] We should not forget, however, that Darwin published *Origin of Species* in the second half of the nineteenth century, a time when progress was on everybody's mind. Progress, be it in science, industry, or business, was interested not in the shadowy sides of life but in the bigger and better. As we can easily notice in the following quotation from a letter of Darwin to Asa Gray, the theory of evolution did not solve, for Darwin, the enigma of cruelty in nature.

> There seems to me too much misery in the world. I cannot persuade myself that a beneficent & omnipotent God would have designedly created the Ichneumonidæ with the express intention of their feeding within the living bodies of caterpillars, or that a cat should play with mice. Not believing this, I see no necessity in the belief that the eye was expressly designed. On the other hand I cannot anyhow be contented to view this wonderful universe & especially the nature of man, & to conclude that everything is the result of brute force. I am inclined to look at everything as resulting from designed laws, with the details, whether good or bad, left to the working out of what we may call chance. Not that this notion at all satisfies me.[16]

For him, the dark sides of life whether in nature or in one's own existence were left without a convincing explanation. We see this also when death hit his own family.

When Darwin's daughter Anne Elizabeth died in 1851, aged ten, evil and suffering moved for Darwin from being a theoretical problem to an agonizingly personal one. In the nineteenth century, most families lost children, and Darwin himself lost three children in infancy, but Anne was his favorite. When Anne got critically ill of tuberculosis, his wife was due to give birth any time. Therefore, she could not travel from their home in Downe to Malvern, where Anne was taken by her father in hope for a cure. Staying with her during her final illness, he witnessed every last, degrading moment of her wasting away. When Anne had died on April 23, 1851, on the same day, Darwin informed his wife, Emma, at Downe, writing, "She went

13. This is the position of Cornelius G. Hunter, *Darwin's God: Evolution and the Problem of Evil* (Grand Rapids, MI: Brazos, 2001), 10.
14. Cf. Hunter, *Darwin's God*, 142.
15. Hunter, *Darwin's God*, 145. Asterisks with dates throughout indicate that at the time of this book's publication, the person being referred to was still alive.
16. Charles Darwin, "Letter to Asa Gray" (May 22, 1860), in *The Correspondence of Charles Darwin*, ed. Frederick H. Burkhardt, vol. 8, 1860 (Cambridge: Cambridge University Press, 1993), 224.

to her final sleep most tranquilly, most sweetly at 12 o'clock today. Our poor dear dear [sic!] child has had a very short life but I trust happy, & God only knows what miseries might have been in store for her. [. . .] God bless her."[17] Though he deeply felt the pain about the loss, he was still confident that Anne's death may have spared her even worse miseries. Though he could not empirically discern the workings of a benevolent God, this notion of "God knows best" was so ingrained even in Darwin that he did not discard it against all odds. But his sentiment slowly changed.

In a letter of May 7, 1879, to John Fordyce, he confessed, "I think that generally (& more and more so as I grow older) but not always, that an agnostic would be the most correct description of my state of mind."[18] This corroborates with his remarks in his *Autobiography of Charles Darwin*, where he writes,

> That there is much suffering in the world no one disputes. Some have attempted to explain this in reference to man by imagining that it serves for his moral improvement. But the number of men in the world is as nothing compared with that of all other sentient beings, and these often suffer greatly without any moral improvement. A being so powerful and so full of knowledge as a God who could create the universe, is to our finite minds omnipotent and omniscient, and it revolts our understanding to suppose that his benevolence is not unbounded, for what advantage can there be in the sufferings of millions of the lower animals throughout almost endless time? This very old argument from the existence of suffering against the existence of an intelligent first cause seems to me a strong one.[19]

Evil mitigates against a benevolent creator. He could have done without inflicting evil on creation. Yet evolution proceeds by natural selection that inflicts suffering. So is there a wise God? Yes. Is there a benevolent God? Yes and no. And with this latter admission, Darwin as a naturalist resigns to agnosticism. He cannot empirically solve the issue of theodicy even if in his personal suffering through the death of his daughter Anne he resorts to an existential "God knows best."

Barth: The Overpowering Goodness of God

Karl Barth (1886–1968), in his *Church Dogmatics*, provided the most interesting as well as perhaps the most confusing proposal as to how to understand the phenomenon of evil. He pursues the line of Reformed theology of Calvin and Paley

17. Charles Darwin, "Letter to Emma Darwin" (April 23, 1851), in *The Correspondence of Charles Darwin*, eds. Frederick H. Burkhardt and Sydney Smith, vol. 5, 1851–1855 (Cambridge: Cambridge University Press, 1989), 24.
18. "Letter to John Fordyce" (May 7, 1879), Darwin Correspondence Project, accessed August 23, 2018, https://tinyurl.com/y2ywnnfg.
19. Charles Darwin, *The Autobiography of Charles Darwin 1809–1882* (90), in *The Works of Charles Darwin*, 29:121–122.

in which one is convinced that God has everything under control, and therefore, evil cannot assert itself as a really threatening phenomenon. Barth speaks here of nothingness as contradiction and opposition, as a "disruptive element" that comes into being as a foreign body under the providence of God. It is, however, of such a unique character that it "can never be considered or mentioned together in the same context as other objects of God's providence."[20]

In the first part of his doctrine of creation, Barth had already mentioned a shadow side of existence. The self-revelation of the creator, however, is not bound to this shadow side of existence as a sort of negative foil needed to hold himself up as positive.[21] It is God's yes to creation that first empowers the no that characterizes the realm of creation. There appears to have been something preexistent within creation that neither belongs to its essence nor stands over against it as something entirely distinct from it but rather finds its continued existence through God's yes to creation. Barth binds this nothingness (*das Nichtige*), or shadow side, very closely to God's activity.

Similar to nothingness is the situation with human sin, through which the person "has covered his own creaturely being with shame."[22] The human being as sinner remains a creature of God. God's word—that is, the testimony of the Holy Scriptures—reveals the human being, however, to be "a betrayer of himself and a sinner against his creaturely existence." According to Barth, one cannot recognize the human being as human or even as sinner when one does not view humanity from the perspective of God's self-revelation. The recognition that the human person is a sinner depends directly upon "the recognition that he shares in divine grace." (CD 3/2:32). To the grace of God belongs the justice of God that is revealed and carried out in the word of God. One recognizes thereby that one is different from what one should be.

It is extremely difficult to reconcile nothingness with the goodness of God. Indeed, creation in its shadow side, in its negative aspect, stands very close to nothingness (CD 3/3:296–97). Yet nothingness is not part of creation, even when it can force itself into creation. Barth calls sin "the concrete form of nothingness because in sin it becomes man's own act, achievement and guilt" (CD 3/3:310). Barth follows thereby the biblical model, for despite the accountability of humans for their behavior, sin as an action is continually described in the Bible as a succumbing to a

---

20. Karl Barth, CD, 3/3, trans. G. Bromiley and R. Ehrlich (Edinburgh: T&T Clark, 1960), 289. Additionally, Karl Barth also treats sin in a detailed fashion within the structure of the doctrine of reconciliation in CD, 4/1 (Edinburgh: T&T Clark, 1956). He emphasizes that sin can be recognized only christologically in the mirror of Jesus Christ (240). Sin is arrogance against God, resistance against following the path that God has indicated and planned, and a lie in that humans seek to know better than God what the real truth is in the salvation process (142–144). The lie is, according to Barth, self-destructive, for humans lie before God and deceive themselves and thus destroy themselves, bringing about death and misery. With these assertions, Barth reveals his commitment to traditional teachings. Through their sinfulness, humans not only alienate themselves from God and other people, but they also create evil for themselves and for others in a destructive sense.

21. Karl Barth, CD, 3/1 (Edinburgh: T&T Clark, 1958), 372–373.

22. For this and the following quotation, see Barth, CD, 3/2 (Edinburgh: T&T Clark, 1960), 27, 26.

foreign power. Sin is, on the one hand, human action, but on the other, it is a result of nothingness. According to Barth, nothingness does not exhaust itself in sin, for then it would simply be a part of creation.

What is then this nothingness? According to Barth, one cannot say of nothingness that it "is," as one might say, for example, that God or a created being "is."[23] Yet we would be playing down the significance of this nothingness if we thus concluded that nothingness is simply nothing. Rather, God takes account of it, is occupied with it, struggles against it, bears it, and overcomes it. It is not simply identical with that which does not exist, and it is also neither the counterpart to God nor a created being, but it is rather *the other* "from which God separates himself and in the face of which He asserts Himself and exerts His positive will." Nothingness, according to Barth, has no existence or recognizability except as the object of God's activity. This means that God's affirmation implies a no toward that to which he does not say yes—that is, to nothingness. God is Lord, both on the right hand and on the left. Precisely because he is also Lord on the left, "he is the basis and Lord of nothingness too." Nothingness is not merely an accident, an oversight of God, but rather, under his no, it is the object of his wrath and judgment. "Nothingness 'is,' therefore, in its connexion with the activity of God. It 'is' because and as and so long as [sic] God is against it" (CD 3/3:353). A lively debate has been spawned over this statement about the being of nothingness, for it is incomprehensible to our "common logic," and according to such common logic, Barth comes very close to declaring God to be the cause of nothingness.[24]

As we have seen, Barth declined to ascribe to nothingness a self-sufficient existence independent of God. He also denied, however, that one could derive nothingness from the activity of God alone, in which God has the role of one who foreknows and permits. Finally, nothingness does not simply represent a deficiency of good or of perfection, since it is not thereby ascribed a ground of being and is thus not an active power. But how can one then still rule out that nothingness comes from God's own self? If nothingness corresponds with the divine nonwilling, then the divine nonwilling is, as it were, the archetype for nothingness. Nothingness would then have its final parallel in God—namely, in God's negative will.[25] Despite all the attempts to disassociate nothingness from God and still assert God as the overarching power, nothingness seems to be an enigma. We must then agree with Barth that we have to deal here with the "ontic peculiarity" of nothingness.[26]

The gracious will of God is so strongly emphasized by Barth that whatever strives and works against God cannot approach a genuine existence. Ultimately, everything will be received into the salvific scope of God. Barth argues always

---

23. For this and the following, see Barth, CD, 3/3:349–351, quotations 351.
24. Regarding this assessment and for references to further literature, see Wilfried Härle, *Sein und Gnade: Die Ontologie in Karl Barths Kirchliche Dogmatik* (Berlin: Walter de Gruyter, 1974), especially his chapter on "Das Nichtige," 227–269.
25. See in this regard Härle, 241.
26. For this and the following quotation, see Barth, CD, 3/3:353.

from the grace of God, from God's covenant with humanity. Evil is the opposite of that which God wills. Nevertheless, it becomes the object of his *opus alienum*—that is, the work that is not proper to him, that of anger and judgment. The negation of the grace of God is "chaos, the world which He did not choose or will, which He could not and did not create, but which, as He created the actual world, He passed over and set aside, marking and excluding it as the eternal past, the eternal yesterday. And this is evil in the Christian sense, namely, what is alien and adverse to grace, and therefore without it." Nothingness opposes the grace of God inasmuch as it offends God and threatens his creation and breaks into the creation as sin, evil, and death and produces chaos.

Barth emphasizes that one cannot deal with nothingness in a frivolous manner. It is such a threatening power that the conflict with it—its conquest, removal, and settlement—is primarily a matter for God. Therefore, nothingness is, above all, God's own problem (CD 3/3:355). Humans are only affected by nothingness insofar as they fall willingly victim to it and thus become sinners. It is in this way that suffering, want, and destruction come to humanity. Yet Barth is optimistic in the face of the destructive power of nothingness, since the "kingdom of nothingness" is already destroyed. "But its dominion, even though it was only a semblance of dominion, is now objectively defeated as such in Jesus Christ. What it still is in the world, it is in virtue of the blindness of our eyes and the cover which is still over us, obscuring the prospect of the kingdom of God already established as the only kingdom undisputed by evil" (CD 3/3:367).

When one reads these words, one cannot but ask to whom this blindness applies. These lines were published just five years after the end of World War II, in which the satanic power, in its destructive and dehumanizing way, celebrated one victory after another. Barth can, of course, refer to the Gospels in which Jesus comments that Satan has fallen from heaven and has lost his position as our accuser at the right hand of God. Martin Luther too wrote in his hymn "A Mighty Fortress Is Our God" that the "old evil foe" can be subdued by "one little word." But nevertheless, both the Gospel writers and Luther took this nothingness, this propagator of chaos and harm, with utmost seriousness. We hear very little of this from Barth.

Nevertheless, Barth wishes to remain a biblical realist. Thus in connection with nothingness, he also spoke of demons. There he proceeds in a way similar to his treatment of nothingness. He reminds us that we dare not understand demons as the opposite of angels (CD 3/3:519–20). Just as heaven and hell have nothing in common, Barth instructs us that we cannot speak in the same breath of God and the devil, or of angels and demons. "The demons are the opponents of the heavenly ambassadors of God, as the latter are the champions of the kingdom of heaven and therefore the kingdom of God on earth. Angels and demons are related as creation and chaos, as the free grace of God and nothingness, as good and evil, as life and death, as the light of revelation and the darkness which will not receive it, as redemption and perdition, as *kerygma* and myth" (CD 3/3:520). Barth does not want to introduce a dualism here but wishes rather to make clear than one must speak of demons in an entirely different way than of angels. The origin and form of the devil and demons is nothingness, whereby Barth once more makes reference to the left hand of God through which they receive their "improper" existence (CD 3/3:522–23). They are ungodly and against God, and because God did not create them, they are also not creaturely. They are not other than nothingness but rather have their origin in nothingness. Because of the death and resurrection of Jesus and his elevation to the right hand of God, nothingness and demons "have nothing to declare." Therefore, we are able to celebrate with Christ "our liberation from demons" (CD 3/3:530).

Barth demonstrates in an impressive way the whole range of the anti-Godly powers of destruction. He does not limit them to the human realm but rather sees the metaphysical realm included in the battle against the God-opposing powers. The greatest problem with Barth's position occurs, however, in his many attempts to demonstrate that the God-opposing powers do not originate in or from God's creation. Though he declares, in agreement with the Gospel of John, that the devil is from the beginning and is the father of lies (CD 3/3:531), he must pass over in silence the passage in the same Gospel that says that the devil is the ruler of this world (John 14:30). For Barth, the God-opposing powers are so much within the context of the gracious and redemptive activity of God that they are nearly overwhelmed by God's redemptive power. However, this does not do justice to the reality of the negative and perverse within our world. Evil is not an accompanying apparition of the salvific activity of God but rather a power that, from our human perspective, leaves open the question of who will prevail in the end.

While for Barth the question is solved of who wins in the end, the question of whence comes evil receives ambiguous treatment. And why there is evil again receives no satisfactory answer. But perhaps these questions are beyond our reach anyhow, as Kant reminded us, if we want to solve them with reasonable arguments.

Rahner: The Incomprehensibility of Suffering

Karl Rahner (1904–84), the premier theologian of Roman Catholicism in the twentieth century, covered in his numerous writings every facet of the Christian faith. For the issue of theodicy, however, he devoted only a brief paper with the title "Why Does God Allow Us to Suffer?"[27] He starts out to caution us that the absolute holiness and goodness of God does not permit us to trace back to God the suffering that comes from the guilt of a free created being. But then there is the suffering that does not come from the guilt of a created being but is nevertheless present in this world. But what does it mean that God permits it? Without restricting in

---

27. Karl Rahner, "Why Does God Allow Us to Suffer?," in *Theological Investigations*, vol. 19, *Faith and Ministry*, trans. Edward Quinn (New York: Crossroad, 1983), 194–208. The page numbers in parentheses in the following text refer to this publication.

any way human freedom, God could prevent by divine predestination of creaturely freedom that there occurs guilt in the world as a no to God's divine will. There is no insoluble connection between freedom that God granted and willed for the world and creaturely guilt. Rahner does not concede that if God granted freedom in the world, then this necessarily implies guilt and sin. While Rahner does not want to distinguish between God permitting and God causing suffering, he wants to distinguish between suffering stemming from free human guilt and those events that cause suffering without stemming from free human guilt.

After these preliminary considerations, Rahner now goes through four answers that have been given within a theistic framework to discern their validity concerning the question that he raised at the beginning. The first attempt sees suffering as a more or less unavoidable side effect in a world that is pluralistic and developing. According to this view, we live in a complex world in which there is always friction. In the biological realm, for instance, the struggle for existence is unavoidable for the development of the species. What we call pain and death are only means of nature to increase life. Even the morally evil and the resulting suffering is a necessity to develop freedom and moral advancement. Evil is only that good that has not yet been completed. Rahner then counters that though this view has some validity, essentially, it is insufficient and even superficial. While he reminds us of the groaning of the whole creation (Rom 8:22), he is undecided whether in the biological realm we can talk about suffering and evil. Yet when we talk about human freedom and moral development, then this is hardly derived from a material base alone. "Freedom as such itself produces suffering and pain and death" (199). Actual freedom, Rahner reminds us, has caused such immense suffering that it cannot be simply referred to as the material and biological base. We may only think here of the gas chambers in Auschwitz. The immense protest against suffering, rising up from world history is not just an intensification of the noise that always accompanies life and death.

The second attempt to explain suffering tries to derive it exclusively from the freedom of created beings. Pain, suffering, and death always result from evil decisions stemming from the freedom of created beings. Rahner explains that this freedom of created beings is not identical to human freedom. It has created a history that started prior to the human and biological history and therefore determined these histories to some extent and made them histories of suffering. There is the variation of this thesis that asserts that all suffering ultimately stems from the freedom of humans who initially were not made to die. Their freedom as creatures, including humans, is absolutized and in its decision, is not caused by anything else. But according to Christian understanding, Rahner contends, no created being, including humans, are totally independent so that they would have sole responsibility for decisions. Freedom is always created freedom and therefore supported by the sovereign providence of God in its possibilities and in its concrete decisions. "Our freedom is completely embraced in God's supreme providence" (201). At the same time, Rahner reminds us that though we are free and though we cannot point to God with regard to our responsibility for our free decisions, they are at the same time totally embraced by God's disposition, which is founded only in God and in nothing and nobody else. Rahner is confronted here with God's sovereign freedom, on the one hand, and our human freedom, on the other, and he claims that though our freedom depends on God's sovereignty, the decision of how we use our freedom cannot be traced back to God.

The third traditional answer to the issue of suffering is, according to Rahner, that God allows us to suffer in order to test us and to make us more mature. "Suffering it is claimed, is the necessary situation in which alone a mature person can grow in patience, hope, and wisdom, and in the pattern of Christ" (203). Though there is a great deal of truth in this answer, it does not really solve the question of suffering. There is so much terrible suffering in this world, according to Rahner, that is destructive for humans and does not contribute to maturation. When old people suffer from Alzheimer's and young children die of cancer, then this has nothing to do with maturation. It is simply cruel suffering. Of course, one can say that these poor victims follow the crucified Christ in his suffering. But this does not address the issue of why God would permit so much suffering that has no humane educative function.

The last attempt to answer the issue of suffering, Rahner sees in reference to life eternal after death and our history of suffering. Of course, Christians are sure that through God's grace, there is eternal life without death, suffering, and tears. Yet nobody can prove that this suffering is the absolutely necessary means to acquire life eternal and that death is the only gate to that life. From the Christian tradition, we know that death had not been necessary. The same is true for sin. Rahner sums up, "Since it is possible to think of an eternal life achieved without suffering, it can indeed be seen as a conquest of suffering but not as an authorization of the latter" (205). Life eternal does not legitimize suffering as its presupposition.

Having thought through possible answers to the issue of suffering and finding them insufficient, he now addresses this issue himself. He starts from the Christian confession that God is the incomprehensible mystery. Even when we are allowed to see God face-to-face, the unfathomable God remains in his fear-causing splendor. "The incomprehensibility of suffering is part of the incomprehensibility of God" (206). Suffering is a reality that we cannot fathom, and in this way, it is a real appearance of the incomprehensibility of God in his very being and freedom. Suffering is the underivable form of the manifestation of the incomprehensibility of God. As a consequence, there is the possibility to despair in the face of the absurdity of suffering and therefore end up in atheism. The other possibility is the unconditional love and adoration to God that makes us forget our own self and stand before the incomprehensible God in his freedom. Only that God to whom we lovingly consent brings light into the darkness of suffering. In other words, Rahner has no answer to the question that he posed in the beginning, "Why does God allow us to suffer?" Yet he reminds us that God is God, and as humans, we are unable to fathom his ways that also involve immense suffering. The only comfort we have is the love of God, which promised the eschatological resolution that there will be an end to all suffering.

Sölle and Rubenstein: The Weakness of God and the Holocaust

Dorothee Sölle (1929–2003), German liberation theologian and writer, reverses the approach of Rahner. Gleaning from Dietrich Bonhoeffer's last letters before his death, she talks about the omnipotence of God in the world and of the nonreligious interpretation of Christian concepts. "Christ took over God's role in the world, but in the process it was changed into the role of the helpless God."[28] The absent God who is represented by Christ is the powerless one in the world. Atheism that was caused by the insoluble issue of theodicy is still a kind of religion. Its God is being accused because of the suffering of the innocent. It is the God of omnipotence, the king, father, and ruler of the world. As Sölle asserts, this God is rightly accused by modernity, and all theological artistry to silence this accusation cannot muffle the truth of rejecting God almighty. Since one cannot silence this accusation, this leads to deposing a theistically understood God. Modern atheism, according to Sölle, was advanced not just by natural science and historical criticism of the biblical documents but as strongly by the suffering, the injustice, and the pain of the innocent. "In all religions, a question mark has been set against the omnipotent and serene gods by the sufferings of men. But only in Christ does the concept of a suffering God appear. Here alone is it the suffering of God which is shouldered by a man. Only in Christ does it become clear that we can put God to death because he has put himself in our hands. Only since Christ has God become dependent on us."[29] Christ has not identified himself with the suffering as a bystander, but he represented the powerlessness of God in the world through his own suffering.

Sölle then concludes that in the nineteenth century, suffering was "the rock of atheism." Yet in the twentieth century, nothing points more clearly to God than his defeats in the world. "That God in the world has been, and still is, mocked and tortured, burnt and gassed: that is the rock of the Christian faith which rests all its hope on God attaining his identity." This pain cannot be extinguished, and this hope cannot be forgotten. Christians share in God's suffering in Christ, and that is their faith. From this, we know that God is powerless and needs help. God puts himself at risk and makes himself dependent on us and identifies himself with the nonidentical. Therefore, it is time that we do something for God, since long ago God did something for us.

28. Dorothee Sölle, *Christ the Representative: An Essay in Theology after the "Death of God,"* trans. David Lewis (London: SCM, 1967), 150.
29. Sölle, *Christ the Representative*, 151, for this and the following quote.

As a result of the Enlightenment, Sölle sees the death of God already as a secret but vibrant topic in Hegel's thoughts.[30] History is understood not only as God giving up Godself as the utmost distancing from himself but also as his own giving up himself as his own doing. But God does not enter into history to such an extent that nothing of God is still outstanding because if this were the case, we would be in heaven.[31] Since theology after "the death of God" is perceived from God giving up Godself, the suffering is then God's own suffering, and the only question concerning theodicy would be why God gave himself up, suffering with creation. Yet as Sölle contends, this touches on the hiddenness of God, which also contains God's future. She refers then to the cross of Christ, which exemplifies unconditional love to others, leading to sacrificing one's life as the exclusive meaning of existence. Since her thoroughgoing theme is suffering in the world in which God has sacrificed his own self because of his own love for the world, the question of theodicy takes a new turn. In Christ's passion, God identifies himself with human suffering; God becomes powerless but nevertheless shows a liberating perspective beyond suffering. However, in Sölle's Hegelian concept, there is no answer to the question, "Why is there suffering?" If it is only induced by humans, as Sölle seems to imply, then humans should also be able to overcome it.

Richard L. Rubenstein (*b. 1924), a Jewish theologian, stated in the preface of his controversial book *After Auschwitz*, "Although Jewish history is replete with disaster, none has been so radical in its total import as the holocaust. Our images of God, man, and the moral order had been permanently impaired. No Jewish theology will possess even a remote degree of relevance to contemporary Jewish life if it ignores the question of God and the death camps."[32] Similar to Sölle, Rubenstein is closely associated with the death of God theologians. While for the death of God theologians, such as Thomas J. J. Altizer (1927–2018) and William Hamilton (1924–2012), it was modern secularity that caused the collapse of a transcendent order of the universe, for Rubenstein, it was the Holocaust that shattered his belief in a transcendent God.

Rubenstein states that the God who tolerates the suffering of even one innocent child is infinitely cruel or blissfully indifferent. This discrepancy between a good God and the suffering in the world cannot be solved by believing in another world wherein the cruelties of this world will be rectified. How would we know that God will do better in another world than in the present one? Rubenstein surmises. He agrees with Paul Tillich (1886–1965) "that the God of theism (that is, a personal God) is dead and deserves to die," since human moral autonomy is incompatible with the traditional concept of a personal God (87). According to

30. Dorothee Sölle, *Atheistisch an Gott glauben* (Olten, Switzerland: Walter-Verlag, 1968), 57, where she extensively refers to Hegel without citing her sources.
31. So Sölle, *Atheistisch an Gott glauben*, 73.
32. Richard L. Rubenstein, *After Auschwitz: Radical Theology and Contemporary Judaism* (Indianapolis: Bobbs-Merrill, 1966), x. The page numbers in parentheses in the text refer to this publication.

Rubenstein, the real objection against a personal or theistic God comes from the irreconcilability of the claim of God's perfection with the hideous human evil tolerated by such a God. Reflecting on the Holocaust, Rubenstein asserts, "We can neither affirm the myth of the omnipotent God of History nor can we maintain its corollary, the election of Israel" (69). But this does not imply for Rubenstein that there is no God or that the God conception is meaningless.

Since the Father-God is the dead God who died at Auschwitz, Rubenstein insists that "God remains the central mystery against which all partial realities can be measured" (238). In Tillichian fashion, he understands God as the ground of being and the focus of ultimate concern. The influence of Tillich on Rubenstein is not surprising, since Tillich taught at Harvard University (1955–62) while Rubenstein pursued doctoral studies there. God is, for Rubenstein, the infinite measure against which we can see our own limited finite lives in proper perspective. As the ultimate measure of human truth and human potentiality, God calls upon each of us to face both the limitations and the opportunities of our finite predicament without disguise, illusion, or hope. Though Rubenstein concedes that we live in a world of utter secularity, in a world of the death of God, God is not dead. But "the world of the death of God is a world devoid of hope and illusion" (257). Rubenstein elaborates, "Individuals have much reason to hope when they contemplate the possibility of fulfilment in the here and now; there are, however, absolutely no grounds for eschatological hope" (258).

Since there is no transcendent God, there is no hope in a hereafter. Whatever hope is for the resolution of human misery, it must occur in this world. Since God is not beyond this world, God is not the cause of evil. Humans forge their own future. With reference to depth psychology, Rubenstein asserts, "Guilt, ambivalence, human evil, and human aggressiveness are as inescapable as human love, affection, and self-sacrifice. They are inextricably bound together" (89). Therefore, people cannot do without law, tradition, and structure. The need is set for guidelines to enable us to apprehend the limits of appropriate behavior. Since Rubenstein questions whether in the long run we can afford to pay the cumulative cost of the inevitable errors in discovering behavioral norms, he seems to look for religion as help.[33] Religion is the way in which we share and celebrate through the inherited myths, rituals, and traditions of our communities, the dilemmas and the cries of life and death, good and evil. In other words, religion is that which ties us together and also ties us to the past. This is even more necessary, since Rubenstein is convinced that "we live in a malignant universe, in which human existence is filled with anxiety and despair" (262). Since there is no eschatological hope, there is only the tragic acceptance of this world. There is neither an eschatological resolution of human misery nor its accreditation to a transcendent and omnipotent God.

---

33. Cf. Rubenstein, *After Auschwitz*, 260.

Moltmann: Theodicy as the Open Wound of Life in This World

Jürgen Moltmann (*b. 1927), a Reformed theologian, covered almost every facet of theology. While he did not devote a separate publication to the issue of theodicy, he was by no means oblivious to this important topic—quite the opposite; his theology has been largely articulated in the light of the reality of pain and suffering in the world. "In fact, the theodicy question has been a primary shaping influence on Moltmann's theological perspective."[34] In this way, his concerns coincide with those of Sölle and Rubenstein. Yet quite different from them, he has not given up on God the Father, since that God is constitutive for the Trinity of Father, Son, and Holy Spirit. As Moltmann insists, a Christian "believes in God for Christ's sake. God himself is involved in the history of Christ's passion."[35]

Moltmann immediately asked the question of whether God's involvement in Christ's passion would mean that God allowed Christ to suffer for us or that God himself suffered in Christ on our behalf. Of course, he knows that patripassianism—meaning that God suffered—was rejected by Christian theology. God himself cannot suffer. The consequence would be, Moltmann explains, that Christ's suffering and death would only be a human tragedy. Moreover, if God is incapable of suffering in every respect, then he would also be incapable of love. It is exactly God's love that makes him suffer not out of a deficiency but out of his superabundant love. Moltmann refers here to Origen as the only patristic theologian who dared to assert that God suffers out of love, saying, "So God suffers our ways as the Son of God bears our sufferings."[36] It is the suffering of the Father who gives up his Son for the sake of the world. Yet in contrast to patripassianism, Moltmann assures that there is not a divine monarch who suffers in and as Christ, but it is God's suffering in Trinitarian terms. God the Father suffers in and with God the Christ.

With reference to the Old Testament, Moltmann explains the pathos of God and that God is not beyond emotions. Especially important for Moltmann is the Hebrew concept of Shekinah, meaning the indwelling of God. With his Shekinah, God is present in Israel and suffers with Israel persecutions and even goes with the Israelites into exile as a prisoner. According to Moltmann, this concept of God's Shekinah allows us to understand the Jewish history of suffering as the history of the suffering of the divine Shekinah.[37] With God's suffering and the divine pathos, the issue of theodicy is implied. With the factuality of suffering, the question about God arises. Moltmann states, "The suffering of the single innocent child

---

34. So rightly, John David Jaeger, "Jürgen Moltmann and the Problem of Evil," *Asbury Theological Journal* 53 (Fall 1998): 5.
35. Jürgen Moltmann, *The Trinity and the Kingdom of God*, trans. Margaret Kohl (London: SCM, 1981), 21.
36. Moltmann, *Trinity*, 24; Origen, *Homilia VI in Ezechielem*, in MPG, 13:714–715.
37. Cf. Moltmann, *Trinity*, 30. The page numbers in parentheses in the following text refer to this publication.

is an irrefutable rebuttal of the notion of the almighty and kindly God in heaven. For a God who lets the innocent suffering and who permits senseless death is not worthy to be called God at all" (47). Here again we notice the affinity to Sölle and Rubenstein in their analysis. Yet different from them, Moltmann concludes that to abolish God does not alleviate suffering, since "even the abolition of God does not explain suffering and does not assuage pain" (48–49). Of course, the theism of the almighty and kindly God comes to an end on the rock of suffering. But "on the rock of suffering the atheism of the godless person who is left to himself ends too" (48–49). Now the dialectic of theodicy starts, since suffering calls into question the notion of the just and kindly God, but the longing for justice and goodness calls suffering into question and makes it a conscious pain. The experience of suffering in its manifold forms causes us to question whether there is a just God or even God's justice.

Moltmann now asserts, "God and suffering belong together, just as in this life that cry from God and the suffering experienced in pain belong together." (48–49). The question about God and about suffering are one common question. They can only find a common answer. But then Moltmann concedes, "No one can answer the theodicy question in this world and no one can get rid of it" (48–49). We must live with this open question, seeking the future in which suffering will be overcome. This means it is the all-embracing eschatological question. Is there an eschatological resolution of suffering, or is there none? Yet for now, we must live with suffering, which is "the open wound of life in this world" (48–49). A faithful Christian experiences deeply the suffering in the world, and therefore, that person asks fervently about God and the new creation.

While often death and suffering are causally connected with human sinfulness, this is not the whole story. As some church fathers taught, death belongs together with the creation of humanity as a finite being. Yet there is also "innocent suffering," as we see in Job and in many psalms of lament in the Old Testament. Moltmann then connects this innocent suffering with the suffering of love, since he surmises that "for love there is only 'innocent' suffering, because anyone who loves cannot look on at the other person's suffering any longer—he wants to overcome it" (51). This kind of suffering can be discerned in Christ's sufferings by virtue of the passionate love that Christ manifests and reveals. Since God suffers in Christ's passion, Moltmann now moves to the issue of whether God was free in his suffering or whether God was a prisoner of his own history.

If God is love, God cannot be content to be sufficient in God's own self. Since God cannot deny himself, God does not have the choice between being love and not being love. And by loving the world, he is by no means his own prisoner but is entirely free because God is love, and therefore, by loving the world, God is entirely himself. While God in his freedom always chooses the good, for humans, that freedom is no longer predecided by love, but human choice is always threatened by evil and injustice. Moltmann explains, divine "love is a self-evident, unquestionable 'overflowing of goodness' which is therefore never open to choice at any time. We have to understand true freedom is being the self-communication of the good" (55). God can, so to speak, do no wrong, but humans can.

Moltmann distinguishes here between two concepts of freedom. One is the nominalist concept that is derived from the language of domination. There only the Lord is free, and the people are his property, and he can do with them as he likes. The other concept of freedom comes from the language of community and fellowship. Their freedom consists in the mutual and common participation in life and in a communication in which there is neither lordship nor servitude. Since the triune God reveals God's self as love in the fellowship of Father, Son, and Holy Spirit, God's freedom lies in the friendship that he offers to men and women and makes them God's friends. Yet this freedom is vulnerable, as we see in God's suffering and sacrifice through self-giving and patience.

Moltmann exemplifies this with the creation of the world. There God's self-humiliation begins, since as the creator, God has to concede to his creation the space in which to exist, and God must allow it time and freedom. "For God, creation means self-limitation, the withdrawal of himself, that is to say self-humiliation. Creative love is always suffering love as well" (59). God had to open up space for creation and thereby limit himself voluntarily. Moltmann sums up, "The creation of the world and human beings for freedom and fellowship is always bound up with the process of God's deliverance from the sufferings of his love. His love, which liberates, delivers and redeems through suffering, wants to reach its fulfilment in the love that is bliss" (60). For Moltmann, creation is nothing static, but it moves forward always envisioning its eschatological fulfillment. This process entails, however, suffering and pain both for creation and for God's own self.

While the main reference for Moltmann's understanding of theodicy comes from *The Trinity and the Kingdom of God*, his *God in Creation* is also illuminating. He tells us there that "it is advisable to eliminate the concept of causality from the doctrine of creation, and indeed we have to stop thinking in terms of causality at all."[38] Creating the world is something different from causing it, since the creator is present in creation by virtue of the Spirit. Therefore, God's relationship to creation must be viewed as an intricate web of unilateral, reciprocal, and many-sided relationships. There is no antithesis between God and the world so that one could be defined over against the other. The creation lives from God's creative power, and yet God lives in creation. God is transcendent in relation to the world and at the same time immanent in it. Moltmann refers here again to the rabbinic and cabbalistic doctrine of the Shekinah according to which there is a division that takes place in God's own self. Though by remaining God, he gives himself away to his people and suffers along with their sufferings. Then there is the doctrine of the

---

38. Jürgen Moltmann, *God in Creation: A New Theology of Creation and the Spirit of God; The Gifford Lectures 1984–1985*, trans. Margaret Kohl (Minneapolis: Fortress, 1993), 14.

Trinity, in which God creates, reconciles, and redeems creation through the Son and is present in his creation through the power of the Spirit.

God is to some extent the emotive force who propels creation forward, therefore the title *God in Creation*. Yet the knowledge of the world as God's creation does not come from the mere observation of the world itself. It is made possible only through the historical revelation of God the Lord. Therefore, the universe is caught up into the history of God's rule. "Creation in the beginning prepares for this history, and the history itself is consummated in the new creation in the kingdom of God."[39] The creation is both in bondage and open for the future. Nevertheless, creation is an open system, since God's activity in history consists essentially in opening up systems that are closed. Even the eschatological kingdom of glory, which completes the process of creation through the indwelling of God, cannot be conceived "as a system that has finally been brought to completion and is therefore itself now closed."[40] The new creation implies the openness of all finite life systems for the fullness of life. For Moltmann, there is no end, since life through God's indwelling continues to go on, though unbounded and no longer marred by suffering.

Today's world, however, is still a world characterized by immense pain and suffering. For Moltmann, suffering is central to his theological reflections, and he devoted a whole book to it: *The Crucified God*. As he states, "The death of Jesus on the cross is the *center* of all Christian theology. [. . .] All Christian statements about God, about creation, about sin and death have their focal point in the crucified Christ."[41] The cross tells us as much about God as the God of Jesus. The Christ event on the cross is an event of God, since God has acted here and suffered. Moltmann does not advocate the traditional doctrine of two natures in Christ but prefers to start with the whole person of Christ, and therefore, the death of the Son must be understood in relation to the Father and the Spirit. In contrast to the death of God theologians, Moltmann talks about the death of God in terms not of Jesus's death but of the death in God—that is, in the Trinity. While the death of God theologians consider God in theistic terms and distance themselves from this God, Moltmann always conceives God in Trinitarian terms and therefore can adhere to this concept even if God dies on the cross.

According to the Christian faith, God suffered in Jesus's suffering, and God died in the cross of Christ so that we can live and be resurrected in God's future. In Hegelian dialectic, Moltmann asserts, "In the cross of his Son, God took upon himself not only death, so that he might be able to die comforted with the certainty that even death could not separate him from God, but still more, in order to make the crucified Christ the ground of his new creation, in which death itself is swallowed

39. Moltmann, *God in Creation*, 56.
40. Moltmann, *God in Creation*, 214.
41. Jürgen Moltmann, *The Crucified God*, trans. R. A. Wilson and John Bowden (London: SCM, 2009), 210.

up in the victory of life."[42] According to Moltmann, God and suffering are no longer contradictions as they are in theism and in atheism, since God's being is in suffering and suffering is in God's being itself because God is love. A God who cannot suffer is a disinterested being, and who cannot suffer can also not love. Yet "God himself loves and suffers the death of Christ in his love."[43] The Father who abandons and surrenders the Son suffers the death of the Son in immeasurable pain of love. This means the Son suffers dying, and the Father suffers the death of the Son.

Because of the death of the Son and God's suffering in this death, there is a theology possible after Auschwitz contrary to what Rubenstein asserted. Just as the cross of Christ, so also Auschwitz is taken into the pain of the Father. "God in Auschwitz and Auschwitz in the crucified God—that is the basis for the real hope which both embraces and overcomes the world, and the ground for a love which is stronger than death and can sustain death."[44]

It is not without significance that in *The Coming of God: Christian Eschatology* everything is directed toward the final glorification of God. Through Christ, the name of God is sanctified; in him, God's will is done; and with him, God's kingdom will come. "All created beings are drawn into the mutual relationships of the divine life, and into the wide space of the God who is sociality."[45] Moltmann does not overlook the immense misery of this world. Yet "the whole creation participates in Christ's tribulation and in the light of the cross is manifested in its forsakenness and havoc, so that it may be drawn into the cosmic resurrection and new creation."[46] There is an eschatological panentheism through which everything and everybody will be received in God. Yet Moltmann also cautions that "there is no hope without fear."[47] It almost looks as if the suffering and the concomitant fear is a precondition for the final glory. The heavy emphasis on the theology of the cross notwithstanding, the Hegelian dialectic and Calvin's conviction of the world as God's theater of glory are very noticeable. As Moltmann warned, however, at the very beginning, there is no answer to a theodicy. Whence there is evil remains unanswered.

---

42. Moltmann, *Crucified God*, 224.
43. Moltmann, *Crucified God*, 234.
44. Moltmann, *Crucified God*, 288.
45. Jürgen Moltmann, *The Coming of God: Christian Eschatology*, trans. Margaret Kohl (Minneapolis: Fortress, 1996), 336.
46. Moltmann, *Coming of God*, 233.
47. Moltmann, *Coming of God*, 234.

7 The Present Situation

We have traversed a vast territory and so far have not found a satisfying answer to the issue of theodicy. Where does evil come from, and how far does it reach? According to the biblical account, it suddenly emerges. It is only in the intertestamental period that we hear of a fallen angel who turned evil. Is evil only a by-product of evolution, as some have claimed, or is there in the background an evil power that transcends human possibilities? Again, there are numerous answers given at the present scene, but very few, if any, are persuasive. We will only describe and evaluate three of them, since they seem to be representative of those who still claim that answers can be found—namely, the process thought of Alfred North Whitehead, the Irenaean theodicy of John Hick, and finally, the idea of open theism of some evangelical theologians.

Process Thought: The Emerging God

North American process theology is based principally upon the work of the British-American mathematician and philosopher Alfred North Whitehead (1861–1947) and the American philosopher Charles Hartshorne (1897–2000). It is especially propagated by the Center for Process Studies in Claremont, California, which was founded by John B. Cobb Jr. (*b. 1925) and David Ray Griffin in 1973, and is part of the Claremont School of Theology. The question raised here is how evil fits into a universe that is governed by a good God.

David Ray Griffin (*b. 1939) at the very beginning of his considerations in *God, Power, and Evil: A Process Theodicy* (1976) presents the following "formal statement of the problem of evil":

1. God is a perfect reality. (Definition)
2. A perfect reality is an omnipotent being. (By definition)
3. An omnipotent being could unilaterally bring about an actual world without any genuine evil. (By definition)
4. A perfect reality is a morally perfect being. (By definition)
5. A morally perfect being would want to bring about an actual world without any genuine evil. (By definition)
6. If there is genuine evil in the world, then there is no God. (Logical conclusion from 1 through 5)
7. There is genuine evil in the world. (Factual statement)
8. Therefore, there is no God. (Logical conclusion from 6 and 7)[1]

1. David Ray Griffin, *God, Power, and Evil: A Process Theodicy* (Philadelphia: Westminster, 1976), 9.

Griffin, of course, is not willing to accept the conclusion of his theses that there is no God if genuine evil is found to exist in the world. For him, the problem appears to be rooted in our traditional conception of God. In our Western conception, one has usually, according to Griffin, understood God as either controlling or being able to control every detail of the events of our world.[2] This appeared to belong to the nature of God, since God could not be God if he did not possess this power. The logical conclusion of this conception was that nothing happened in the world unless God either caused it or at least permitted it despite the fact that God had the power to prevent it. If God is so almighty that he determines every occurrence, then God is responsible for everything evil.[3] A God, however, who compels and always enforces his will is a despotic God, such as is prevalent in Judaism, Christianity, and Islam and that also gives rise to despotic human beings. This criticism of the conception of God was already brought into sharp focus by Whitehead. According to Griffin, however, this traditional view of God does not correspond to the biblical testimony of the Judeo-Christian tradition.

The biblical testimony suggests the rejection of either thesis 2, "A perfect reality is an omnipotent being," or thesis 3, "An omnipotent being could unilaterally bring about an actual world without any genuine evil."[4] For Griffin, process theology and its view of evil do not contradict the biblical tradition. In Griffin's view, God is not able to fully control every occurrence in the world.[5] The reason for this is to be found not in God's weakness or imperfection but rather in the view of God that is distinctive of process theology. Process theology maintains that "God's power is persuasive, not controlling."[6] Thus in an important sense, God is responsible for the evil in the world, but in Griffin's view, God cannot be indicted or held accountable for evil. The potential for genuine evil is grounded in the metaphysical—that is, the necessary features of the world. The willing or permitting of evil is not determined by the divine will but rests ultimately upon the essential being of God and the world.

The world, as process theology in the tradition of Whitehead has claimed, is not created out of nothing, but creation means rather "the creation of order out of chaos."[7] There is thus a real world that stands over against God and upon which God's purposes are brought to bear. God, however, does not possess a monopoly of power, for the actual world necessarily contains potent actualities through which a certain amount of self-determination and influence upon the future is affected. Thus God cannot fully control the becoming within each actuality, since every actuality will always in part be determined by that which has preceded it as well as through its own inherent potency. Evil can, for instance, arise out of this

---

2. Griffin, 17.
3. Cf. in this regard Dalton DeVere Baldwin, "A Whiteheadian Solution to the Problem of Evil" (PhD diss., Claremont Graduate School, 1975), 314–315, who adopts this thesis of Whitehead.
4. Griffin, *God, Power, and Evil*, 53.
5. Griffin, 275.
6. Griffin, 276.
7. Griffin, 279.

potency without corresponding to divine intention. Genuine evil is described as disharmony, as when, for example, varying elements of an experience conflict with one another so that there is a feeling of a mutual destruction or when bodily pain or mental evil, such as sorrow, fear, or dislike, is produced.[8] This is intrinsic to the structure of reality. It is also argued in this connection that sometimes morally responsible freedom turns consciously from its goal and introduces genuine evil.[9]

If one asks why such an evil exists, one is told that voluntary love without morally responsible freedom is not possible. The freedom to decide in a morally responsible manner must always contain an alternative, otherwise it is not genuine freedom. Thus the possibility of evil as a worse alternative is necessarily presupposed. One is reminded here of Augustine, who also maintained that evil was necessary as a contrast to good so that good could distinguish itself from it. In Augustine's thought, however, this is presented only as a possibility in order to make the existence of evil plausible. In process theology, on the other hand, the necessity of evil constitutes a fundamental assumption about the structure of reality. Behind this view lies Whitehead's dipolar conception of God who both precedes and follows. God is "preceding" in his eternal aim and "following" in the power of his persuasion and in the process character of all genuine being. Whitehead "shows how evil arises without making God responsible for any evil which cannot be justified. Excess evil which cannot be justified results from the wrong use of responsible freedom."[10] Thus God is freed from the suspicion of being unjust. Also, in this view, evil does not detract from the divinity of God. Yet how is the structure of evil itself to be viewed?

Although process theology seldom reflects on the structure of evil, Marjorie Hewitt Suchocki (*b. 1933) took up this theme in her well-informed dissertation. She writes, "The world, in its freedom, transcends God, even as God in his freedom transcends the world. But in this transcendence the world becomes truly responsible for its good and its evil. The metaphysical structure within which good or evil relationships take place is one which must pronounce the individual occasion itself as good. [...] The relationships which must develop in the interrelated community of being are the arena of relative good and evil. But given this structure of interrelationships, no evil is ever final: the structure is ultimately redemptive."[11] This does not mean that evil is not real, but rather, it means that it anticipates its

---

8. Griffin, 282.
9. For this and the following, see Baldwin, *Whiteheadian Solution*, 317.
10. Baldwin, ii, in the summary of his work.
11. For this and the following quotation, see Majorie Hewitt Suchocki, "The Correlation between Good and Evil" (PhD diss., Claremont Graduate School, 1974), 249–250. In a revised version of her dissertation ("The End of Evil: Process Eschatology in Historical Context" [Albany: SUNY Press, 1988], esp. 154), she once again emphasizes that our finite existence reveals a fundamental ambiguity in which good and evil are intertwined with one another and that this ambiguity produces evil as well as redemption. Thus redemption as the triumph of good over evil is seen as a historical process. Evil as a destructive power, which not only is active in this process but also opposes it, is not, however, taken into account.

transformation. Evil will be overcome either already before the end of time or at the very least in the eschaton. Through God's providence, the power of evil is already broken. Hence evil stands under the influence of grace, which extends itself into the whole world so that the world might be redeemed. "God is the future of the world in every fresh moment; as the future of the world he is sheerly grace."

One is here reminded of the triumph of grace in the theology of Karl Barth. Similar to Barth, the activity of evil is relatively faint, and it has lost its God-opposing and destructive dynamic. It is part of the evolutionary process that finally ends within this process when all things find their completion in God. Is this optimism, however, justified? And why would God allow so much evil in this world? Moreover, evil continues within our world without any signs of weariness. In light of its persistent wickedness, evil will not enter into any kind of pact with good and is not ready for any transformation. It is certainly correct that God is not an omnipotent despot who determines every minute detail. It is, however, the conviction of the biblical documents that God not only has compassion and steadfastly desires to move everything toward his goal but also judges and punishes evildoers. Despite the many correct perspectives of process theology, one cannot escape the suspicion that it has been neatly outlined in theory on a drawing board but often overlooks the living reality of this world.

We should not forget that Whitehead, the main mentor of process thought, was a mathematician and only late in life pursued philosophy. We notice this also in the deliberations of the philosopher Lewis Ford (1933–2018). He distinguishes between persuasive and coercive power, explaining that coercive power directly influences the outcome, whereas persuasive power operates more indirectly. "It is effective in determining the outcome only to the extent that the process appropriates and reaffirms for itself the aims envisioned in the persuasion."[12] Coercive power exercised by God would restrict creaturely freedom and therefore would impoverish God, since God could have no genuine social existence. Yet God has elected to enter into dialogue with sinful, yet free, human beings. God is neither a craftsman nor a cosmic watchmaker. God's persuasive power "maximizes creaturely freedom, respecting the integrity of each creature in the very act of guiding that creature's development toward greater freedom."[13] This freedom presupposes that the world as a whole or its individual parts possess a self-activity of their own.

Ford then reflects on evolution and states that over the past several billion years, there has been an increasing complexity of order that cannot be satisfactorily accounted for simply in terms of the chance juxtaposition of component elements. It calls for a transcendent directing power constantly introducing richer possibilities of order for the world to actualize. God as the persuasive power proposes, and the world as the receptive power disposes. The response of the creature is

---

12. Lewis Ford, "Divine Persuasion and the Triumph of Good," in *The Problem of Evil: Selected Readings*, ed. Michael L. Peterson (Notre Dame, IN: University of Notre Dame Press, 1992), 248.
13. Ford, 249.

the necessary self-activity that ensures spontaneity. This holds true for the whole created order. No creature is left to itself. As Ford explains, "God thus serves as a dynamic source of value, personally responding anew to the concrete situation confronting each creature in turn, and providing it individually with its own particular initial aim."[14] If this initial aim were actualized, evil will be avoided. But is there then any ultimate triumph of good?

While in classical theism God's omnipotence in terms of God's coercive power guarantees the ultimate triumph of the good, in process theism, the future is an open risk. "God is continuously directing the creation toward the good, but his persuasive power is effective only insofar as the creatures themselves affirm that good."[15] While the future is risky and uncertain, we may hope that the grace of God may be received and permeate all beings. This hope calls upon us to redouble our efforts to achieve the good in this world with all its ambiguities for good and evil. Since God and the world are cojoined, the world must trust God to provide the aim for its efforts, and God must trust the world for the achievement of that aim. Ford then concludes, "The world is a risky affair for God as well as for us. God has taken that risk upon himself in creating us with freedom through persuasion. He has faith in us, and it is up to us to respond in faith to him."[16] Ford even admits that the good will not triumph unless we achieve that victory. But this victory does not come without God.

Since in his primordial nature God's conceptual feelings are inexhaustible, God has the necessary resources to achieve the maximum harmonious intensity from any situation. We wonder here how this conception of God differs from God's omnipotence. But what is even more disturbing is the scant attention that is given to the magnitude of evil. Especially in the last one hundred years, we have seen so much evil in the world induced by humans on each other and on nature and also the destructiveness in nature itself, from tsunamis to earthquakes wiping out hundreds of thousands human lives, that it is difficult to believe that divine persuasion has made any progress. The resolution of evil seems shakier than ever. The philosophers Peter Hare (1935–2008) and Edward Madden (*b. 1925) rightly observe, "Process theists have not taken the problem of the large number that remains unpersuaded seriously."[17] Mere persuasion does not suffice to overcome evil.

The Irenaean Theodicy of John Hick

John Hick (1922–2012), British philosopher of religion, states at the outset, "The fact of evil constitutes the most serious objection there is to the Christian belief

---

14. Ford, 252.
15. Ford, 257.
16. Ford, 257–258.
17. Peter Hare and Edward Madden, "Evil and Persuasive Power," in *Problem of Evil*, 270.

in a God of love. It is also probably the hardest objection to write about."[18] Nevertheless, he wrote a massive volume on this topic that is still noteworthy today. He distinguishes between an Augustinian and an Irenaean type of theodicy and follows the latter but with modifications and corrections suggested by the study of the Augustinian tradition. Hick carefully goes through the history of theology and philosophy of Western thinking, outlining first the Augustinian type of theology and then the Irenaean type before he presents his own "theodicy for today."

Hick finds in the Bible an implicit theodicy, since the Bible, on the one hand, expresses a profound faith in God and, on the other, shows the realities of sin and suffering, be it cruelty, violence, poverty, disease, or just human folly. "The climax of this biblical history of evil was the execution of Jesus of Nazareth" (279). Yet even through the darkest point in the biblical history of evil, God's purpose was moving physically or invisibly toward its far-distant fulfillment. The Christian faith, however, found in this climax of evil the greatest good of all that the history of Jesus would end in tragedy. This paradoxical understanding of evil betrays an implicit Christian theodicy. Divine providence cannot be inferred from the evidences of nature, as William Paley had still thought, but it preserves an already existing faith from being overcome by the darkness of evil. Hick therefore concludes, "The aim of the Christian theodicy must thus be the relatively modest and defensive one of showing that the mystery of evil, largely incomprehensible though it remains, does not render irrational a faith that has arisen, not from the inferences of natural theology but from participation in the stream of religious experience which is continuous with that recorded in the Bible" (281). Faith arises not from natural theology but from the religious experience that is in line with the experience of the faithful in the biblical record. The Christian faith is then a distinctive consciousness of the world and of our existence in this world that comes from our consciousness of God in Christ. Hick then terms the historical events upon which the Christian faith is based *Christian mythology*. They convey in a universally understandable way the special importance and meaning of certain items of mundane experience, such as the life and destiny of Jesus. Christian theology then speaks systematically about God on the basis of these data that are provided by the Christian experience. Hick claims that in the past, theology and myth have been closely intertwined because the less people knew about the character of the physical universe, the more difficult it was for them to identify myth as myth being distinct from history and science. Therefore, the dominant Christian theodicy was based on the ancient myth of the origin of evil and the fall of humanity, which then was reasonably assumed to be actual history. In this way, the great creation-fall-redemption myth became the official Christian myth of Christ standing at the center of the universe and being of crucial importance for all people. Yet Hick contends that we can no longer share the

---

18. John Hick, *Evil and the God of Love* (London: Macmillan, 1966), xi, in his preface. The page numbers in parentheses in the following text refer to this publication.

assumption that the creation-fall myth is basically authentic history, and therefore, we look at the theodicy critically that is based on this assumption.

Since the religious movements are not adapted to solve problems, the Christian mythology only presents but does not resolve the mystery of evil. For instance, the Augustinian theory that the fall is both the beginning of sin and its punishment is simply not true when we see that in nature, the "evils" of earthquakes, floods, and pestilence originated quite independent of human sinning. Moreover, there is the tension between creaturely freedom and divine predestination, since in the absence of any temptation, creaturely freedom cannot lead to sin, and to assume divine predestination impedes creaturely freedom. Hick then concludes that if we accept the creation-fall myth, we must also accept that there must be some flaw in creation that cannot be traced back to any other ultimate source than to the creator of all that is.

Next to this majority report of the Augustinian tradition that Hick finds unacceptable, there is the minority report of the Irenaean tradition. Hick points out that for Irenaeus, there is a distinction between image and likeness of God referred to in Genesis 1:26: "Then God said, let us make man in our image, after our likeness." The view of Irenaeus was "that man as a personal and moral being already exists in the image, but has not yet been formed into the finite likeness of God" (290). The image then was the raw material for further and more difficult creative work of God in humans. The features of this likeness were revealed in the person of Christ, but for humans in general, the second phase of the creative process was not attained, since the fall intervened. This failure multiplied the perils and complicated the route to the likeness of God. In the light of present-day anthropological knowledge, we must assume two distinguishable stages in the evolutionary process. In the first stage, through the creative power of God, the physical universe brought forth a creature who has the possibility of existing in conscious fellowship with God. But the second stage, Hick contends, is very different. Since personal life is essentially free and self-directing, human individuals only through the uncompelled responses and willing cooperation in the world with God may eventually become that perfected persons that the New Testament calls "children of God."

Hick presents here a developmental and teleological picture of humanity. While he admits that he cannot demonstrate it, "human goodness slowly built up through personal histories of moral effort," and this "has the value in the eyes of the Creator which justifies even the long travail of the soul-making process" (292). In individual freedom, humans are in the process of becoming those perfected beings who God is seeking to create. Since this progress pertains to each individual, this does not necessarily entail a corresponding progressive improvement in the moral state of the world. While human individuality shows an accumulation of evil as well as of good, Hick claims that there is no doubt a development in our ethical situation from generation to generation. We are not put into a paradise at the end, but in analogy to the children, we grow to adulthood in an environment whose primary and overriding purpose is the realization of the most valuable potentialities of human personality. Hick explains, "We have to recognize that the presence of pleasure and the absence of pain cannot be the supreme and overriding end for which the world exists. Rather, this world must be a place of soul-making. And its value is to be judged, not primarily by the quantity of pleasure and pain occurring in it at any particular moment, but by its fitness for its primary purpose, the purpose of soul-making" (295). "Soul making" is a phrase Hick gleaned from the poet John Keats (1795–1821). For Keats, the world is "the vale of Soul-making."[19] It needs to be a vale of pains and troubles in order to school an intelligence and make it a soul by becoming personally itself. While in the medieval worldview humans are seen as insignificant creatures because of the existence of the angelic world, nowadays, humans are dwarfed by the vastness of the physical universe. Yet Hick reminds us that humans are organic to the world, and the acts and thoughts are conditioned by space and time. God has set us in a creaturely environment, and the final fulfillment of our nature in relation to God will accordingly take the form of an embodied life within this environment. As we move slowly toward that fulfillment through the pilgrimage of our earthly life, so is the whole creation groaning in travail and waiting for the time when it will be set free from its bondage to decay, as Paul described it.

Apart from all developmental thinking, Hick insists upon the special character of humanity as a personal creature made in the image of God. Theodicy must center on the soul-making process that is taking place within human life. For Hick, this is the starting point to relate the realities of sin and suffering to the perfect love of an omnipotent creator. Instead of looking to the past for a clue to the mystery of evil, we must look to the future in an eschatological scope. Hick then treats moral evil, pain, and suffering.

Hick understands by sin that there is a disorientation at the very center of our being. The question then concerning theodicy is, "Why has an omnipotent, omniscient, and infinitely good and loving Creator permitted sin in His universe?" (301). The usual answer was focused on our human freedom and responsibility as finite personal beings. Since automatic goodness cannot be described as being morally good, humans must be mutable creatures who are at least subject to some forms of temptation. God could have created humans so resistant to temptation that they did not fall. Yet God did not do this, since this would have meant that God preselected our responses to our environment. But it does not seem feasible for the creature to be in a perfectly neutral position over against God. Either humans are so intimately conscious of God as to be held in God's presence and service by the overwhelming immensity of the divine reality and goodness or else they are not thus conscious of God's presence and are self-centered rather than God centered. Yet for the latter possibility, humans can hardly bear the virtually unlimited guilt attributed to them.

---

19. "Letter to George and Georgiana Keats" (April 21, 1819), in *Selected Letters of John Keats*, ed. Grant F. Scott, rev. ed. (Cambridge, MA: Harvard University Press, 2002), 290.

Hick, however, does not claim that God is responsible for evil. Granted that God created in absolute freedom all the conditions of creaturely existence, including goals out of which sin and suffering ensue. Yet this does not make God responsible for evil, since there are both differences and similarities in the way in which humans and God are said to be responsible. Hick explains, "Human responsibility occurs within the context of an existing moral law and an existing society of moral beings. But God is Himself the source of the moral law and the Creator of all beings other than Himself. In His original decision to create He was accordingly not responsible *under* any moral law or *to* any existing person. Nevertheless, there is a technical sense of 'responsible' that can be applied to God as well as to man" (326). This means that God's ultimate omniresponsibility does not take away our individual accountability for our own deliberate actions. Divine and human responsibilities operate on different levels. We are responsible for our life within this world, while God is responsible for the existence of this world and for the fact that we live responsibly in it.

Having shown that we are responsible for our lives and for the moral evil connected with it, Hick now focuses on suffering that is caused by physical pain. He contends that the kind of goodness that God desires in his creatures will not have been created except through a long process of creaturely experience in response to challenges and disciplines of various kinds. This, of course, involves at least occasional pains for the sentient creatures in this world. The evolutionary process is, for Hick, here the guiding paradigm. He asks why there must be so much physical pain as there is for the "purpose of soul-making" (345). Yet before he treats this under the rubric of suffering, he scrutinizes the pain suffered in the animal kingdom.

We remember how Darwin wrestled with the issue of suffering among living beings. While the subject of pain in animals remains largely a field for speculation, there is no denying that some animals do indeed experience pain. Hick argues that animals are steered away from danger by means of pain sensations. This means that pain has a positive value. When he considers that most animals are violently killed and devoured by others, he states that "death is not a problem to the animals, as it is to us" (349). With this statement, Hick is mistaken, since animals also have a death awareness, which we notice when animals are encountering a slaughterhouse. Hick then maintains that human forms of suffering are very different from those of animals. Yet the important question with regard to theodicy is, for Hick, not why animals are liable to pain as well as to pleasure but rather why these lower forms of life should exist at all. Such thoughts seem strange when Hick, on the other side, advocates an evolutionary concept of life.

But Hick continues in an evolutionary trend and asks whether a world from which suffering was excluded would serve what we are supposing to be in the divine purpose of soul-making. Since we are created through the long evolutionary process and made in the image of God, would we be able to grow without suffering toward the finite likeness of God? Hick also surmises that when we are endowed with freedom in relation to God, it is essential that there is also a certain distance from God. This makes possible, nay even makes virtually inevitable, that we center our lives upon ourselves than upon God. This means that sinfulness is inevitable, and it also has its own paradoxical place in divine providence. Therefore, we naturally bring suffering upon ourselves and upon others. Hick concludes that the possibility of revolt without pain would lack the stimuli to develop a human civilization and culture. "Not only would there be no way in which anyone could injure anyone else, but there would also be no way in which anyone could benefit anyone else, since there would be no possibility of any lack or danger. It would be a world without need for the virtues of self-sacrifice, care for others, devotion to the public good, courage, perseverance, skill, or honesty" (361). In other words, there must be suffering so that personal qualities can be developed. A world without suffering and pain, according to Hick, would be a sterile world.

While Hick does not have an idealistic view of this world, he is convinced that only because of this world with its dangers and challenges can the more valuable human characteristics emerge. Yet now he turns to the amount of suffering in this world and still argues that if God would have eliminated all the horrors such as Hiroshima and the American Civil War, there would have been "a divinely arranged paradise in which human freedom would be narrowly circumscribed, moral responsibility largely eliminated, and in which the drama of man's story would be reduced to the level of a television serial" (363–64). According to Hick, even the worst calamities seem to contribute to soul-making. Of course, he also knows about the opposite, that affliction may crush the character and take away from it whatever virtues it possessed. Nevertheless, optimism seems to prevail with Hick.

Hick does not see the problem in pain and suffering; rather, he views it in the fact that they do not seem to serve the constructive purpose but are distributed in random and meaningless ways. Suffering is often undeserved and rationally unintended. But then Hick objects that "in a world that is to be scene of compassionate love and self-giving for others, suffering must fall upon mankind with something of the haphazardness and inequity that we now experience" (370). Yet Hick does not reject this excessive and underserved suffering. It remains, for him, a real mystery impenetrable to the rationalizing human mind. Therefore, he concludes "that this world, with all its unjust and apparently wasted suffering, may nevertheless be what the Irenaean strand of Christian thought affirms that it is, namely a divinely created sphere of soul-making" (372).

Hick finally arrives at the eschatological fulfillment that he tenaciously defends against any kind of naturalism. He explains, "the question whether human sin and suffering are finally evil and inimical to good depends upon their eventual furtherance or prevention of the fulfilment of God's plan for His creation" (374). This means in the ultimate reckoning that suffering and evil are only evil if they do not contribute to the good in the ultimate perspective. God is gradually forming perfected members of humanity whose fuller nature we can see in Christ. An answer to theodicy is only given in the eschaton, when the interplay between good and evil will be resolved. Although we do not know how God will eventually free all created souls from their bondage to sin, the probability of God's success to do so amounts to practical certainty according to Hick. The Christian hope is hope not just in one's own salvation but in the salvation of the whole human race. "Within faith and hope we may confidently affirm the ultimate salvation of all God's children" (381).

In conclusion, Hick argues "that pain and suffering are a necessary feature of the world that is to be the scene of a process of soul-making; and that even the haphazard and unjust distribution and the often destructive and dysteleological effects of suffering have a positive significance in that they call forth human sympathy and self-sacrifice, and create a human situation within which the right must be done for its own sake rather than for a reward" (389). This leads us back to the early Old Testament conviction that God metes out both evil and good so that ultimately God's promises will be redeemed. Yet we have noticed in the Old Testament that this conviction of God being the author of both good and evil could not be maintained unless God becomes a trickster. Therefore, evil was excluded from God's portfolio and attributed to an evil force that attempts to thwart God's ways. In Hicks perception, however, evil ultimately contributes to God's educational advancement of humanity. Here the severity of evil as an anti-Godly force is diminished. This shows especially when he talks about the millions of Jewish men women and children that were deliberately and scientifically murdered. He suggests that God saw with anger and grief the suffering so willfully inflicted upon these people. But Hick is convinced that God's good purpose for each individual has not been defeated by the efforts of wicked tormentors. Beyond our world, they are alive and will have their place in the final fulfillment of God's creation. If God sees these atrocious actions with anger and grief, one can only wonder why God did not render such actions impossible. Is God then not finally a trickster? Though Hick is very careful in his argumentation, he seems to know more about the working out of history than is biblically warranted. It is not surprising that his theodicy encountered considerable skepticism.

The Openness of God

In evangelical quarters, the view has been proposed that there is a certain openness in God. Decisive was the year 1994, when Clark Pinnock (1937–2010) along with four other scholars published The Openness of God, which laid out a new evangelical vision of God. The omnipotence of God who foreknows everything and controls every detail was perceived to be too stifling. It was also felt that it did not render accurately the biblical testimony. These scholars asserted that God grants humans a certain amount of freedom to cooperate with God or to stand up against God. There is a certain dynamic give-and-take relationship between God and us. We respond to God's initiatives, and God in turn responds to our responses. At times, God decides to accomplish our goals, and at other times, God changes them to fit them into God's own purposes. This means God does not control everything that happens but is open to receive input from us. Of course, such give-and-take between God's creatures and the creator is somewhat akin to process theism, and therefore, it is not surprising that the two theological schools, evangelical open theists and process theologians, came into dialogue. Yet before we pursue that dialogue, we need to outline more the claims of evangelical open theists.

Since love is central to both the revelation and the reality of God, this means that there is an interaction between God and the created world, including humans. While God's anger is temporary, God's love is permanent (Ps 30:5). If love is that important in the biblical understanding of God, then other attributes, such as omnipotence or omniscience, come into second place. When we read the Bible, especially the Old Testament, we are confronted with the whole gamut of divine emotions, such as suffering and sorrow, repentance and anger, rejoicing and regret. God is depicted as a father, as a mother, and as a husband. This means not that God was made in the image of humans but that he is involved in human history and intimately affected by the events of this history. This can also be seen in the bargaining of Abraham with the heavenly visitors concerning the fate of Sodom (Gen 19:1–29). Although Sodom was ultimately destroyed, "this story reveals that God sometimes reconsidered his plans in response to human requests."[20] This means that human intercessions can influence God's actions.

But God also has plans and brings them to fruition. However, they are not cast-iron molds to which history must conform. Sometimes God acts unilaterally, as in the beginning of creation, and then God interacts with humans to bring about his purposes. This means that not all the time God acts as an irresistible, all-determining force. There are other agents too with whom God interacts. Since God's love is central, God is completely reliable and in this way unchanging. Yet it does not mean that God predetermines every last detail. "Even if he determines one event, it does not necessarily follow that he determines all events."[21] God is active in human history and pursues these objectives for creation while taking into account their decisions and actions.

When Christianity entered the Hellenistic world, it applied the classical divine attributes of impassibility, immutability, timelessness, and simplicity to the God of the Bible. This God then became self-sufficient, unrelated, and changeless. "Though the tradition, with good intentions, employed immutability and impassibility in order to protect God's freedom, they were taken too far and left no room

---

20. Richard Rice, "Biblical Support for a New Perspective," in *The Openness of God: A Biblical Challenge to the Traditional Understanding of God*, ed. Clark Pinnock et al. (Downers Grove, IL: InterVarsity, 1994), 29.
21. Rice, 56.

for speaking of divine openness where God, in vulnerability, finds himself to others in love."[22] Christian theology needs to reevaluate classical theism to develop more relational metaphysics so that the living, personal, responsive, and loving God of the Bible can be rediscovered.

In contrast to classical theism, open theism is introduced to overcome distortions caused by excessive Hellenization and allow biblical insights to operate more normatively. There are basically two models of God that are most influential—namely, to think of God primarily in a monarchic way in which God is removed from the contingencies of the world. God is unchangeable in every respect and all-determining and irresistible. The other model understands God "as a caring parent with qualities of love and responsiveness, generosity and sensitivity, openness and vulnerability, a person (rather than a metaphysical principle) who experiences the world, responds to what happens, relates to us and interacts dynamically with humans."[23]

Pinnock, the most widely known proponent of open theism, depicts God as the sovereign creator who voluntarily brought into existence a world with significantly free personal agents in it, agents who can respond positively to God or reject God's plans for them. Since God gives liberty to his creatures, God accepts the future as open and not as closed and has a relationship with the world that is dynamic and not static. Pinnock is convinced that the Bible presents such an open view of God as living and active. God is open to the changing realities of history and is delighted when we trust God and saddened when we rebel against God. It is important to recognize that God depicted in the biblical witness is both transcendent as the self-sufficient creator of the world who is sovereign and eternal. But at the same time, God is immanent, present in the world, active within history, involved, relational, and temporal. God is so transcendent that he creates room for others to exist and maintains a relationship with them. God is also so powerful that he can humble God's self, and God is so secure that he can suffer and change. Immanence and transcendence of God must be kept in proper balance so that God does not become an elevated human being or, on the other hand, a transcendent snob. Through the Hellenization of the Christian faith, "the God of promise who acts in history tended to be replaced by a metaphysical statement about abstract being" (106).

Since God created the world out of nothing, each being owes its existence to God, whose being is independent of any world, making any relationship with the world voluntary and not necessitated. Pinnock makes sure that this act of creation does not entail that God controls and determines everything. There is some capacity for choice. "Being socially triune, God has made a world with freedom, in which loving relationships can flourish" (110). Yet the relation between God and creation is asymmetrical because the creator gives life and freedom to the creature and

---

22. John Sanders, "Historical Considerations," in *Openness of God*, 100.
23. So Clark H. Pinnock, "Systematic Theology," in *Openness of God*, 103. The page numbers in parentheses in the following text refer to this article.

voluntarily limits the exercise of the creator's power in relation to it. God has the power to control all things but does not cling to his rights to dominate and control. God voluntarily gives creatures room for freedom. "Creating free creatures and working with them does not contradict God's omnipotence but requires it. Only omnipotence has the requisite degree and quality of power to undertake such a project."[24] God is not dependent on the creaturely activities but can always adapt to them so that his set goals can be achieved. God's omnipotence means not that God determines everything but that God has the power to deal with any situation that arises. God does not totally control all activities but has the power to deal with them according to God's plans.

The all-powerful God in turn negates power to the creatures so that God becomes vulnerable, as we see in the fact of the emergence of sin. Pinnock talks here about the "vulnerability of God," which is somewhat misleading: not that God is vulnerable but that only his plans that have to be adjusted to the new situation created by sinful creatures are vulnerable.[25] Leaving room to the creatures allows them not only to become covenant partners but also to move away from God and indulge in rebellion and sinfulness. Pinnock explains, "At present, God's will is resisted by powers of darkness, but the day will come when his will shall triumph. At present, evil is mounting a challenge to God's rule with considerable effects." By creating a world like ours, God took the risk that history might become unpredictable. "Understanding God's power gives us some help with the vexed problem of evil. If this is a world in which evil is possible but not inevitable, then it can be seen as stemming primarily from the misuse of freedom. The full display of God's sovereignty would not be a present reality but something to come at the end of history, when his glory is revealed rather then at the present time when the spirit suffers with us and the universe groans" (117). Though in the present history, there is a give-and-take between God and humanity, since God is a relational God. But on account of God's sovereignty, there is no doubt that in the end, God's ends will prevail. Such reasoning does limit God's omniscience. Pinnock reminds us that according to the biblical witness, God does not have exhaustive foreknowledge. He cites many instances where God does not possess complete knowledge of the future. To the contrary, God gave the creatures freedom and allowed for an open future that to a degree can be shaped by their decisions. The future is not already determined in every detail. Otherwise, God could not experience surprise and delight. World history would be boring, since nothing unexpected would ever happen. "God is a person and deals with us as persons. This means that God understands us, has intuition into every situation we face and is able to deal appropriately with every situation" (123). God does not foreknow every future choice or the outcome of every human decision, but God

24. Pinnock, 113.
25. Cf. Pinnock, 115, for this and the following quote.

is all-knowing in that he knows all that is possible and is powerful enough to do whatever is needed.

This open theism emphasizes, on the one hand, the continuous interaction between God and humans without jeopardizing the final fulfillment of creation. In such a view of God, evil is a reality that emerges on account of human freedom and the freedom of the created in general. Yet Pinnock focuses exclusively on the relationship between God and humans and the freedom involved in this relationship. He does not consider evil in terms of natural calamities or the suffering that ensues from diseases and mishaps. Again, to be a theodicy in a complete sense of the word would require he answers why God allows pain, suffering, and natural calamities. Perhaps, according to Pinnock, it cannot be answered, since "God controls some things but not everything."[26] Since God created other powers, God is not the only power in the universe. Though no other power can match God's influence, he has to contend with these powers and therefore is not completely in control of everything, exercising exhaustive sovereignty. But according to Pinnock, this does not imply that God is the author of evil. "With the fall into sin, a clash occurred between God and the creature, and God had to adjust to it. God exercises power in ways appropriate to the creation project" (93). The fall into sin becomes a by-product of human freedom. One might then ask whether God deliberately allowed humans to fall into sin or whether he was unable to avoid the fall.

Pinnock claims that God has chosen to be a vulnerable, superior power—he lets sinners challenge his rights, and they seem to take the initiative away from him. The reason for this is that God wants to love and not overpower. Pinnock sees the vulnerability of God manifested in Jesus's renunciation of power and letting himself become a victim. Pinnock points to the cross of Christ to understand the power of God who voluntarily limits his power so that God can relate to the world in self-sacrificing ways. Yet even if we would grant all of this, the atrocities committed in this world and the calamities produced by tsunamis, hurricanes, and tornadoes remain unanswered. This also shows when Pinnock explicitly addresses the problem of evil. He claims that the open view of God helps with the problem of evil because it yields "a logic of love" theodicy. He sketches that out in six points:

(a) God created for the sake of loving relationships.
(b) This required giving real freedom to the creature that it not be a robot.
(c) Freedom, however entails risk in the event that love is not reciprocated.
(d) Herein lies the possibility of moral and certain natural evils—those which appear irredeemably malicious and demonic.

26. Clark H. Pinnock, *Most Moved Mover: A Theology of God's Openness* (Grand Rapids, MI: Baker Academic, 2001), 53. The page numbers in parentheses in the following text refer to this publication.

(e) God does not abandon the world but pledges a victory over the powers of darkness. In such a theodicy, God does not will evil but wills love and, therefore, freedom that opens the door to things going right or wrong.

(f) Though God does not protect us from ourselves, God is there redeeming every situation, though exactly how, we may not yet always know. (131–32)

Through the freedom that God granted, moral and certain natural evils came into the world, as Pinnock states. While he affirms that God does not will evil, by granting freedom, God implicitly condones evil. The natural calamities go unaccounted. Yet Pinnock does not see it that way. He claims, "The open view of God lets one affirm the reality of genuine evil because it does not see God as the only source of power and does not have to figure out why, in God's mysterious providence, horrors come upon us. The openness model accepts that certain evils ought not to be. God is not in control of the powers of evil at this time in history, so they do not always play into the hands of God" (133).

Pinnock even seems to have an answer for calamities in nature, since he claims that some natural evils are an inherent part of the natural order. Some of them are even needed for life, such as the killing of one life in order to sustain another life. Furthermore, there is also a diabolic dimension to natural evil, and the innocent are savagely killed by tornadoes and plagues. Pinnock even contends that "some evils originate in the kingdom of Satan, and the reason that the world looks at times like a war zone is that it is a war zone" (134). Nature at present does not unambiguously reflect the will of God. Yet in relation to the problem of evil and the demonic, Pinnock refers to the power of God to deliver us from evil here and now. In Jesus's ministry, his works of power signaled the inauguration of the kingdom of God. They portrayed the end of Satan's reign and the coming transformation of the world. "Signs and wonders signal a new phase of history, which will culminate in the new creation" (135). Yet this is somewhere in the future. But what about the present where evil raises its ugly head? Pinnock himself asks, "Why does God tolerate the ongoing activities of evil agents so liberally?" (135).

Pinnock's answer is that God's power to act can be obstructed in ways we do not readily understand. God's power can at least be temporarily blocked. Moreover, since God has created free patrons, God cannot simply terminate them and their evil deeds. God made a kind of covenant of noncooperation with creatures, and therefore, God must endure the decisions of these free agents at least for a time. If he were to revoke the freedom he gave, this would show that God was not serious in giving it in the first place. Since God has decided to make this kind of world, this decision constrains God's freedom to act. There is a certain self-limitation of God that began with creation. "Some evils are the unavoidable by-products of an orderly natural process which is life giving and at the same time gives opportunity for noble responses" (136). Yet Pinnock even concedes, "It is possible to question

God's wisdom in the ways in which he is employing his power" (137). Such concession would almost imply that we know better how God should run the world. This is certainly not what Pinnock intended to say.

While open theism certainly is closer to the biblical witness than process thought in portraying God as the relational power who is closely involved with the affairs of the world, open theism seems to know more about the constrains on God's power than is biblically warranted. After all, God is God, and therefore, his ways are not always our ways. As Paul conceded, we still see in a mirror dimly.

Excursus: Open Theism and Process Theology

Open theism with its emphasis on the relational aspect of God and the give-and-take between the creator and the created bears a decided affinity to process theology. Pinnock concedes that open theism has often been charged with being "a thinly disguised version of process theology" (141). Indeed, he finds process theism attractive and notes that there are certain convictions that process theism and open theism hold in common, such as the priority of the love of God, the criticism of conventional theism, the more dynamic model of God, and the restriction on divine foreknowledge, to mention just a few points. It is therefore not surprising that representatives of process theology and of open theism collaborated on a book with the fitting title *Searching for an Adequate God*.

Central for the dialogue between process theology and open theism is the understanding of God. For process theology, God's power in the world is always persuasive and never coercive in the sense of unilateral control. This at once comes to the fore with humanity because, as David Ray Griffin asserts, "with the rise of human beings, it became possible for creaturely power to become demonic."[27] Because of human creativity, the possible emergence of demonic power was an inevitable by-product of the creation of human beings. For open theism, human freedom also involves the possibility of evil, as we have noted. But according to open theism, God created the world out of absolutely nothing, and therefore, this world and all its creatures are contingent and absolutely dependent on God. Their power is ultimately a gift of God and can be overridden, as we noted with the confidence of the elimination of all evil in the eschatological fulfillment. In process theology, "God lacks the inherent capacity to control the self-determining power of others."[28] We are confronted here with the alternative of the power of control, a power that is not continuously exercised, and the thoroughgoing power of persuasion.

---

27. David Griffin, "Process Theology and the Christian Good News," in *Searching for an Adequate God: A Dialogue between Process and Free Will Theists*, ed. John B. Cobb Jr. and Clark H. Pinnock (Grand Rapids, MI: William B. Eerdmans, 2000), 34.
28. So correctly Richard Rice, "Process Theism and the Open View of God," in *Searching for an Adequate God*, 187, for this and the following quote.

According to process theology, God decides the general features of reality, and he sets the conditions necessary for good things to happen. Yet the actual course of the universe depends on the decisions of others, and God can only persuade. This also relieves God of the responsibility for all the specific problems in the world. God is ultimately not responsible for evil, since he is at no point in total control of the world. While this provides a theodicy, "the process view of God departs from traditional Christianity," as Richard Rice perceptively notes, and, as we must add, also from the biblical witness. Open theism, on the other hand, upholds the biblical conviction that God is the sole fundamental reality, the one and only ultimate explanatory principle. Yet with that assertion, the problem of evil would be handed back to God. An actual theodicy is not provided either by open theism, especially when we remember the almost anthropomorphic depiction of God's moods and activities.

8 The God Who Cares

We have traversed an immense intellectual and theological landscape and have not received a satisfactory answer to the question of who is really in control of the affairs in this world. As we said in the beginning, for most people, the answer to the question of whether there is somebody in this world who controls it and who cares about us is of utmost importance. All other theological issues, such as faith, grace, or justification, occupy second place. If there is nobody in control and nobody who cares about us, these issues recede into oblivion. According to the Christian understanding, theodicy is primarily a question about God and God's working in the world.

Who or What Is God?

When we ask who or what God is, usually the so-called attributes of God are adduced, which say that God is omnipotent, omniscient, omnipresent, and eternal. But these are essentially philosophical concepts that are rarely found in the Bible. Neither the Israelites nor the Christians later on were much interested in who God is but what God does. Philosophical concepts about God's being entered the horizon of both Judaism and Christianity once they were confronted with the prevailing Hellenism of their time. Then they had to defend their faith in the arena of philosophical reasoning. Paul could still claim, "For Jews demand signs and Greeks desire wisdom, but we proclaim Christ crucified, a stumbling block to Jews and foolishness to Gentiles" (1 Cor 1:22–23). He juxtaposes the Christian message and the desire for wisdom. But soon the sentiment changed and the Christian message was clothed into the language of wisdom. We can already notice this in writings that were composed toward the end of the New Testament era. For example, the domestic codes or household codes in Ephesians 5:21–6:9, Colossians 3:18–4:1, and 1 Peter 2:18–3:7 are based on the philosophical genre of the *oikonomia*. Already Aristotle referred to this genre of practical philosophy, and it was also picked up by other philosophers.[1] How important the Hellenistic world was for Christianity can be seen in the New Testament, which was written in koine, meaning in the common language of that time—namely, a simplified version of classical Greek. If Christianity wanted to penetrate the Hellenistic world with its message, it had to adopt not just the prevailing language but also the concepts of that world.

---

1. Cf. for more details, Gerhard Sellin, *Der Brief an die Epheser* (Göttingen, Germany: Vandenhoeck & Ruprecht, 2008), 428, to this passage.

We can notice this intention with the early Christian apologists of the second century, such as Quadratus († ca. 130 CE) and Aristides of Athens († ca. 125 CE). Both dedicated their apologies to the emperor Hadrian and attempted to defend Christianity against various attacks. Quadratus, for instance, showed that the deeds of Jesus had indeed occurred and were no fairy tales, while Aristides pointed out the exemplary lifestyle of the Christians.[2] He attempted to portray Christians as a new race that led humanity from its decay to new life. This strategy of defense became necessary, since in the second century, more and more people accepted the Christian faith, and the secular authorities became increasingly suspicious of this new religion. Justin Martyr, who died in Lyons in 165 CE during a persecution of Christians, showed in two apologies that the Christian faith is the true philosophy in contrast to the pagan philosophies in which one cannot sense God's spirit at work.

The most important apologist of early Christianity was Origen, who was born in Alexandria, Egypt, and lived from ca. 185 CE to ca. 253 CE. Around 246 CE, Origen attacked the eclectic Platonist Celsus, who had claimed that a reasonable Christian theology is a contradiction in itself because Christianity is hostile to all human values. Origen defended the Christian faith as intellectually credible and showed that Christians are at least as decent a people as pagans or are even better. While Christians at that time did not serve as soldiers of the pagan state and refused to function in various public offices, Origen emphasized that they helped the country by offering prayers and by teaching the people to lead honest lives. His work *On First Principles* was the first comprehensive exposition of the Christian faith. In the introduction, he claimed that the apostles had rendered only that which was necessary for salvation, while the rest was up to later theologians to expound. Origen was convinced that the Christian faith offered a new and comprehensive understanding of the world that was superior to that offered by Hellenistic culture, but it was not necessarily opposed to that culture.

In showing that the Christian faith was intellectually credible, one had to use concepts that bore only remote similarity to those used in the Christian message. We can see this best with Pseudo-Dionysius (ca. 500 CE), who influenced many philosophers and theologians in their God talk up to the present time. Though he was actually a disciple of the Neoplatonic philosopher Plotinus, he wrote under the pseudonym Dionysius the Areopagite, a convert of Saint Paul in Athens (Acts 17:34), and consequently gained almost apostolic authority. In his treatise *The Divine Names*, he outlines his methodology, saying,

> Furthermore, we must ask how it is that we know God when He cannot be perceived by the mind or the senses and is not a particular Being. Perhaps 'tis true to say that we know not God by His Nature (for this is unknowable and beyond the reach of all Reason and Intuition), yet by means of that

2. Cf. Maier, *Eusebius*, 136; and Leslie William Barnard, "Apologetik I," in TRE, 3:375–376.

ordering of all things which (being as it were projected out of Him) possesses certain images and semblances of His Divine Exemplars, we mount upwards (so far as our feet can tread that ordered path), advancing through the Negation and Transcendence of all things and through a conception of a Universal Cause, towards That Which is beyond all things.[3]

Pseudo-Dionysius advocates here a threefold way to arrive at a God: the negative way (via negativa), the superlative way (via eminentia), and the way of causal inference (via causalitatis). According to the negative way, we negate attributes that are usually consigned to human beings, such as finite, mortal, and comprehensible, and then attribute to God adjectives such as infinite, immortal, incomprehensible. According to the superlative way, we confer upon God adjectives such as omnipotent, omniscient, or omnipresent by attempting to surpass attributes that are usually associated with human beings, such as potency, knowledge, or presence. Finally, according to the way of causal inference, God is referred to as the first uncaused cause or the creator of all things. Even statements such as God as the moral order of the world (Kant) or the holy (Rudolf Otto) or the pure act (scholasticism) are ultimately related to one of the three ways that Pseudo-Dionysius lined out.

When we follow Pseudo-Dionysius, we start with us and then try to describe who God is making God in our image in a Feuerbachian fashion by projecting how we think God ought to be. While there is certainly some truth in these attributes that we accord to God, we dare not forget that they are not derived from our experience of God but are intellectual constructs. But this is not the way the biblical documents talk about God. For instance, what is traditionally called God's omnipotence comes to the fore in God's promise to Abraham and Sarah that they will have a son. When Sarah doubted this, God asked her, "Is anything too wonderful for the Lord?" (Gen 18:14). Similarly, in announcing the birth of Jesus, the angel says to Mary, "Nothing will be impossible with God" (Luke 1:37). In both cases, the emphasis on God's omnipotence serves only to assure that God can fulfill the promises God has made but not to state that God can do or wants to do whatever God pleases. However, when we start with human possibilities and confer them in one way or another to God, how can we still avoid the charge of Feuerbach that God is a product of our human desires? Here the Bible presents just the opposite approach. God's promises come first, and then people reflect on how they discerned the materialization of these promises as God's activity in history. These reflections are then rendered in the biblical documents, and we are invited to participate in these reflections.

The first and continuous experience of God in the Bible involves God's personal quality. God is not a person that one can depict. The Israelite prohibition of making pictures of God (Exod 20:4) attests to this, a prohibition that was later adopted

---

3. Dionysius the Areopagite, The Divine Names (VII, 3), in On the Divine Names and the Mystical Theology, trans. C. E. Rolt (New York: Macmillan, 1951), 151–152.

by the Muslims. Yet God is an addressable and a responding "Thou," as we clearly see in the Psalms. The experience of God is rendered predominately with male attributes, but feminine attributes are interspersed—for example, in the verse, "All people may take refuge in the shadow of your wings" (Ps 36:7). Since God was not considered a fertility god, a sexual definition of God as being male or female was foreign to the Israelites. God can be experienced in a personal way but is no actual person. In contrast to an actual person, God is not confined by the categories of space and time. As Psalm 139 poetically expressed, God is from eternity to eternity, and from God, nothing is hidden; God is everywhere present, and in God's majesty, God is experienced as the holy one.

God's holiness can be gleaned from the injunction in Leviticus 11:44: "Sanctify yourselves therefore, and be holy, for I am holy." Holiness is an attribute of God that we should emulate, not a projection of a human attribute. Of course, in every religion holiness is considered a trademark of God's majesty. In Leviticus, however, it does not serve to demarcate God from us, but it should incite us to godlike conduct. God's holiness also implies that we are not equal to God, and therefore, we dare not encounter him in a casual way. The Israelites even shied away from addressing him with his proper name, Yahweh, and instead called him in Hebrew *Adonai* (My Lords). Even in the English Bible translations, Yahweh is usually replaced by "the Lord." We must always be mindful that in God, we are confronted with the creator and Lord of the universe. Holiness also means that God is just.

The biblical emphasis on God's justice is not so much on the penal or judicial aspect, though God will mete out what is right, but on that there is a certain divine way of action that we should emulate. The psalmist therefore says, "For the Lord is righteous; he loves righteous deeds; the upright shall behold his face" (Ps 11:7). Justice is paired with God's wrath, primarily over those who are unjust. Therefore, we read in the New Testament, "It is a fearful thing to fall into the hands of the living God" (Heb 10:31). Yet something decisive has occurred: "In Christ God was reconciling the world to himself, not counting their trespasses against them, and entrusting the message of reconciliation to us" (2 Cor 5:19).

This readiness of God toward reconciliation is not something totally new. Already the psalmist recognized, "But you, O Lord, are a God merciful and gracious, slow to anger and abounding in steadfast love and faithfulness" (Ps 86:15). It is a thorough-going characteristic of God's history with humanity that God is merciful. The Old Testament history can be seen as one of the apostasies of God's chosen people, yet God, even in threatening Israel with the day of wrath, ultimately does not reject them. Instead, God promises to make "an everlasting covenant" with Israel (Isa 55:3). The Christians realized that this promise found its fulfillment in Jesus, who was called the Christ, the human face of God. Through his sacrificial death, Christ made a new covenant, a new testament, with humanity (cf. Mark 14:24).

Yet do God's mercy and the willingness to reconcile the transgressors not imply that God condones evil instead of eliminating it? Even putting things in an eschatological perspective—saying that in the end, things will come out all right—is of little comfort to those who suffer under present evils and injustice. Furthermore, if God is the one according to whose will everything ultimately occurs, how can there be so much evil in this world? This issue of theodicy, of God's justice, has always occupied the minds of people. We noted that in the Old Testament, Job already posed the question as to why so many bad things can happen to a good person. He finally arrived at the insight that in confrontation with God's majesty, it makes no sense to demand that God should justify his own actions (cf. Job 38–40). God is God, and this means he cannot be judged by our categories of good and evil. Moreover, God is beyond our understanding and "is ultimately in control of human affairs."[4] Kant, too, recognized that theodicy is "at bottom no more than that of our presumptuous reason failing to recognize its limitations."[5]

In his treatise *The Bondage of the Will* (1525), Luther talks about the unsearchable will of God, or the hidden God who does not want to be known by us and whose ways are none of our business. "God must therefore be left to himself in his own majesty, for in this regard we have nothing to do with him."[6] The distinction between the hidden and the revealed wills of God, which is most pointedly stated by Luther in *The Bondage of the Will*, is closely connected to Luther's understanding of God's Godhead and the hiddenness of God's actions. Since God is God, we cannot discern God's activity unless he points us to that activity. God is active in a way that we do not expect or understand. Luther writes, "For the works of God must be hidden and never understood, even when it happens. But it is never hidden in any other way than under that which appears contrary to our conceptions and our ideas."[7] If we ponder why and how God has done something or why he allows this or that, then we always end up in despair. We should not search for the hidden will of God. "This will is not to be inquired into, but reverently adored, as by far the most awe-inspiring secret of the Divine Majesty, reserved for himself alone."[8] Instead, we should cling to the preached and revealed will of God, through which we experience God as gracious and merciful. With these thoughts, Luther wants to put an end to all the speculations about God and point to the Gospel alone.

As the German Lutheran theologian Paul Althaus (1888–1966) reminded us, God's hiddenness "presupposes his self-attestation."[9] Hiddenness always presupposes a prior presence of some kind. This is also true for God, since the God question is present in every human being. Everybody needs something to which he or she ultimately clings and that serves him or her for God. As finite beings, we

4. So Anthony C. Thiselton, *Doubt, Faith, Certainty* (Grand Rapids, MI: William B. Eerdmans, 2017), 40.
5. Immanuel Kant, "On the Miscarriage of All Philosophical Trials in Theodicy" (8.255), in *Religion and Rational Theology*, trans. Allen W. Wood and George Di Giovanni (Cambridge: Cambridge University Press, 1996), 24, accessed April 15, 2019, https://tinyurl.com/y2ql5kqc.
6. Martin Luther, *The Bondage of the Will*, in LW, 33:139.
7. Martin Luther, in a *scholium* or comment on Rom 8:26, in LW, 25:366.
8. Luther, *Bondage of the Will*, 33:139.
9. Paul Althaus, *Die christliche Wahrheit: Lehrbuch der Dogmatik*, 5th ed. (Gütersloh, Germany: Bertelsmann, 1959), 93.

need something that has infinite validity. Therefore, Luther writes in his *Large Catechism*, "Anything on which your heart relies and depends, I say, that is really your God. [. . .] A 'god' is the term for that to which we are to look for all good and in which we are to find refuge in all need."[10] But then he adds, "If your faith and trust are right, then your God is the true one. Conversely, where your trust is false and wrong, there you do not have the true God." Decisive is not that everybody has a God or something or someone that is regarded as a god but that this God can be at our side regardless of what comes and therefore be a right God, or rather *the* right God.

But by returning again to the issue of theodicy, how does it show itself that God is the one who is in control if there is so much evil in this world? Are these ancient documents of the Bible really reliable when they tell us that God is superior to everyone and everything else, that he is merciful and that he will provide for God's people a new heaven and a new earth in which righteousness rules? Here the issue of divine providence needs to be addressed. Are our world and its history a conglomeration of accidents, or is there really something or someone in control?

God's Providential Care

Divine providence seems to have lost its persuasive power. Science has demonstrated that the laws of nature control the universe. Moreover, evolution seems to be the overarching concept for most people. Yet when disasters strike, either caused by nature or by ruthless humans, at least in the West, people still seek metaphysical comfort regardless of whether they are religious or not. This seems to indicate that the question is not dead of whether there is still someone or something beyond ourselves who cares about what is going on in this world.

Moreover, as we increasingly make this planet our own, this domestication seems to turn against us and threatens us and the world in which we live with ever-greater dangers, such as global warming, mass migrations, and depletion of natural resources. More and more people are truly frightened and ask whether the future will eventually suffocate us. In their concern, they yearn for the comforting assertion not that the future confronts us as an inescapable fate of a doomsday but that there are meaning and fulfillment for our lives and for the cosmos in general. The German astronaut Alexander Gerst released on December 2018, the day before he returned to earth from the International Space Station, a video message in which he addressed himself to the not-yet-born generation of his grandchildren and apologized in the name of his generation that with regard to the human-caused global warming, the various destructions of the environment, and the wars, it seems

---

10. Martin Luther, *The Large Catechism*, in *The Book of Concord, The Confessions of the Evangelical Lutheran Church*, ed. Robert Kolb and Timothy J. Wengert (Minneapolis: Fortress, 2000), 386, in his explanation of the first commandment (2).

that we do not leave the earth in good condition.[11] And he hopes that we are not remembered as that generation that has egotistically and ruthlessly destroyed the foundation for the lives of future generations.

Confronted with this dire warning, we cannot close our eyes to modern critical rationality and resort to higher powers that come to our rescue. Living in the twenty-first century, we have been used to shouldering our own fate, and we have learned that all events have causes that can be rationally explained. But would this also mean that divine providence and divine preservation of the world have become untenable today? The scientist and Episcopalian priest William Pollard (1911–89) seemed to answer this question in the affirmative when he wrote, "To speak of an event as an act of God, or to say that it happened because God willed that it should, seems a violation of the whole spirit of science."[12] We remember that this kind of reasoning—that for every phenomenon, there is a this-worldly explanation—turned Charles Darwin into an agnostic.

Not only secular rationalism makes it difficult for us to talk about divine providence. Modern technology has given us ever-greater possibilities of changing the world for good and for bad. The experiences of Auschwitz and Hiroshima compel us to disagree with Gottfried Wilhelm Leibniz, who optimistically declared that our world is the best possible one. Even Augustine's Neoplatonic idea that evil is only a deficiency of the good no longer seems credible. Some would go so far as to agree with Richard Rubenstein when he ponders that if there were God, he could not have permitted Auschwitz to happen, and if he had, we would have to strip him of his divine office.[13] A few might even be inclined to agree with the pessimistic philosopher Arthur Schopenhauer (1788–1860). He rejected Leibniz's assertion that our world is the best possible one and claimed that this is "the worst of all possible worlds."[14] It is not only God's special providence or God's miracle-working activity that is being challenged today. The general providence that God is benevolently present with creation is being questioned too. How can God interact with the creative process or accompany it in a benevolent way if ultimately everything occurs "naturally"?

Surprisingly, scientists today are raising again the question of teleology, assuming a directedness of nature, while theologians and many other people have largely abandoned the assertion that there is an empirically discernible teleology. Scientists, for instance, point out that the fundamental laws in physics would only have

---

11. "Nachricht an meine Enkelkinder [with Closed Captions]" You Tube, December 19, 2018, https://tinyurl.com/ycbkocb7.

12. William Pollard, *Chance and Providence: God's Action in a World Governed by Scientific Law* (New York: Charles Scribner's, 1958), 7.

13. Cf. Rubenstein, *After Auschwitz*, 87, 153–154. In the second edition, he comes to a pantheistic understanding of God according to which God either creates or destroys. Cf. Richard Rubenstein, *After Auschwitz: History, Theology, and Contemporary Judaism*, 2nd ed. (Baltimore, MD: Johns Hopkins University Press, 1992), 306.

14. Arthur Schopenhauer, *The World as Will and Idea*, trans. R. B. Haldane and J. Kemp (London: Routledge & Kegan Paul, 1957), 3:395.

to be a little different from the way they are and life, as it is today, would have never arisen. It seems therefore that "a life-giving factor lies at the center of the whole machinery and design of the world."[15] The scientists John D. Barrow (*b. 1952) and Frank J. Tipler (*b. 1947) therefore introduced the weak anthropic principle in which they reasoned that taking into account the cosmological context, life could and indeed has evolved. Not everything in our world can be left to chance, but some things must be designed in such a way that life could evolve on the basis of carbon and that the universe is old enough that this development took place. Barrow and Tipler even ventured the claim in the strong form of the anthropic principle that the universe must have those properties that allow life to develop within it.

The British theoretical physicist and theologian John Polkinghorne (*b. 1930) summarizes the main scientific insights assembled under the rubric of the anthropic principle as follows:

> Although life only began to appear on the cosmic scene when the universe was 11 billion years old, and self-conscious life when it was 15 billion years old, there is a real sense in which the cosmos was pregnant with life from the Big Bang onwards. The laws of nature were finely tuned in a way that alone made the evolution of carbon-based life a possibility. Only if the forces of nature were exactly what they are could there have been stars capable of burning reliably for the billions of years necessary to fuel the development of life on a planet. Only if the nuclear forces were exactly what they are would the first generation of stars have been able to make the chemical elements that are the basis of life, so that in the death throes of a supernova explosion there spewed out the stardust of which we are made.[16]

As with all scientific explanations, the anthropic principle is derived from the past. Life in our universe has evolved, and therefore, so the assertion, there must be certain constants that made the origin and development of life possible. In retrospect, the historical and evolutionary process is interpreted as a strictly immanent event. But what has actually happened, and what took place at that point when it took place? And did this have anything to do with God? The answer to these questions is disclosed neither by the anthropic principle nor by scientific research.

When we talk about divine providence, however, we do not turn to the past. Our attention is directed toward the present. The conviction is uttered that God has the present in God's hands here and now, and therefore, our future is decided too. The assertion is made that the future will not open itself in any possible way. It will open only in the manner that is sanctioned by God. With this assertion, we

---

15. John A. Wheeler in the foreword to John D. Barrow and Frank J. Tipler, *The Anthropic Cosmological Principle*, 2nd ed. (Oxford: Clarendon, 1988), vii.
16. John Polkinghorne, "Science and Theology in the Twenty-First Century," *Zygon* 35 (December 2000): 945.

do focus not just on the cosmos but also on humanity and its conduct and history. Divine providence therefore extends to nature, to human conduct, and to history.[17] When we first turn to nature, we remember that all natural processes presuppose nature and matter or energy. Yet these presuppositions cannot be taken for granted because there is insufficient reason to suppose that an initial singularity occurred. The world is contingent, it is not absolute, and God is not in need of it. The world was created out of nothingness and is continuously threatened by it. Divine providence therefore asserts first of all that God continues to preserve his creation. God upholds creation against falling back into nothingness. Martin Luther, for instance, was much more impressed by the continuous preservation of God's creation than by the initial creative act. He remarked that many people start something, but most do not have the energy to continue it.[18] God, however, maintains his creation and is with it in every single moment. Nothing is exempt from his caring providence, whether it is the oscillations of electrons or the encounter of two people that ends up in marriage.

We are talking here about God who, as a Spiritual expresses, has "got the whole world in his hands." In a panentheistic way, the world is enveloped by God who is present to the whole world as well as to its individual entities. In perceiving God's relation with the world in this way, the British theologian and biochemist Arthur Peacocke (1924–2006) particularly talked about a "top-down" causality in which God could be causatively effective without abrogating the laws and regularities that are operative in the world.

> Particular events could occur in the world and be what they are because God intends them to be so, without at any point any contravention of the laws of physics, biology, psychology, sociology, or whatever is the pertinent science for the level of description in question. [. . .]
> In thus speaking of God, it has not been possible to avoid talk of God "intending," of God's "freedom," that is, to avoid using the language of personal agency. For these ideas of "top-down" causation by God cannot be expounded without relating them to the concept of God as, in some sense, an agent, least misleadingly described as personal.[19]

God's preserving and life-furthering power is illustrated well by the Old Testament understanding of spirit (ruah).[20] When God gives his spirit, something

---

17. These three areas of divine providence were also mentioned by Michael J. Langford, *Providence* (London: SCM, 1981).
18. Cf. Martin Luther, "Randbemerkungen Luthers zu den Sentenzen des Petrus Lombardus" (1510/11), in WA, 9:66.29–34.
19. Arthur Peacocke, *Theology for a Scientific Age: Being and Becoming—Natural, Divine, and Human* (Minneapolis: Fortress, 1993), 159.
20. To the following, cf. Hans Schwarz, *The Trinity: The Central Mystery of Christianity* (Minneapolis: Fortress, 2017), 4–5.

becomes alive and lives as long as God's spirit works in it. When God, however, takes away his spirit, then people or things perish. Therefore, the psalmist pleads with Yahweh, saying, "Do not cast me away from your presence, and do not take your holy spirit from me" (Ps 51:11). But if nothing can exist or occur without God, if God makes possible the earthquake as much as the life-giving spring rain, the destructive floods as much as a beautiful sunrise, do we then not equate divine providence with the laws of nature or with all natural occurrences? Are we then not in danger to pantheistically identify God with nature itself? Would then not nature become interchangeable with God?

Such danger could arise only if we forget that God makes the difference between something and nothing. As Georg Wilhelm Friedrich Hegel, for instance, emphasized, God is not equal with nature, but nature is dependent on God—it is contingent. If we do not understand God as the one who is behind *all* natural events, we run the risk of limiting God to ever-fewer events for which we do not yet have a natural explanation. God then would become a cosmic jack-in-the-box. Yet Polkinghorne cautioned that "the one god who is well and truly dead is the god of the gaps."[21] Much earlier, Dietrich Bonhoeffer (1906–45) had warned us of the fate that such a God would encounter. He would be edged out of the world through our increasing knowledge of the natural causes and effects.[22] To avoid this danger, Bonhoeffer emphasized that we must affirm God in the midst of life, in those places where we seemingly already know all the natural causes. This affirmation of God as the all-preserving power seems to be consequent and necessary for trusting in divine providence once we are confronted with the laws of nature and the natural causes of all processes.

But if it is so, would we not affirm a demonic God, a God who plays dice with our future and who in dispassionate equanimity builds up and destroys? Indeed, the Old Testament occasionally compares God and us with the potter and the clay, indicating that we are fashioned by God's hands (Isa 64:8; Jer 18:6). At this point, the issue of theodicy or of God's justice emerges. In answering this question, we must remember that the biblical witnesses do not advocate a metaphysical dualism. They do not divide historical and natural events into two categories: a category of evil for which Satan is responsible and a category of good that is ascribed to God. They are much more interested in emphasizing that ultimately all processes serve to help God's kingdom triumph. This does not mean however that we are only informed about the journey itself, while the individual events up until the end are dark and enigmatic. While some events will indeed defy explanation, others "joyfully declare the glory of God's working." Altogether, we can discern three areas with different parameters for explanations: nature, human conduct, and history.

---

21. Polkinghorne, "Science and Theology," 35:944.
22. Cf. Dietrich Bonhoeffer, *Letters and Papers from Prison*, ed. Eberhard Bethge, rev. and enlarged ed. (New York: Macmillan, 1968), 188, in a letter dated July 16, 1944.

Providence in Nature

Nature serves as the foundation for all life and provides us with varying degrees of dependability that can be understood as the result of the caring activity of God.[23]

(1). The first kind of dependability is represented in the rising and setting of the sun and in the cycles of the seasons. They provide the foundation for the development of life on earth,* and as far as we know, they are fully reliable. Of course, the movements of the planets, which can be calculated in advance, cannot be presupposed as being absolutely reliable. In our calculations, we tacitly assume that what we have observed in the past will also hold true for the future. Yet the probability for ultimate modes of behavior besides those that we have observed over thousands of years is virtually zero.

We remember that the reliability of the cycles of day and night and of the seasons is also reflected in God's covenant with Noah. Yahweh assures, "As long as the earth endures, seedtime and harvest, cold and heat, summer and winter, day and night, shall not cease" (Gen 8:22). While we have not interfered with the cosmic constellations, we must be mindful that we have considerably changed things on our earth by deforestation of primal woodlands, the heavy output of carbon dioxide into the atmosphere, and the pollution of air and water. Thus the cycles of seasons have been thrown out of sync, and new cycles will establish themselves. For instance, in midlatitudes, the summers will be warmer and drier and the winters less cold and wetter. On a global scale, the weather extremes of wind and rain will increase. This means even human interference cannot ultimately prohibit a certain dependability and predictability of nature. Even with earthquakes and floods, we assume a certain predictability when we talk, for example, about a once-in-a-century event.

(2). A different kind of reliability arises when several alternatives and large numbers of repeated incidences are involved. We encounter this, for example, in chemical reactions when wood or other fuels are burnt, in nuclear reactions in the core of the sun, and in the functioning of our body cells. Without the dependability of these processes, there would be no life on earth and no human history. Our very lives depend on the reliability of a huge number of these processes. For instance, our body cells must be precisely duplicated when we grow or when old cells are replaced by new ones. The mutation of a single cell can lead to a dangerous cancer that spreads throughout our body and damages our life severely or even cuts it short. Again, the biblical witnesses remind us that God provides this kind of dependability. We hear that no sparrow falls to the ground without God's permission (Matt 10:29), and all the hairs on our head are numbered (Matt 10:30), and God sends rain on the just and on the unjust (Matt 5:45).

(3). There is, however, a third kind of dependability, which we encounter primarily in the evolutionary process of the universe and of life itself. "So far as the

23. To the following, cf. Pollard, *Chance and Providence*, 74–78.

laws of nature and the structure of things in space and time are concerned, the universe *could* have had many histories than the one it has had. At the same time, however, it is equally true, under the stern requirements of the necessity of choice in temporal existence, that it *can* have only one of these histories."[24]

Once the choice has occurred, all other possibilities are gone and lost forever. The whole evolutionary process, especially of life on earth, is so accidental that the American vertebrate paleontologist George G. Simpson (1902–84) could rightly claim that "there is no automatism that will carry him [humanity] upward without choice or effort and there is no trend solely in the right direction. Evolution has no purpose."[25] Speaking from the perspective of evolution, there was no need for humans to evolve. And in the biblical creation account, we do not read that God commanded the earth to bring forth humans, as he did with other living creatures (cf. Gen 1:24). We could say that the emergence of humans on earth resulted solely from God's solitary decision. Even Charles Darwin wished that he could see a little more divine guidance in the evolutionary process. At the same time, he emphasized that the evolutionary process proceeded by natural selection. Thereby, he advanced rather strict rules according to which life and the evolution of new species advanced. Scientific research has since then refined Darwin's findings considerably, but it has not repudiated them. The French biochemist Jacques Monod (1910–76) also claimed that there is chance and necessity in the evolutionary process. Therefore, this third kind of dependability tells us, on the one hand, that the natural process is trustworthy, since it is ongoing, but it tells us, on the other, that it is open and undetermined.[26]

The evolutionary process characterized by both chance and necessity also allows us to talk about God's continuing activity in the world.[27] In so doing, we dare not identify God with the physical processes lest we end up with a Spinozean equation of God and the world. God should also be not mistaken "as some kind of *additional* factor added on to the processes of the world."[28] Such a transcendent God would give the world too much independence. We should rather acknowledge that God works through the evolutionary process by being the provider of both continuity

---

24. Pollard, *Chance and Providence*, 68.
25. George G. Simpson, *The Meaning of Evolution: A Study of the History of Life and of Its Significance for Man* (New Haven, CT: Yale University Press, 1960), 310. Of course, we do not want to say herewith—and neither does Simpson—that everything was completely unforeseeable in the evolutionary process. There are always covariances within this process and certain boundaries that cannot be passed or below which a certain species does not come (e.g., the minimum weight for mammals). This leads to an inner equilibrium within the evolutionary system with the goal of optimizing the conditions for existence and survival. Cf., for example, the paper of Paul Overhage, "Gebundene Mannigfaltigkeit," in *Gott in Welt: Festgabe für Karl Rahner*, ed. Herbert Vorgrimmler (Herder, Germany: Freiburg, 1964), esp. 842–844.
26. Simpson, *Meaning of Evolution*, 311, even states that this "new evolution involves knowledge, including the knowledge of good and evil." Humanity again is confronted with the basic choice between good and evil similar to the beginning in paradise.
27. For the issues relating to God's continuous creation, cf. the insightful analysis provided by Mark Worthing, *God, Creation, and Contemporary Physics* (Minneapolis: Fortress, 1996), 130–138, 156–157.
28. Peacocke, *Theology for a Scientific Age*, 176.

and openness. As Polkinghorne appropriately asserts, God is present "in the chance as well as in the necessity of an evolving world."[29] God's continuous activity in the world does not mean that God simply determines what is to be. It also allows for freedom that creation can evolve in its own way. God does not determine the outcome of every scientifically random event "but instead controls randomness by setting broad boundaries. God thereafter allows organisms to interact according to natural laws within these boundaries, producing a wide range of beautiful and complex results."[30] We therefore conclude that God is not a primordial tyrant, at whose decree things come into being or proceed, but a supporting and trusting God.

While the natural sciences have traditionally been seen as presenting a world that is predictable and governed by ironclad laws, we have noticed that this perception has been severely shaken, especially in the twentieth century. "There are systems, at every level of complexity, whose future development is unpredictable. These were: subatomic systems, at the ('Heisenberg') micro-level; many-bodied Newtonian systems at the micro-level of description; and non-linear dynamical systems at the macroscopic level."[31] This new awareness of the unpredictability, open-endedness, and flexibility inherent in many natural processes and systems should not lead us to assume that this provides avenues for God interfering with natural causes. Instead, it gives us a new appreciation for God's continuing creation. Not everything was predetermined from the very beginning. Creation, as it presents itself to us today, is indeed a miracle, not a necessity. The open-endedness also implies a certain precariousness, since it allows for human interference.

Some conclude from the openness of the evolutionary process that humanity should take this process into its own hands. Since scientists have deciphered the genetic code, biotechnology has given us more and more opportunities to manipulate the genetic makeup of living beings. Yet even before this discovery to change genetic makeup, humanity has interacted with the evolutionary process through agriculture, animal breeding, and so on. These interactions, however, have not changed the overall impression of the process. Our own choices in the evolutionary process become again part of the natural process and are thereby not exempt from accidental occurrences, for instance, in determining where and how we interact with nature. If chance would not have played a role in the great contributions for the future of humanity, many Nobel Prizes in the natural sciences would not have been awarded to certain persons. We delude ourselves if we hope to be able to control the natural processes in such a way that they become totally predictable. It is not our lack of insight that makes this undertaking impossible but the processes of nature that are "fundamentally uncontrollable."[32]

29. John Polkinghorne, "The Life and Works of a Bottom-Up Thinker," *Zygon* 35 (December 2000): 960.
30. So very persuasively Bradford McCall, "The God of Chance and Purpose," *Theology and Science* 17, no. 1 (February 2019): 137.
31. Peacocke, *Theology for a Scientific Age*, 152.
32. So Pollard, *Chance and Providence*, 178.

It is exactly with regard to this kind of dependability, this trustworthiness of the natural process, that we discern a peculiar train of thought in the biblical creation accounts. We hear that God initially said and it was so (Gen 1:9). This is followed by the command for humanity to assume a certain responsibility (Gen 1:28). And finally, we are told that God takes protective care of humanity (Gen 3:21: "And the Lord God made garments of skins for the man and for his wife, and clothed them"). This means that the creative process and humanity's function within it do not suffice to make it dependable. Beyond initiating and maintaining his creation, God also has to abide with it. We are reminded here of Luther's observation that we should not think that God has retired and is sleeping on a pillow in heaven; instead, he watches and guides everything. Luther was also much impressed with the fact that God did not abandon his creation after he made it. Luther wrote, "He [God] has not created the world like a carpenter builds a house and then leaves it and let it be the way it is, but he stays with it and sustains it the way he has made it, otherwise it would not remain."[33]

God's care for humanity as expressed in the natural process is not uniform. It proceeds on several layers of dependability involving greater or lesser freedom. Within this freedom, adverse constellations have their place too, such as earthquakes and floods, or human management and mismanagement of the earth, and even to some extent, the seductive and devastating anti-Godly powers. Of course, we could ask why God allows for freedom that does not preclude negative possibilities. Yet what kind of freedom would that be if it only contains good? If there were only freedom for good, it would just be another name for coercion. There would be no actual freedom to choose between good and bad. God would be the primordial tyrant at whose fiat everything occurs. Since the overpowering providence expressed in Stoic and Islamic thought is foreign to the biblical experience, we arrive at a notion of providence that sets forth but does not compel, a notion of providence that accomplishes and does not dehumanize. The final goal and degree of dependability are known, and therefore, the natural process is trustworthy though not always rectilinear.

In talking about the natural process, we acknowledge that there is a dynamic drive in nature. Scientific investigation has shown us that nature moves consistently with and in space and time. Since, phenomenologically speaking, space and time are also nature's outermost parameters, we have no reference point with which we can clearly discern the teleological direction of this movement. Yet when this drive is related to God, such a direction is provided. Now we recognize the eschatological dimension of nature and hear that "the creation waits with eager longing for the revealing of the children of God" (Rom 8:19). We also realize that nature is not an isolated phenomenon. It is tied to and expressive of the phenomenon of

---

33. Martin Luther, *Kaspar Crucigers Sommerpostille* (1544), in WA, 21:521.20–25, in a meditation on Rom 11:33–36.

life and therefore of humanity. Knowing about God, who cares for us through the processes of nature, we can approach the future confidently.

Providence in Moral Discernment

Besides natural events, there is another important way in which God's general providence expresses itself. In the natural process, God's continuous creative activity is dominant, while in the moral process, God's preserving creative activity rules supreme. Through moral discernment, God maintains and guides his creation, and within creation, God takes special care of humanity so as to avoid creation's destruction and human self-annihilation. God did not abandon the world once God had created it. God continues to accompany it in a caring way. Similarly, God does not let humanity go on its own once it appears on the scene. Even when humans stray away from God's precepts, God still cares for them (cf. Gen 3:21). Moreover, God endows humanity with certain guidelines within which it can unfold itself and that may aid it in finding its proper place within creation. Yet where do we find these guidelines?

The most obvious place to seek moral guidance is in one's conscience. The name "conscience" is derived from the Latin *conscire* and means "being a witness to" or "knowing with" someone. In other words, the conscience was originally understood as a kind of moral self-reflection that scrutinizes one's activities. When we remember how many crimes have been committed in nationalistic and fascist countries in the name of conscience, we wonder what kind of normative and autonomous voice this conscience is. We realize that our conscience itself is not a moral norm; rather, it attests to norms that it attempts to enforce.[34] Yet the extent to which these norms are perceived and enforced differs greatly. For some, they seem to be hardly existent, while for others, they are torturous, as they were, for instance, for young Luther in his monastery cell. If we want to address ourselves to the trustworthiness of the moral process, we cannot just look at the conscience as the expression of moral norms. We must search behind the conscience for those very norms.

A promising way in our search for normative forces of human behavior opens up when we investigate the so-called natural law. The *natural law* concerning morality should not be confused with the *laws of nature* that natural science investigates. The notion of a natural law dates back to the ancient idea that the gods gave people rules and regulations according to which people could and should conduct their lives. Aristotle cast this into a philosophical framework by claiming that basic to all human law is the divine law. The fundamental divine law is that which is just by

---

34. Cf. the important collection of papers by Charles E. Curran ed., *Absolutes in Moral Theology?* (Cleveland: Corpus, 1968), which contains Robert H. Springer's paper "Conscience, Behavioral Science and Absolutes," 19–56, in which he states that "greater relativity in the abstract will yield sounder moral conclusions in the concrete" (56).

nature and "which is the criterion and creative foundation of all human legislation and jurisdiction."[35]

At first, the Christian community was rather hesitant to adopt the idea of a natural law, which was especially prevalent among the Stoics. It was primarily Origen who paved the way for the reception of natural law in the Christian community when he identified Christ, the Logos, with the rational—that is, reasonable structure of the world. In Hellenism, this rational structure was called Logos also. At the same time, however, Origen pointed out that the existing positive law of the state could easily conflict with natural law. For instance, he claimed, "When the law of nature, that is, the law of God, commands what is opposed to the written law, observe whether reason will not tell us to bid a long farewell to the written code, and to the desires of its legislators, and to give ourselves up to the legislator God, and to choose a life agreeable to His word, although in doing so, it may be necessary to encounter dangers, and countless labors, and even death and dishonor."[36]

Soon Origen and other theologians (such as Lactantius) referred to the world reason and argued that to outlaw Christian congregations and to demand sacrifices to the gods was contrary to the natural divine law.[37] Lactantius equates the divine law with the natural law, stating, "Therefore the law of God must be undertaken, which may direct us to this path; that sacred, that heavenly law, which Marcus Tullius [Cicero], in his third book respecting the Republic, has described almost with a divine voice."[38] Here an attempt was made to found and limit state laws through the divine natural law.

In Augustine, we find a more explicit understanding of the natural law. He asserts that we consider something just and right because nature teaches us and not because we might have arrived at it through human convention. With this statement, he refuted the heavy critique of the natural law a thousand years later by English empiricists, such as Thomas Hobbes (1588–1679), who understood the natural law primarily from the perspective of a contract or a mutual agreement. He reasons that while every person has the right to everything, "the law of the Gospel" tells him "*whatsoever you require that others should do to you, that do ye to them.*"[39] Therefore, a person renounces the right to anything so that the condition of war of everyone against everyone else is avoided. Yet for Augustine, this order or law is derived not from human reason but from God's will. Augustine claims, "The eternal law is the divine order or will of God, which requires the preservation of natural order, and forbids the breach of it."[40] The eternal law is not temporal but is concomitant with order, peace, and harmony. At the same time, this law is

---

35. So Emil Brunner, *Justice and Social Order*, trans. M. Hottinger (New York: Harper, 1945), 6.
36. Origen, *Against Celsus* (5.37), in ANF, 4:560.
37. Cf. Lactantius, *The Divine Institutes* (5.13), in ANF, 7:148.
38. Lactantius, *Divine Institutes* (6.8), 7:170; Cicero, *Republic*, 3.22.16.
39. Thomas Hobbes, *Leviathan*, in Hobbes, *Selections*, ed. Frederick J. E. Woodbridge (New York: Charles Scribner's, 1930), 271.
40. Augustine, *Reply to Faustus the Manichaean* (22.27), in NPNF FS, 4:283.

equal to the wisdom and will of God. The eternal law must be distinguished from the temporal law regardless of whether it was given in paradise or implanted in our hearts or promulgated in writings.[41] The eternal law is eternally unchangeable and applies to the whole creation.[42] Animals however are subjugated under this law in such a way that they have no part in it, while angels participate in it fully. Animals are simply driven by their instinct. Humanity stands in the middle, in part subjugated to it like animals and in part participating in it like angels. Natural law belongs essentially to our humanity. It is therefore made concrete and present in many ways, as the specific natural law, for instance, in the Golden Rule, the Mosaic law, and the law inscribed in our hearts. In these forms, the temporal law is the reflection of the eternal law.[43]

Thomas Aquinas largely followed Augustine in his understanding of the natural law. For him, "The Eternal Law is nothing other than the exemplar of divine wisdom as directing the motions and acts of everything" (ST 1a2ae.93.1). Contrary to Augustine, Thomas does not think that the term law (*lex*) is derived from reading (*legere*) or choosing (*eligere*), but it "comes from *ligando*, because it is binding on how we should act."[44] He therefore emphasizes the normative element in the law. "The Law is nought else than an ordinance of reason for the common good made and promulgated by the authority who has care of the community."[45]

Thomas distinguishes four different kinds of laws: (1) divinely revealed laws directed toward supernatural purposes, (2) positive human laws based on natural law, (3) natural law itself, and (4) the world law from which natural law follows. Natural law then "is this sharing in the Eternal Law by intelligent creatures."[46] This means that natural law is connected with both the eternal law and the natural judgment of human reason. Through human reason, the eternal law gains binding power as a reasonable prescript. The natural law is therefore essentially reasonable.[47]

By basing the natural law on the eternal law *and* reason, Thomas not only ensured its binding character but also allowed for a dangerous bifurcation: human reason and God's precepts. Once reason took its own path, as happened during the Enlightenment, many things were introduced as reasonable that were clearly against the divine (eternal) law. We notice this to some extent already with Thomas himself when, following Aristotle, he argued for slavery as something given by nature. For him, slavery follows from the fact that "it is expedient for him [the slave] to be ruled by a wiser whom he serves."[48] Thereby, Thomas sanctioned

---

41. Cf. Augustine, *On the Psalms* (119.117), in NPNF FS, 8:580.
42. To the following, cf. Augustine, *Reply to Faustus* (22.28), in NPNF FS, 4:284.
43. Cf. Augustine, *Letters* (157), in FaCh, 20:331.
44. Aquinas (1a2ae.90.1), 28:7.
45. Aquinas (1a2ae.90.4), 28:17.
46. Aquinas (1a2ae.91.2), 28:23.
47. Aquinas (3a2ae.93.5), 28:65–67.
48. Aquinas (2a2ae.57.3). Cf. also the comprehensive study by Bénézet Bujo, *Moralautonomie und Normenfindung bei Thomas von Aquin: Unter Einbeziehung der neutestamentlichen Kommentare* (Paderborn, Germany: Schöningh, 1979), 293–295.

the feudal society in existence at his time. Though he could have designed a very different order of society, Thomas has not yet developed a universally applicable natural law of human freedom. Since natural law results primarily in reasonable action according to body, soul, and mind, humanity sets up natural laws on the basis of the drive to self-preservation. It establishes natural laws according to its animal nature—which it shares with all other sentient beings—for the purpose of procreation and nurture of its descendants. According to its reasonable nature, humanity has a natural inclination to recognize God and to live in community. Once it has been determined what the essence of humanity is, the law must be developed accordingly to further our humanity. Of course, besides the natural law of the individual, Thomas does not neglect the natural law of the community as it applies to family, state, and church.

When Martin Luther says in his *Lectures on Romans* that "we make up many stories about the Law of nature," we might conclude that he did not much appreciate this time-honored concept.[49] When we also remember that he called reason a whore, this might reinforce our picture of Luther's low esteem of humans as reasonable beings.[50] But Luther did not reject reason and natural law. He simply wanted to point out the problems contained in both.

Luther was convinced that God had ordered everything in the world, from the largest events to the smallest details. In his *Lectures on Galatians* of 1531, Luther stated with reference to Deuteronomy 22:5, "The male was not created for spinning; the woman was not created for warfare."[51] God has established a certain order in creation according to which each member has its specific place and function. Let the king rule, the bishop teach, and the people obey the magistrate. "In this way let every creature serve in its own order and place."[52] This order extends over the whole of creation from nature to humanity. If God has ordered nature, it is only logical that even interhuman relationships are not arbitrary. Indeed, Luther is pointing out framework type of structures for family, government, and other interhuman relationships. For instance, God has instilled in the hearts of parents that they serve their children to the best of their ability, nourish them, care for them, and bring them up with great diligence.[53]

Luther claims that these orders of relationships between people are best expressed in natural law. For instance, everybody knows that we should obey our parents, since we are from the same blood and they bring us up.[54] Likewise, reason

49. Martin Luther, Lectures on Romans: Glosses and Scholia (1515–1516), in LW, 25:344, in his interpretation of Rom 8:3.
50. Cf. Martin Luther, Predigten des Jahres 1546, in WA, 51:126.9–10, where Luther says that reason is "the biggest whore that the devil has."
51. Martin Luther, Lectures on Galatians (1535), in LW, 26:307, in his explanation of Gal 3:19.
52. Luther, 308.
53. Martin Luther, A Simple Way to Pray (1535), in LW, 43:203, in his explanation of the fourth commandment.
54. Martin Luther, Predigten über das 2. Buch Mose (1524–1527), in WA, 16:512.3–6, in his explanation of the third commandment.

tells us that we should not kill anybody. From passages such as Matt 7:12 and Romans 2:15, Luther concludes that the natural law contains all the precepts of the prophets and all other commandments.[55] To a large extent, Luther thinks of natural law as identical with the Mosaic law. Since the Mosaic law, however, was given to the Jewish people, only that part of this law that is congruous with the natural law is obligatory for everyone. The matter is different from the commandment of love. Luther rightly recognizes that it is part of the natural law.

Since the "natural law is inborn in us like the heat in fire and the fire in flint, [. . .] it cannot be separated from divine law."[56] It is a natural gift of God that was not lost through the fall. It enables and facilitates communal life and serves as the basis and corrective for all other forms of law. Luther states that if natural law and reason were inherent and available to all, all people would be equal in their conduct.[57] However, he concedes that natural law is no longer available in its absolutely normative form. Though it is still inscribed into our hearts, on account of our sinfulness, its words do not have compelling power.[58]

Luther similarly assesses the power of reason. For instance, he admonishes a prince to "determine in his own mind when and where the law is to be applied strictly or with moderation, so that law may prevail at all times and in all cases, and reason may be the highest law and the master of all administration of law."[59] But reason does not function independently as the norm for natural law, though Luther admits that the written law stems from reason as the wellspring of all law.[60] Natural law can fulfill its normative function only insofar as it is embedded in the ordering activity of God that surrounds and maintains it and that reason continuously presupposes.[61] Reason does not inaugurate the trustworthy moral process, but it discovers and forms the legal process according to God's ordering action. As long as reason and natural law are sustained by the ordering activity of God, they are the normative and formative forces of the moral process.

In the Enlightenment, however, Luther's admonition concerning the relationship between God's ordering activity and the natural law was discarded. Thomas Hobbes, for instance, sees in the natural law "a precept of general rule, found out by reason."[62] Then he argues on a strictly rational basis about liberty, justice, and peace without any reference to God. Jean Jacques Rousseau (1712–78) then claimed that humanity is good by nature. Furthermore, humanity could regain this natural state if it would turn away from the corrupting influences of society and civilization and be itself, instead of simply being citizens whose value

55. To the following, cf. Martin Luther, *Against the Heavenly Prophets, in the Matter of Images and Sacraments* (1525), in LW, 40:97–98.
56. Martin Luther, "Table Talk" (2119 B; 1531), in WATR, 2:374, 17–19.
57. Martin Luther, *Psalm 101* (1534–1535), in LW, 13:161, in his explanation of Ps 101:1.
58. Martin Luther, *Lectures on Deuteronomy* (1525), in LW, 9:108, in his exegesis of Deut 10.
59. Martin Luther, *On Temporal Authority: To What Extent It Should Be Obeyed* (1523), in LW, 45:119.
60. Luther, 45:129.
61. Cf. Luther's argument in *The Judgment of Martin Luther on Monastic Vows* (1521), in LW, 44:336.
62. Hobbes, *Leviathan*.

depends on the community in which they live.[63] This idea is pursued further in his *Social Contract* (1762). While he realizes that human society is threatened by the tyranny of the people themselves, he is convinced that a true and just society cannot be based on mere force; it must rather be consistent with people as free and rational beings. Therefore, he suggested that humanity be liberated from the tyranny of the individual human will. Rousseau insisted that "each one of us puts into the community his person and all his powers under the supreme direction of the general will; and as a body, we incorporate every member as an indivisible part of the whole."[64] Freed from the narrow confines of its own being, a human being will find fulfillment in a truly social experience of fraternity and equality with citizens who share the same ideals.

The question that must be posed is whether one can count on such agreement by nature. Is the foundation for Rousseau's "social contract" really to be found in nature? In his *Essay concerning Human Understanding* (1690), John Locke had already asserted that all our knowledge only stems from sense perception.[65] Following this empirical trend, David Hume (1711–76) finally discarded all metaphysics. Though he still allowed for an original moral sense in humanity, he distinguished between matters of fact, which rest on certain conventions of experience, and truths of reason, which are based on certain conventions of reason. There is no longer an eternal norm of justice. Law becomes a matter of convention.[66] Yet if there is no longer a directing moral influence, how can sinfully inclined human beings, whom Rousseau portrays, become citizens who strive for fraternity and equality? Humanity seems to be on a course leading to enslavement rather than to freedom.

When ontologically grounded natural law was abandoned, not only its normative character but also its outdated manifestations were discarded. For instance, the idea was increasingly challenged that there were different classes of people with different rights and privileges. Undeniable progress could now be made by instituting inalienable human rights for all people and democratic procedures for dealing with each other. Yet in doing away with the metaphysically grounded natural law, one was also prone to consider the natural law as an expression of circumstances and mere convention. The natural law separated from its divine ground became time bound. This allowed for its continuous development, for

---

63. Jean Jacques Rousseau, *Emile or Education*, trans. Barbara Foxley (New York: E. P. Dutton, 1948), 5–7; cf. also William Boyd, *The Educational Theory of Jean Jacques Rousseau* (New York: Russell & Russell, 1963), 190, who rightly claims that in *Emile*, Rousseau does not neglect nature: "He is merely seeking for a method of keeping men as near nature as possible under existing social conditions."

64. Jean Jacques Rousseau, *The Social Contract* (1.6), trans., ed., and with an introduction by Maurice Cranston (Baltimore, MD: Penguin, 1969), 61.

65. Cf. John Locke, *An Essay concerning Human Understanding* (2.1.2), ed. Alexander C. Fraser (Oxford: Clarendon, 1894), 1:64, after having rejected the concept of innate ideas.

66. For the empirical foundation of laws, cf. David Hume, *A Treatise of Human Nature* (3.3.1), ed. L. A. Selby-Bigge (Oxford: Clarendon, 1896), 591.

instance, in regard to gender and sexual orientation, but it also turned it into an expression of its respective age. As the Reformed theologian Emil Brunner (1889–1966) has cautioned, if there is nothing that is universally valid and no justice beyond ourselves that meets all of us as an undeniable demand, then there is no actual justice "but only power organized in one fashion or another and setting itself up as law."[67] The alarming frequency with which totalitarian systems have emerged during the last one hundred years should make us wonder whether reason itself is a sufficient foundation for the moral process. Even the strong pressure on political correctness in speech and manners sometimes assumes a form of totalitarianism. For instance, the majority of the people in Germany feel that they must be very careful about what they say in public. While during the height of absolutism, kings and princes understood that they enjoyed their rule through the grace of God, today's dictators exercise their rule in their own name. They no longer feel subject to higher powers. The individual human being has become its own ultimate measure for right and wrong.

But already Charles Darwin asserted that human moral and mental faculties differ in degree rather in kind from the capacities of animals.[68] If there is indeed a moral continuity between animals and humans, there should be even more reason to assume that such continuity exists between one human being and another. There is a common moral bond that assures our survival. Perhaps the reason we tend to deny the basic unity of the human moral process lies in the fact of our sinful estrangement from each other. We have become individualized human beings that are turned in on themselves without recognizing our actual neighbors and their needs. Symptomatic for this situation seems that people are so busy with their iPhones that they are oblivious to their immediate environment. We are so far apart from each other that we tend to forget our common history and common destiny.

The German behavioral scientist Wolfgang Wickler (*b. 1931), a former student of Konrad Lorenz (1903–89), points out our common moral history in his insightful book *The Biology of the Ten Commandments*. He claims that the Ten Commandments (specifically the fourth to the tenth) are demands that have not just emerged on the human level. For instance, inhibition against killing members of one's own group and against theft and lying and the summon to honor older members of the same social group are already present among animals.[69] This does not mean that these commandments are immutable. As a foundation and summary of appropriate moral behavior, they show a development even within the human family.

67. Brunner, *Justice and Social Order*, 8.
68. Cf. Charles Darwin, *The Descent of Man, and Selection in Relation to Sex* (124.126), in *The Works of Charles Darwin* (London: Pickering, 1989), 21:128–130, where he talks about "social instincts" in both animals and humans that serve "the good of the community" and "the difference in mind between man and the higher animals" that is "one of degree and not of kind."
69. Cf. Wolfgang Wickler, *The Biology of the Ten Commandments*, trans. D. Smith (New York: McGraw-Hill, 1972), 76, 12, 160–161.

There are Decalogue-like collections of commandments known in Egypt, in India, and among the Maasai in Kenya.[70] Especially the latter are instructive, since they portray a nomadic existence that necessitated significant changes in the Decalogue to adjust to the peculiarities of this form of life.[71] We are reminded here of Luther's insight: "What God has given from heaven to the Jews through Moses, he has also inscribed in the hearts of all humanity."[72] Luther recognized the Decalogue as a basic norm that is known to everyone even without the Mosaic law. Ethnological research has adduced more and more evidence that indeed there are some basic norms of human behavior. The biologist Arnold W. Ravin from the University of Chicago expressed this very appropriately when he said, "Every culture has a concept of murder, that is, a specification of conditions under which homicide is unjustifiable. Every culture has a taboo upon incest and usually other regulations upon sexual behavior. Similarly, all cultures hold untruth to be abhorrent, at least under most conditions. Finally, all have a notion of reciprocal obligation between parents and their children. These universal or near-universal ethics [. . .] do indicate some profound and fundamental needs in all men to behave within certain limits or ethical boundaries."[73] This means that by nature, the behavior of human beings is not as free and unspecified as we might initially assume. To be a human being means to act according to certain norms that enable us to live together and further our own species. For Ravin as well as for Konrad Lorenz and his followers, morality is natural. Sociobiology, however, cautioned against such optimism and showed that altruism among members of the same species is the result of the fact that the actual carriers of biological evolution are not individuals, whether species or single members, but the genes that cooperate in order to survive. The biologist Edward O. Wilson (*b. 1929) therefore writes, "The genes hold culture on a leash. The leash is very long, but inevitably values will be constrained in accordance with the effects on the human gene pool."[74] The findings of behavioral genetics are not, however, totally void of moral implications.[75] It is still concerned with survival. Yet in contrast to Darwin, who considered the survival of individuals and of groups, behavioral geneticists have realized that individuals certainly do not survive, and groups quite often do not survive either.

70. Cf. Siegfried Morenz, *Egyptian Religion*, trans. A. E. Keep (London: Methuen, 1973), esp. 112 and 121–123, where he refers to the so-called Book of the Dead and classifies the commandments in ancient Egypt as wisdom literature. This comment is especially telling, since it attests to the acquisition of right conduct through insight and not just divine revelation. Cf. also Saddhatissa, 87; and Kashi Nath Upadhyaya, *Early Buddhism and the Bhagavadgita* (Delhi: Motilal Banarsidass, 1971), 413–414. Cf. also Moritz Merker, *Die Maasai* (New York: Johnson Reprints, 1968), 335–336. Of course, the Maasai are a Semitic tribe, which Merker emphasizes, pointing to their common heritage with the Israelites.

71. Cf. Wickler, *Biology*, 44–5, who refers here to Merker's study of the Maasai.

72. Martin Luther, *Predigten über das 2. Buch Mose* (1524–1527), in WA, 16:380, 19–20, in a sermon on Exod 19.

73. Arnold W. Ravin, "Science, Values, and Human Evolution," *Zygon* 11 (June 1976): 151.

74. Edward O. Wilson, *On Human Nature* (Cambridge, MA: Harvard University Press, 1978), 167.

75. Cf. Hans Schwarz, "The Interplay between Science and Theology in Uncovering the Matrix of Human Morality," *Zygon* 28 (March 1993): 69–70.

In an evolutionary scheme, only genetic units have an inherent tendency to last long enough to survive, and these units have evolved to survive by helping their copies reproduce wherever they may live. In order to succeed with propagation, certain behavioral traits are favored, while others are abandoned as being unsuccessful. For humanity, this would mean that the explicit forms of behavior depend on the environment in which the social behavior takes place.

The trustworthiness of the moral process, which is maintained by living according to these norms, depends on our ability to develop these norms in such a way that they continue to be normative for interactions with the environment in which we live. If these norms are not developed in accordance with the changes we encounter and inaugurate, we will become helpless victims of the developments that surround us.[76] For instance, if we do not adjust our conduct to the crowded conditions in our modern anonymous mass society, this will lead to a deterioration of individual partner relationships.[77] We will "get on each other's nerves" to such an extent that either society completely disintegrates or new individual protective areas are created. Therefore, we often have become immune to what happens around us. For instance, in an elevator, people have their eyes directed to the floor, waiting until their floor arrives instead of looking the others in the eyes and starting a conversation, as one would do in a small village where everybody knows everybody else. Yet this isolation also has its drawbacks. When one encounters street violence, often people ignore it instead of coming to help. German politicians therefore urge people not to look the other way when they notice such violence or some other crime but to get involved and at least call the police or other help. Contrary to our obligation of governing the world and using it in accordance with the moral norms appropriate to us and our situation, we can easily become helpless victims or immune bystanders.

These insights and conclusions have important implications for our understanding of the traditional theology of the orders of creation. The Lutheran theologian Werner Elert (1885–1954) is certainly right when he claims that they are presupposed in the Decalogue with words of command and prohibition and are orders to which we belong as created beings. Therefore, he calls them "orders of creation."[78] We wonder however whether Elert is correct when he asserts that they are always orders that already exist and not those that we should maintain. Truly, the sixth commandment does not constitute marriage but presupposes it. But adultery was committed through acts that were considerably different in King David's Israel from those in Luther's Germany or in puritan England. Needless to say, in each epoch, marriage was also understood quite differently. This does not mean that the underlying norm "thou shalt not commit adultery" had no binding value. But if we

---

76. Cf. Wickler, Biology, 171–173.
77. Cf. Wickler, 179.
78. Cf. Werner Elert, The Christian Ethos, trans. Carl J. Schindler (Philadelphia: Muhlenberg, 1957), 77–79.

want to maintain the goal of durable pair relationships, which is envisioned in this commandment, then the exact interpretation of their normative ought-character must be reconsidered with each changing situation.

Since moral norms are goal oriented, intended to preserve the species rather than to constitute it, it might be good to follow the suggestion of Walter Künneth (1901–97). He speaks of orders of preservation instead of orders of creation. Künneth does not intend to diminish the creational character of these orders, but he objects to their static interpretation and maintains that creation must be perceived from the perspective of God's conserving activity.[79] This is even more necessary, since we know God's creation only in its fallen condition, under the aspect of preservation. According to Künneth, the orders of preservation counteract the tendencies of the destructive anti-Godly powers. They are a sign that God does not want to destroy the world but conserves it for Christ's sake and toward Christ. The orders of preservation therefore ultimately have eschatological character; they point to the eschatological fulfillment in the new creation.

Since these orders are no longer evident in their original divine creational intention, they assume the character of a law. But as law, they enable and facilitate the living together of people. They express a mutual obligation and therefore have basically the character of mutual service. Yet they are also susceptible to sinful distortion and can be misused to perpetuate injustice and inequality. Therefore, they should never be separated from God as the originator and granter of these orders. This does not mean that we should go as far as Karl Barth, who claims that through its sinful existence, humanity is in such depravity that it cannot, by its own power, know anything about these fundamental moral laws of nature. Barth therefore insists that this order cannot be found anywhere in the world. It has "sought us out in the grace of God in Jesus Christ revealed in His Word, disclosing itself to us as such where we for our part could neither perceive nor find it."[80]

Dietrich Bonhoeffer attempts a similar christomonistic foundation of these orders, as does Barth. Bonhoeffer claims that it is an empty abstraction to talk about the world if one does not relate it to Christ.[81] The relationship "of the world to Christ assumes concrete form in certain mandates of God in the world. The Scriptures name four such mandates: labor, marriage, government and the Church." The term *mandates* is very apt, for it points to the obligatory aspect of these orders. Yet we are afraid that an exclusively christocentric approach to these orders—whether we accept their foundation in Christ or not—obscures the fact that the acknowledgment of certain moral norms is a necessary condition for human existence

---

79. For the following, cf. Walter Künneth, *Politik zwischen Dämon und Gott: Eine christliche Ethik des Politischen* (Berlin: Lutherisches Verlagshaus, 1954), 139–140.
80. Barth, CD, 3/4:45.
81. Cf. Dietrich Bonhoeffer, *Ethics*, ed. Eberhard Bethge and trans. N. H. Smith (New York: Macmillan, 1965), 207, including the quote.

as such.[82] Since they are binding for both atheists and Christians, they are not a source of revelation.

Atheists can recognize these norms of moral behavior as partly inborn and partly handed on by tradition. In the light of God's self-disclosure in Jesus Christ, however, Christians perceive in these norms the preserving activity of God. They realize that through the evolving moral process, God is preserving the human community against human self-destruction and against the destructive and seductive tendencies of the anti-Godly powers. Luther expressed this very picturesquely when he said, "If God were to withdraw his protective hand and leave room to the devil you would become blind, or an adulterer and murderer like David. You would fall and break your leg and drown."[83] Through God's self-disclosure in Jesus Christ, we are also reminded of the trustworthiness yet transitory character of the moral process. It will find its fulfillment and completion in the eschatological new creation, when the moral norms will be unimpaired and self-evident. Then our moral behavior will be characterized by complete harmony with God.

It has not been difficult for us to assert the trustworthiness of the natural process. We know that the universe has evolved in an amazing way over the course of its existence, and there is little doubt that this process of unfolding will continue. Yet amid all the present-day uncertainties, it has been more difficult for us to assert that there are basic moral norms that we can trust and that we must continuously develop. When we consider the historical process, then its trustworthiness is even more difficult to maintain. We are informed by the Christian tradition that God is the Lord of history, but when talking about human history the question immediately emerges, Whose side is God on?

Preservation through the Historical Process

In World War I (1914–18) the churches called upon God to bless the weapons on both sides of the trenches. After the Allies had dictated to Germany the terms of peace in the Treaty of Versailles (1919), the "German Christians" saw the special finger of God in Hitler's rise to power in 1933. Even in 1934, when many had discovered that Hitler was not a blessing, a group of theologians in Württemberg, Germany, wrote the following statement: "We are full of thanks to God that he, as Lord of history, has given our country Adolf Hitler, as leader and savior from our difficult lot. We acknowledge that we are bound and dedicated with body and soul to the German state and to its *Führer*. This bondage and this duty contain for us, as Protestant

---

82. Immanuel Kant in his *Metaphysical Foundations of Morals*, in *The Philosophy of Kant: Immanuel Kant's Moral and Political Writings*, ed. and with an introduction by Carl J. Friedrich (New York: Random House, 1949), 150–151, argues on the basis of "pure reason" that there are certain moral norms that, when universalized, will support human existence, while others, once universalized, will impede it.

83. Martin Luther, *Predigten des Jahres 1531*, in WA, 34/2:237.16–19, in a sermon on the festival of Saint Michael.

Christians, their deepest and most holy demand in the fact that it is obedience to the commandment of God."[84]

Even Gerhard Kittel (1888–1948)—the former editor of the *Theological Dictionary of the New Testament* and who as a theologian was never a member of the so-called German Christians—confessed that he had prayed for years that the German people might be saved from their distress and disgrace.[85] Should the emergence of Adolf Hitler not be regarded as God's answer to such prayers? Had not Adolf Hitler himself invoked the power of "providence" when he was amazingly spared from assassination attempts, claiming "that he was a man chosen by Providence to act as the agent of the 'World Historical Process'"?[86]

But it was not only Christians in Nazi Germany who ventured such "providential" interpretations of history. In 1941, when the invasion of the German Army in Russia was most threatening, Metropolitan and later Patriarch Sergius (1867–1944), of the Russian Orthodox Church of Moscow and All Russia, confidently wrote in a circular addressed to the laity and clergy of his district that, as on previous occasions, "with the help of God, they [i.e., our people] will once again chase away the troops of the enemy."[87] Of course, we could argue with Luther that God simply "uses one rascal to punish the other."[88] That is, God does not condone either of them but simply uses them in his providential activity to restore order and justice. The factor of historical survival or eminence does not legitimate a certain power or authority as providential.

There are still amazing historical events, however, that invite true theological evaluation. For instance, when the Gothic hordes of King Alaric (ca. 370–410 CE) ransacked Rome in 410 CE, many pagans claimed that the ransacking signaled the wrath of the ancient gods.[89] These gods were angry because the people had forsaken the ancient cults and adopted Christianity. However, Augustine attempted to show in his book *The City of God* that this was not the case. He claimed that the decline and fall of Rome were due to the moral depravity of paganism. A generation later, the presbyter Salvian of Marseille (ca. 400–75 CE) explained in his book *On the Government of God* that the decline of Rome was a judgment on the Christians due to their neglect of God's commandments and not on the heathen.[90] The fall of

---

84. "Zwölf Thesen der Kirchlichen Einheitsfront in Württemberg" (May 11, 1934), in *Die Bekenntnisse und grundsätzliche Äußerungen zur Kirchenfrage*, vol. 2, *Das Jahr 1934*, ed. Kurt Dietrich Schmidt (Göttingen, Germany: Vandenhoeck & Ruprecht, 1935), 73.

85. Cf. Gerhard Kittel in Karl Barth and Gerhard Kittel, *Ein theologischer Briefwechsel* (Stuttgart, Germany: W. Kohlhammer, 1934), 12.

86. Alan Bullock, *Hitler: A Study in Tyranny*, rev. ed. (New York: Harper Torchbook, 1964), 723. Bullock comments, "Anything, however trivial, which went right in the last two years of the war served Hitler as a further evidence that he had only to trust in Providence and all would be well."

87. Sergius, *Die Wahrheit über die Religion in Russland*, trans. Laure Wyss (Zollikon-Zürich: Evangelischer Verlag, 1944), 16.

88. Cf. Martin Luther, *Admonition to Peace: A Reply to the Twelve Articles of the Peasants in Swabia* (1525), in LW, 46:32.

89. Cf. Etienne Gilson in his introduction to Augustine, *The City of God*, ed. Vernon J. Bourke (Garden City, NY: Doubleday Image, 1958), 16.

90. Salvian, *The Governance of God* (6.12 and 7.1), in FaCh, 3:172, 185.

Rome was God's punishment for the unrighteousness of the Christians in church and society. Whom should we then trust in the assessment of history: the pagans, Augustine, or Salvian? Perhaps we should keep in mind what the Reformed theologian Gerrit C. Berkouwer (1903–96) once wrote "that the interpretation of an historical event as a special revelation of Providence too easily becomes a piously disguised form of self-justification."[91] It is one thing to believe that through God's providential action, even in the historical process, his kingdom will finally triumph, but it is yet another to conceive divine providence atomistically as a fragmentary demonstration of God's power.

We do not agree with the German poet Friedrich Schiller that "world history is world judgment."[92] It is also difficult for us to approve the attempt of Georg Wilhelm Friedrich Hegel to conceive of world history as a theodicy of God in which the thinking spirit is "reconciled with the fact of the existence of evil."[93] Yet should we follow Dorothee Sölle when she claims that the pain, injustice, and suffering of the innocent lead to the dethronement of God almighty, the king, father, and ruler of the whole world?[94] Has not Bonhoeffer claimed that "God lets himself to be pushed out of the world" so that "God is weak and powerless in the world"?[95] Was William Hamilton right when he claimed that he carried out the legacy of Bonhoeffer in asserting that the traditional sovereign and omnipotent God is difficult to perceive or meet? Hamilton suggested that "in place of this God, the impotent God, suffering with men, seems to be emerging."[96] Finally, Thomas J. J. Altizer speaks of the death of God as an event in history. "We must realize," he states, "that the death of God is an historical event, that God has died in our cosmos, in our history, in our *Existenz*."[97]

It would indeed be futile to attempt a justification of the historical process as a result of God's providential activity. Luther's emphasis on the theology of the cross should serve as a warning against such endeavors. In the *Heidelberg Disputation* (1518), he asserts, "True theology and recognition of God are in the crucified Christ."[98] Luther realized that God completes when he destroys, "that he makes alive when he puts one on the cross, that he saves when he judges," that he discloses

91. Gerrit C. Berkouwer, *The Providence of God*, trans. L. Smedes (Grand Rapids, MI: William B. Eerdmans, 1952), 180.
92. See Friedrich Schiller's poem "Resignation" (1786), in *Gesammelte Werke in fünf Bänden*, ed. Reinhold Netolitzky (Gütersloh, Germany: Bertelsmann, 1959), 3:394.
93. Georg Wilhelm Friedrich Hegel, *The Philosophy of History*, with a preface by Charles Hegel and an introduction by C.J. Friedrich, trans. J. Sibree (New York: Dover, 1956), 15. It is also difficult to agree with him when he writes, "God governs the world; the actual working of his government—the carrying out of his plan—is the History of the World" (36).
94. Cf. Dorothee Sölle, *Christ the Representative: An Essay in Theology after the "Death of God,"* trans. David Lewis (London: SCM, 1967), 150–151, where she quotes Bonhoeffer's statement in our following quotation.
95. Bonhoeffer, *Letters and Papers*, 188, in a letter of July 16, 1944.
96. William Hamilton, *The New Essence of Christianity* (New York: Association, 1966), 54, where he refers to Bonhoeffer's quotation mentioned in the previous footnote.
97. Thomas J. J. Altizer and William Hamilton, "America and the Future of Theology," in *Radical Theology and the Death of God* (Indianapolis: Bobbs-Merrill, 1966), 11.
98. Cf. Martin Luther's explanation to thesis 20 of the *Heidelberg Disputation of 1517*, in LW, 31:53.

himself when he disguises himself.[99] This means there is no rectilinear connection between historical events and God so that we could trace God's working in history. Luther consequently concluded that God works under the appearance of the opposite. This means he always works different from the way we would expect him to work. Bonhoeffer emphasized this "weakness" of God too. But unlike some of his followers, he also confessed in his *Letters and Papers from Prison* very much like Luther: "I believe that God is no timeless fate, but that he waits for and answers sincere prayers and responsible actions."[100] Though we cannot empirically discern God's ways in history, we know from his embodiment in Jesus that God is active in history in general and in our own personal history in particular. Therefore, Jesus encouraged his followers to engage in a dialogue with God and address and consider God as their father.

From what has been written so far, we might conclude that acknowledging God's providential involvement in the historical process is simply a matter of faith. If this were so, it could easily lead to credulity and to an attitude of regarding any historical oddity as the result of God's will. This could be even more the case when we relate God and history than when we relate God and nature. This is due to the fact that historical events are more multifaceted. They are singular and depend on a unique space and time. Their causal explanations contain a significantly higher degree of subjectivity than those in the natural sciences.[101]

(1). In the natural sciences, an established causal connection between two stages of experience can be repeated by anyone at any place and any time. Historical events however are singular, and their presumed sequence cannot be subjected to experimental scrutiny (e.g., Does World War I always lead to World War II?).

(2). In the natural sciences, paradoxical phenomena (e.g., duality of wave and corpuscle) can be explained as complementary. Differing historical perspectives however usually exclude each other (e.g., the attempts to explain the reason for the devastation of Rome in 410 CE).

(3). In the natural sciences, the causal sequence between two stages of experience can always be established. If hypothetical forces have to be assumed to establish such a sequence, such procedure usually leads to new advancements in science. With historical events, the causal sequence is often not evident, and history appears as a sequence of accidents (e.g., the legal phrase "an act of God").

Since we can justify God's providence neither by pointing to historical accidents nor by simply equating in deterministic fashion the historical process with God's providence, a criterion to assess the trustworthiness of God's providential activity in the historical process must be gained from other sources.

99. So Erich Seeberg, *Grundzüge der Theologie Luthers*, 2nd ed. (Stuttgart, Germany: W. Kohlhammer, 1950), 54–55.
100. Bonhoeffer, *Letters and Papers* (1943), 11.
101. For the following, cf. Albert C. Outler, *Who Trusts in God: Musings on the Meaning of Providence* (New York: Oxford University Press, 1968), 45–46.

It is important here to remember that God is introduced in Scripture as the one for whom nothing is impossible and who determines the course of history. This confession of God's almighty power and his governing of history however only serves to emphasize the conviction that God will bring his plan of salvation to completion (Gen 18:14; Luke 1:37). This confession does not impress the notion upon us that all of history runs according to God's preconceived plan. When Jesus was asked for a theological interpretation of the death of the Galileans that Pilate had slain or the eighteen men who were killed by the tower that collapsed at Siloam (Luke 13:1–5), he did not equate the course of history with God's judgment. He reacted similarly when his disciples asked him why a man was born blind (John 9:3). At the same time, Jesus did not simply shrug his shoulders and declare that history is without meaning. In the first two instances, he answered in existential fashion that events like these remind us of our own mortality and sinfulness. In the latter case, he commented, according to the Evangelist, that this case serves to manifest God's works.[102]

In other words, historical events are not an end in themselves. They are also not just part of the larger context of world history. Ultimately, historical events have eschatological significance. They are "a living reminder of the End, speaking sometimes with certainty and more often in utter ambiguity."[103] Though the New Testament alerts us to watch for the signs of the end, it is obvious to the New Testament writers that history does not provide us with a timetable for events leading to the eschatological fulfillment of history and creation (Matt 24:32–33; 36–37).

While we must agree with the biblical testimony that the historical process will find its fulfillment and completion in the eschaton, we must refrain from the temptation to identify God with one of the causes of the historical process or with the cause. Friedrich Gogarten (1887–1967) offered a more convincing suggestion. He reminded us that God has accepted us in his sonship. In so doing, God has granted us the freedom to lead our lives responsibly without interfering in our lives through divine providence.[104] God wants us to be his governors in the world. A governor without freedom and responsibility would be a mere puppet and not a responsive and responsible being. Yet responsibility does not exclude divine providence. On the contrary, it necessitates providence. We should be God's governors and because of this responsible God relationship, we need God's guidance. This can be illustrated by the Old Testament understanding of *berith* (covenant), which also plays an essential role in the Christian faith. We see how important the notion of covenant is when we remember that "testament," as used in the Old or the New Testaments,

---

102. Cf. Rudolf Bultmann, *The Gospel of John*, trans. G. R. Beasley-Murray (Philadelphia: Westminster, 1971), 331, esp. n. 3, in his exegesis of John 9:1–7.
103. Evgenii Lampert, *The Apocalypse of History: Problems of Providence and Human Destiny* (London: Faber and Faber, 1948), 176, who convincingly asserts an apocalyptic and eschatological interpretation of history.
104. Cf. Friedrich Gogarten, *The Reality of Faith: The Problem of Subjectivism in Theology*, trans. Carl Michalson (Philadelphia: Westminster, 1959), 55–57.

really means covenant. In Old Testament thinking, a covenant "mostly involves a promise by the master or suzerain to take his vassal under protection," but it is not an "agreement or settlement between two parties" or "a mutual agreement."[105] Finite humanity attempting to fulfill its task as God's governor is this inferior agent who needs God's assistance and guiding providence.

God is not a puppeteer who simply pulls strings or who preordains every detail of history. While God is above and beyond the details of this world, allowing creation and humans freedom and a degree of independence, God is also in his creation and in history providing, where necessary, predictability in the natural processes and help from self-destruction through moral norms. While some of these "laws" are almost rigidly enforced, others allow for such freedom that they can even be ignored. Yet opting out of them also brings divine providence to naught. Concomitant with such opting out is a relinquishing of our responsibility to be God's governors in this world.

We have seen that God grants his assistance and guiding providence in providing the trustworthiness of both the natural and the moral process. He also grants the trustworthiness of the historical process. However, human life and history in any form are unwarranted. The believer perceives them not as accidental but as the result of God's creative and sustaining activity. The believer receives them as a gift, unmerited and undeservedly. Yet the unbeliever does not understand this trustworthiness (of the historical process) to result from the God who provides order. While the impact of the natural and moral processes maintains order and averts chaos, the primary thrust of the historical process is directed toward grace and fulfillment, not toward order and sustenance. The unresolved tensions of history illustrate this especially well. God reminds us that we "groan inwardly while we wait for adoption" and that the whole of creation still waits "with eager longing for the revealing of the children of God" (Rom 8:19–23). We recognize that our world is in transition from "in the beginning God created heaven and earth" to "and God will be all in all." Consequently, our position as God's administrators of this world and as the executors of the historical process is not a permanent one.

That special piece of history, called salvation history, continually reminds us that we are created not just by God but toward God. Thus the unresolved contradictions of our historical existence will find their resolution in the larger context of salvation. While God in his general providence "provides both order and grace as the matrix of existence," (human) existence is not a self-contained phenomenon.[106] It is open toward its future, which is foreshadowed in the Christ event as the promise and the proleptic anticipation of a new creation. Therefore, we now turn to God's special providence.

---

105. Moshe Weinfeld, "Berith," in TDOT, 2:255–256.
106. Outler, Who Trusts in God, 52.

God's Special Providence

In our survey of God's general providence, we have seen how God provides a trustworthy basis for human activity. In granting order to our existence, God primarily sanctions natural constellations, which already prevail in our world. Only in the eschatological provision of a new creation do we notice that God's providential activity will extend beyond the presently available. Does this mean that within the historical context we cannot expect anything new? Will the phenomenon of a new world in which justice will rule only emerge when the eschaton commences?

We remember that already in the present there is genuine newness in the evolutionary processes of life. The evolution of life in its present form was not something simply to be expected, but it included both novelty and predictability. Turning to God's self-disclosure as it culminated in Jesus Christ, we notice too that there are constancy and surprise. God's involvement with humanity developed along certain lines (e.g., covenant, promise and fulfilment, law and Gospel, etc.). At the same time, there are events that were totally unexpected, such as the crossing of the Red Sea, the election of David, and the coming of the Messiah. Even Christian existence stands under the same dialectic. On the one hand, it is as predictable as any other human existence. But at the same time, Christians have a vision of a new creation and are encouraged to proleptically anticipate something of the eschatologically envisioned goal. As Christians, they enjoy already here and now an existence in the new creation. The eschaton as something genuinely new is not just a future phenomenon; it is to some extent already a present experience. To realistically affirm this eschatological newness, we must remember that God's general providence extends beyond the provision of order. Just as God's self-disclosure is unexpected, so is God's special providence as God's provision of newness in his miraculous activity. We must deal here primarily with the problem and significance of miracles as well as with the issue of prayer as a response to and a request for God's providential care.

Miracles

In order to talk about miracles, we must first clarify what we mean by this term. In everyday language, a miracle is something totally unexpected that in a positive way enters our world. Somebody miraculously escaped unscathed a tragedy such as a horrible car crash or was miraculously healed of cancer against the expectations of the medical personal. For a Christian, however, it is intimately connected with God's working in the world. Therefore, a miracle is theologically understood as an unexpected act of God that contradicts our usual experience and becomes visible as an occurrence in the objective world. A miracle is an exception. We do not call something that occurs every day a miracle or unexpected newness. The feeding of the five thousand (John 6:1–14) has often been called a miracle. Augustine rightly commented, "For certainly the government of the whole world is a greater miracle than the satisfying of five thousand men with five loaves; and yet no man wonders at the former; but the latter men wonder at, not because it is greater, but because it is rare."[107] The problem posed by a miracle however is not its exceptional character but that it becomes visible in the objective world. Thus miracles are erratic blocks and are in danger of becoming stumbling blocks. The reason for this is that as an act of God, they pertain to the metaphysical dimension, while as something that has become visible, they belong to the dimension of the natural or the physical.

Through the dominance of the natural sciences, a more and more stringent distinction was made between the natural (the object matter of the natural sciences) and the supernatural (the realm of God). If God is the agent of a miracle, one commonly assumed that God could proceed not in a natural manner but in a supernatural one. Thus a potential conflict was laid between those who felt that the natural context of events does not allow for divine disruptions and those who asserted that an all-powerful God can at any time interfere with the natural. It is important to remember that the distinction between the natural and the supernatural is relatively recent. For example, Augustine was still free to say, "A portent, therefore, happens not contrary to nature, but contrary to what we know as nature."[108] This is also in line with the biblical worldview where the natural and the supernatural permeated each other. Therefore, miracles as unusual events were commonplace. But the strict distinction between the natural and the supernatural restricts—if not outright precludes—the possibility of a miracle.

It was only in the ninth century, after the Greek neo-Platonic works of Dionysius the Areopagite had been translated into Latin, that the term *supernatural* finally made its appearance in Western theology.[109] Yet it was only after the thirteenth century, primarily with the help of Thomas Aquinas, that *supernatural* became a commonly accepted theological term. Aquinas, for instance, clearly distinguished between the natural and the supernatural in a miraculous event when he wrote, "Firstly, there is natural change, which is done in the natural way by the appropriate agent. Secondly, there is miraculous change, which is done by a supernatural agent, above the normal order and course of nature—as for instance the raising of the dead to life."[110] Yet Thomas did not want to see the natural in opposition to the supernatural. Like most people in the Middle Ages, Thomas perceived God as the one who connects the natural with the supernatural so that the natural order is enveloped in the supernatural, which provides origin, sustenance, and goal for the natural.[111]

Aquinas agreed with Augustine that a miracle is "*something difficult and unusual.*" But then he added that it is also something "*surpassing the capabilities*

107. Augustine, *Lectures or Tractates on the Gospel according to St. John* (24.1), in NPNF FS, 7:158.
108. Augustine, *City of God* (21.8), in NPNF FS, 2:459.
109. For the following, cf. John P. Kenny, *The Supernatural: Medieval Theological Concepts to Modern* (Staten Island: Alba House, 1972), 94–95.
110. Aquinas, *Summa Theologiae* (3a.13.2r).
111. Cf. Aquinas, *Summa Theologiae* (1a.105.5r).

of nature [*supra facultatem naturae*] and the expectations of those who wonder at it."[112] A miracle therefore is not simply something unusual and unexpected. It is something altogether wondrous, having God as its cause totally hidden. Since Thomas defined a miracle as an act of God that is outside the normal pattern of nature and surpasses its capabilities, he even went so far as to say, "Creation and the justifying of the sinner, while they are acts of God alone, are strictly speaking not miracles, because they are acts not meant to be accomplished by other causes." Thus a miracle, as an act of God, takes place not outside the natural realm but within it, replacing the natural course of things.

Such a definition rightly emphasizes that at certain points, God is present in nature in an unusual way. Yet the conclusion could easily be drawn that God is significantly less present in the usual proceedings of nature. Putting the natural in opposition to the supernatural, as had become more and more customary in medieval scholastic theology, was intended to emphasize the supremacy of God. God is above and beyond nature. By reserving the supernatural as God's unique and separate realm or mode of action, God was inadvertently placed into a rather aloof position. God usually let things run their course unless his special miraculous involvement was called forth. The general acceptance of the distinction between natural and supernatural coincided with the growing significance and independence attributed to the natural sciences. Thus unintentionally, God was relegated more and more to the realm of the supernatural, and eventually, God was completely divorced from the realm of the natural. Nature was gradually perceived as running independently according to its own laws. In the fifteenth century, eminent scholars such as Nicholas of Cusa (1401–64) still attempted to bridge the widening chasm between theology and science by assuming "the coincidence of opposites," in which all finite contradictions would merge into an infinite unity.[113] But his influence was not lasting; natural science dominated more and more, eventually excluding supernatural possibilities.

Until fairly recently in Roman Catholic theology, God's involvement in the world followed the reasoning advanced by Aquinas. God was active in the world through the laws of nature and through human reason, which meant through secondary causes. A miracle was then an exception, so to speak, a divine intervention. It could only be asserted if a certain phenomenon (e.g., the healing of a sick person) could not be sufficiently explained by assuming only natural causes.[114] God's involvement in

---

112. For this and the following quotation, see Aquinas, *Summa Theologiae* (1a.105.7).
113. Cf. Nicholas of Cusa, *The Vision of God* (9), in *Unity and Reform: Selected Writings of Nicholas de Casa*, ed. John P. Dolan (Notre Dame, IN: Notre Dame University Press, 1962), 149.
114. Cf. the extensive study by Louis Monden, *Signs and Wonders: A Study of the Miraculous Element in Religion* (New York: Desclee, 1966). Cf. also the five characteristics of a miraculous healing in Lourdes that were cited in Ruth Cranston, *The Miracle of Lourdes*, updated and expanded ed. by the Medical Bureau of Lourdes (New York: Doubleday Image, 1988), 125–126. The five characteristics are the following: "1: Absence of curative agent (such as drugs or injections, special treatments, etc.), 2. Instantaneousness, 3. Suppression of convalescence, 4. Irregularity of the method of healing, 5. Function restored without action of the organ—still incapable of accomplishing it."

a miracle was thus conceived as an action separate from the workings of other (natural) forces. However, two dangers could arise from this kind of thinking.

(1). God disrupts occasionally the processes in this world at specific, unusual points through miraculous actions. Here the potential conflict was laid between God and the laws of nature. How can God interfere if, as science shows us, the laws of nature rule supreme? Since many people still today consider a miracle as a divine interference, they doubt that such interferences are possible.

(2). The occasions for divine interventions become fewer and fewer as our natural knowledge of the world increases. This latter point is demonstrated by the decreasing number of miracles officially admitted by the Roman Catholic Church. Gradually, God becomes so transcendent that in more and more cases we only confront the natural events by themselves. The more we know about how nature proceeds, the less there is a need to resort to divine or miraculous explanations. God is relegated to a supernatural sphere that has no bearing on our everyday life, and as Bonhoeffer has claimed, God is edged out of the world.

Protestant theology too had its problems with miracles. Some theologians attempted a similar distinction between the natural and the supernatural, as Aquinas, and arrived at comparable results. Most theologians however, in response to the rising dominance of science, attempted to "reconcile" the biblical miracles with the scientific knowledge of their time. For instance, in the seventeenth century, when German Protestantism no longer found the worldview of Jesus tenable, a theory of accommodation was developed. This theory attempted to distinguish between the conceptuality with which Jesus proclaimed his message and the actual intent of his proclamation. The German enlightenment theologian Johann Salomo Semler (1725–91) further refined this theory in the eighteenth century. For example, he claimed that the Jews of Jesus's time believed that all unusual and extraordinary physical evils were caused by evil spirits.[115] Though Jesus did not share this belief, he accommodated himself to the thinking of his contemporaries, and in the eyes of the Jews of his time, he performed miraculous exorcisms. The intention of the "miraculous" expulsions of demons was to free these people from their fears of these evil spirits.

A generation earlier, the English deist Thomas Woolston (1670–1733) claimed that the New Testament miracles could not have occurred in the way they were depicted by the Evangelists. If visualized, these events would lead to numerous contradictions.[116] Yet like Semler, Woolston did not want to suggest that the New Testament miracles were fictitious. According to Woolston, some miracles, such as the story of the empty tomb, were most likely bare of historical content, but

115. Cf. Anonymous, *Versuch einer biblischen Dämonologie oder Untersuchung der Lehre der heil. Schrift vom Teufel und seiner Macht*, with a preface and an appendix by Johann Salomo Semler, new ed. (Halle, Germany: Carl Hermann Hemmerde, 1776; Waltrop, Germany: Hartmut Spenner, 1998), esp. 335–336 and 341–342, in Semler's appendix.

116. Cf. Emanuel Hirsch, *Geschichte der neuern evangelischen Theologie* (Gütersloh, Germany: Gerd Mohn, 1964), 1:316–318.

others certainly did contain a historical kernel. Woolston however left it open as to what this historical kernel was. He suggested that in the form in which they were told by the Evangelists, the New Testament miracles were at best only allegorical or mystical.

In the eighteenth century, many natural explanations of the New Testament miracles were advanced. For instance, Jesus's walking on water acquired a natural explanation. He was merely wading in shallow water. Since his disciples had their view obstructed by a haze, they believed that he was actually walking on water. The feeding of the five thousand was interpreted as the result of Jesus's powerful preaching. His audience was so fascinated by him that they forgot about their hunger. For a short while, eating was secondary. Of course, not everyone was satisfied with such compromising explanations. To the dismay of Semler, Hermann Samuel Reimarus (1694–1768), for example, denounced the New Testament miracles as pious fraud deliberately invented by the authors. "Only thirty to sixty years after the death of Jesus, people appear who write down these miracles as if they happened in the world."[117] Our scientific knowledge of the world had now become the norm for what God could do. What was naturally possible according to the then available scientific knowledge was also regarded as supernaturally conceivable. In the twentieth century, the New Testament scholar Rudolf Bultmann (1884–1976) still followed this line of thinking when he claimed, "It is impossible to use electric light and the wireless and to avail ourselves of modern medical and surgical discoveries, and at the same time to believe in the New Testament world of demons and spirits."[118]

Yet in the same century, scientists pointed out that the order and structure we discover in nature is not something that is there as a given, but it is partly something we introduce into nature. The English astronomer Sir Arthur S. Eddington (1882–1944) expressed most eloquently when he said, "We have found that where science has progressed the farthest, the mind has but regained from nature that which the mind has put into nature. We have found a strange foot-print on the shores of the unknown. We have devised profound theories, one after another, to account for its origin. At last, we have succeeded in reconstructing the creature that made the foot-print. And Lo! it is our own."[119]

We should remember that the so-called laws of nature are not laws according to which events must occur, though we usually expect this, but they are laws patterned according to our experience of the way events generally happen. Furthermore, we must keep in mind that the substructure of reality is undetermined. It allows for the kind of novelty that, for instance, characterizes the evolutionary process.

117. Hermann Samuel Reimarus, *The Goal of Jesus and His Disciples*, trans. and with an introduction by George W. Buchanan (Leiden, Netherlands: E. J. Brill, 1970), 119.
118. So Rudolf Bultmann in his famous essay "New Testament and Mythology," in *Kerygma and Myth*, ed. Hans Werner Bartsch, trans. Reginald H. Fuller (London: SPCK, 1953), 5.
119. Arthur S. Eddington, *Space, Time, and Gravitation: An Outline of the General Relativity Theory* (Cambridge: Cambridge University Press, 1921), 200–201.

It would be wrong however to assume that our present understanding of nature again allows for God's miraculous interference. The idea of God interfering with nature is also foreign to the biblical understanding of God's working. When we look to the biblical witness, we notice that God's miraculous activity is not viewed as something contrary to or superimposed on nature. "There is no talk of a sealed-in world or of iron-clad laws which must be broken through."[120] Since the biblical witness is convinced that God is involved in the totality of the world, miracles are viewed then as a new and surprising mode of God's ongoing activity. In other words, God's special providence is a peculiar but important case of his general providential activity. Paul Tillich stated this succinctly: "Providence is not inter-ference; it is creation. It uses all factors, both those given by freedom and those given by destiny, in creatively directing everything toward its fulfilment. [. . .] It is not an additional factor, a miraculous physical or mental interference in terms of supranaturalism."[121]

Arthur Peacocke explains this in more detail:

> *Particular* events or cluster of events, whether natural, individual and personal, or social and historical, (a) can be specially and significantly revelatory of the presence of God and of the nature of his purposes to human beings; and (b) can be intentionally and specifically brought about by the interaction of God with the world in a top-down causative way that does not abrogate the scientifically observed relationships operating at the levels of the events in question. The combination of (a) and (b) renders the concept of God's special providential action intelligible and believable within the context of the perspective of the sciences.[122]

God's miraculous activity occurs within and through the present structure of nature. This does not imply, however, that a miracle as miracle becomes evident in the natural context. While God is equally and totally present to all times and places in nature and history, human awareness of that presence does not always have the same intensity. There are certain events that are more revealing of God's activity than others. Therefore, a miracle has special revelatory significance. Yet this significance is not demonstrable. What become visible are two significant consequences of a miracle.

(1). We observe that something ran counter to our usual sensory experience.[123] It may just be a striking constellation of causes, conforming to the laws of nature and occurring at the appropriate moment. For instance, such a constellation would be the strong east winds that according to Exodus 14:21 began to blow at exactly the

---

120. Gerrit C. Berkouwer, *Providence of God*, 222.
121. Paul Tillich, *Systematic Theology* (Chicago: University of Chicago Press, 1951), 1:267.
122. Peacocke, *Theology for a Scientific Age*, 182.
123. See also Mark Pontifex, *Freedom and Providence* (New York: Hawthorn, 1960), 114.

right moment and enabled the Israelites to escape through the Red Sea, while their cessation did not allow the pursuing Egyptians to take the same route. However, our observation that something ran counter to our usual sense experience could also be due to a special (causal) act that overrides the normal sequence of cause and effect in human affairs. An example of this kind of event would be the healing of the paralytic (Mark 2:11). Though medical science knows of exceptional instances in which paralyzed persons can regain the function of their limbs, there is no law that says that and when it will indeed be so. At most, one can hope for such an event, but one cannot expect that it occurs. A miracle stands in contrast to other events that occur with regularity.

(2). The other consequence of a miracle is that the miraculous event is perceived as an item of the past. Once the miracle had occurred, we would have seen that the Israelites had arrived at the other side of the sea, and we would have watched how the formerly paralyzed person was walking again. Once these results are visible, we can enlist the help of all available expertise to bring the states prior to and after the miracle into a causal relationship. Being in charge of the natural context in which we live, we will also want to find the natural causes that made the miraculous event possible. The causal nexus that we establish therefore does not say anything about God's workings. Even totally unexpected, the events appear totally natural, as scientific investigation will tell us.

But our Christian faith will inform us that it was not just nature that made this "miraculous" change possible. It was, at the same time, the result of God's mighty hand through his special providential activity. We encounter this twofold explanation already in the bible. When the disciples at Pentecost were filled with the Holy Spirit and began to speak in other languages, some bystanders commented, "They are filled with new wine" (Acts 2:13). Yet is such a twofold view of reality possible? Or does it simply give the same constellation a different name? We remember here the dilemma that scientists initially faced when they wanted to determine the exact nature of elementary particles. They were confronted with the seemingly exclusive duality between wave and corpuscle until the Danish physicist Niels Bohr (1885–1962) introduced the principle of complementarity, suggesting that wave and particle properties are complementary aspects of a single reality. This principle allows for a twofold view of reality, a view that is not based on a temporary deadlock in scientific research but reflects "an essential characteristic of reality."[124] We should apply this insight to the binary components of a miracle—namely, the natural cause and effect sequence—and God's miraculous activity of using these causes in an unusual or unprecedented way. We can then conclude that though the visible presence of the one (e.g., nature) seems to exclude the presence of the

---

124. Pollard, *Chance and Providence*, 141; and cf. Günter Howe, "Zu den Äußerungen von Niels Bohr über religiöse Fragen," *Kerygma und Dogma* 4 (January 1958): 26–27, where Howe points out the implications of Bohr's principle of complementarity for our understanding of reality.

other (e.g., God), both aspects, God and nature, complement each other and point to the whole of reality.

A miracle does not replace faith by demonstrating the presence of God through sign language. Rather, it necessitates faith so that we allow for and affirm the total twofold reality that encounters us. William Pollard has captured this situation very aptly when he said, "What to the faithful is an act of divine mercy showing forth our Lord's restorative power is for the pagan merely a piece of extraordinarily good luck. What to the faithful is a manifestation of divine judgment is to the pagan only a misfortune."[125] But with this evaluative remark, we are already touching upon the significance of miracles for God's process of saving the world from misery and imperfection.

According to the biblical witness, miracles are intrinsically related to the process of salvation from anguish and imperfection. Today, even the most critical analysts of the New Testament sources admit that Jesus did indeed perform acts that his contemporaries regarded as miraculous and that we still consider highly unusual.[126] The Gospel writers show that Jesus accompanied his teaching ministry with a ministry of healing. He healed people, such as the paralytic (Mark 2:11), Peter's mother-in-law (Mark 1:31), and people obsessed with unclean spirits (Mark 1:26).

But Jesus's miraculous activity is not without analogies. There are accounts of miracles performed by contemporaries of Jesus. These accounts show an astounding similarity to Jesus's own miracles. Apollonius of Tyana (ca. 3–97 CE), for instance, an itinerant neo-Pythagorean teacher and contemporary of Jesus, is supposed to have raised people from the dead and healed many who were sick.[127] Though some of the miracles may simply have been attributed to persons in antiquity to emphasize their importance, it would be overreacting to conclude that none of these miracles actually took place that was allegedly performed. Even the similar structure of miracle stories of the Gospels and of miracle stories in other literary sources of antiquity would not disprove their factuality.[128] There are not many variations possible of how a miracle can be effectively told. Since, however, the power to perform miracles was at that point also considered a status symbol, symbolizing a special relationship with the gods, each claim to truth must be carefully analyzed. The possibility cannot be excluded that even some of the miracles attributed to Jesus are without historical basis, merely serving to underscore his exceptional status.

The New Testament writers did not seem to be threatened by the existence of other miracle stories. They were even convinced that the performance of miracles

---

125. Pollard, *Chance and Providence*, 66.
126. Cf. Herbert Braun, *Jesus of Nazareth: The Man and His Time*, trans. Everett R. Kalin (Philadelphia: Fortress, 1979), 29.
127. Cf. Gerd Petzke, *Die Traditionen über Apollonius von Tyana und das Neue Testament* (Leiden, Netherlands: E. J. Brill, 1970), 125–137; cf. also Philostratus, *The Life of Apollonius of Tyana* (4.6), trans. F. C. Conybeare (Cambridge, MA: Harvard University Press, 1969), 1:367.
128. Rudolf Bultmann, *The History of the Synoptic Tradition*, trans. J. Marsh, rev. ed. (New York: Harper & Row, 1968), 210, 231–233, who tries to explain their similar structure through the hypothesis of a common origin.

was not the exclusive prerogative of Jesus. They tell us that Jesus himself warned of false Christs and prophets of the end-times who would perform great signs and wonders (Mark 13:22). The apostles also knew of people who used sorcery to perform miraculous deeds (cf. Acts 8:9). If we want to obtain a complete picture of the significance of the miracles of Jesus, it is insufficient to interpret them exclusively in the light of Near Eastern or Greco-Roman religious thought.

Since Jesus's miracles were part and parcel with his mission, we must understand them primarily from the perspective of the purpose and destiny of his life. If we can agree with the New Testament writers that Jesus announced the kingdom of God and brought it about through his life and destiny (Mark 1:14–15), then Jesus "was creating the future by his wonders; the forces of the world to come were already being manifested in and by him."[129] Miracles are therefore never used by Jesus to demonstrate his power and to legitimate himself (cf. Matt 12:38–39). They are rather signs to illustrate his message. They show that God is not a distant and far off God but a God actively involved in the creative process. God does not simply confirm present tendencies but is willing to give them a new and unprecedented turn. This creative activity of God results in a decisive confrontation with the anti-Godly powers. According to the New Testament writers, Jesus did not perform his miracles aloof and detached from affairs of the day. Authorized by God, he fought and overcame the destructive anti-Godly powers, and each of his victories became visible in a miracle. In a vivid and dramatic way, the Evangelists tell us that these powers recognized Jesus and exclaimed in anguish, "What have you to do with me, Jesus, Son of the Most High God? I adjure you by God, do not torment me" (Mark 5:7).

Since the miracles that Jesus performed were primarily used to illustrate his message, he did not perform miracles indiscriminately or "on stage" in contrast to some modern-day Evangelists. Often, "faith healers" simply use Christian vocabulary to advance their own reputation and to mislead innocent believers. Their actions have very little to do with God pushing back the advances of evil and misery. Frequently, they are self-induced.

We have seen that God fends off the destructive anti-Godly powers through his orders of preservation in natural, moral, and historical processes. Through his miracles, however, he not just maintains order but, in a creative act, initiates a completely new order. The anti-Godly powers are not merely kept in check, but at one specific point, they are overcome; they have to retreat. Therefore, miracles are signs of the commencing kingdom and reign of God.[130] We obtain a glimpse of an

---

129. Anton Friedrichsen, *The Problem of Miracle in Primitive Christianity*, trans. Roy Harrisville and John S. Hanson (Minneapolis: Augsburg, 1972), 73. Cf. also Rudolf Bultmann, *Theology of the New Testament*, trans. Kendrick Grobel (New York: Charles Scribner's, 1955), 1:7, who shows that Jesus sees the fulfilment of the prophetic predictions of salvation "is already beginning in his own miracles."

130. Cf. Joachim Jeremias, *New Testament Theology: The Proclamation of Jesus*, trans. John Bowden (New York: Charles Scribner's, 1971), 95, who rightly claims that the victories over the power of Satan "are a foretaste of the eschaton."

entirely new creation, when sick people are restored to health, the dead are brought back to life, biologically impairing phenomena (such as hunger) are overcome, and physically limiting phenomena (such as space and gravity) are eliminated. The seer in the book of Revelation, envisioning the eschatological perfection, conveys a similar picture when he says, "Death will be no more; mourning and crying and pain will be no more, for the first things have passed away" (Rev 21:4). Those phenomena that people cause to doubt that God is in control of the affairs in this world are either alleviated or held in check. Miracles are bulwarks against evil.

Of course, Jesus's miracles are only temporary points of victory over evil procured by the anti-Godly powers. Those who are healed may become sick again, those who are brought back to life will die again, and those who are fed will once again be hungry. Does this mean that the present structure of reality is so overpowering that even miracles would at best provide a temporary escape and not an indication that the present structure of reality will be taken up into a new structure, the new world to come? Is God unable or unwilling to eliminate evil forever? We could only answer these questions in the affirmative if we were to neglect the resurrection of Jesus Christ as the miracle through which all other miracles of Jesus are endowed with ultimate validity. Jesus's resurrection was not a resuscitation or a return to life after which another and final death followed. As Paul victoriously exclaimed, "Death has been swallowed up in victory" (1 Cor 15:54). In Jesus's resurrection, death was permanently overcome through a new form of life. Here the promised transformation of the whole cosmos had commenced.

The reality shown to us in the resurrection of Jesus Christ was not a restoration of our present cosmos back to its original state. It was an indication and anticipation of a new cosmos.[131] Since this miracle, the inauguration of a new reality, happened with and because of Jesus, we are allowed to accept all the miracles that he himself performed and all miracles that are still performed in his authority as signposts foreshadowing and pointing to a new world to come. Miracles have eschatological significance. They point to the promised eschaton, and they anticipate it proleptically. They indicate that our present world is not endowed with permanence but on its course to a new world. Through his special providence, God reminds us that the orders of preservation are just that, orders that preserve the world for its fulfillment and perfection in the new world to come. In his special providence, God also shows us that these orders are only of penultimate quality. Though they are usually reliable, they are not so restrictive as to exclude genuine newness, even in the sense of the ultimate and universal newness of the new creation. Negativity and imperfection will finally be overcome through God's redemptive power.

We must refrain, however, from the utopian assumption that there is a developmental continuity between our present structure of reality and salvation in and

---

131. Cf. William Manson, "Eschatology in the New Testament," in *Eschatology: Four Papers Read to the Society for the Study of Theology*, ed. William Manson et al. (Edinburgh: Oliver and Boyd, 1952), 6.

through Christ. As the Jesuit priest and paleontologist Pierre Teilhard de Chardin has shown, evolutionary pressure provides, at best, the elements for the christo-genesis, but by itself, this pressure will not bring about the christogenesis, the new world indicated by Jesus Christ. To achieve salvation, neither evolution nor revolution will suffice. Salvation can only be brought about by something unprecedented and new, by the creative activity of God as foreshadowed in the Christ event.

It should be noted, at least parenthetically, that a miracle taken by itself does not necessarily have convincing power. It does not necessitate the conclusion that we are confronted here with God's salvific activity. For instance, many of those who saw that the sick were restored to health were amazed and glorified God (Mark 2:12). Even Jesus's "friends" and the scribes consented that Jesus had performed unusual deeds. But they concluded that he was either "beside himself" or connected with "Beelzebul, and by the ruler of the demons he casts out demons" (Mark 3:21–22). A miraculous act by itself is silent. It does not disclose whether (1) it is endowed by God with eschatological significance; (2) it is a sign that we are confronted with an especially gifted person, such as a true miracle worker; or (3) it is a seductive act of anti-Godly powers. For Jesus, however, sign and proclamation go together. As we can see with his "friends" and the scribes, those who rejected his message did not change their minds once they were confronted with his miracles. They had heard the miraculous message of the commencement of the salvational process and rejected it together with its signs. Here the conclusion of the parable of the rich man and Lazarus conveys a most telling insight: "If they do not listen to Moses and the prophets, neither will they be convinced even if someone rises from the dead" (Luke 16:31).

Both general providence and special providence do not demonstrate that God is in control, the one who keeps evil in check or even eliminates it at some points. In both instances, the good that results can be traced back to nature and its laws. The awareness that God is active in these constellations has to come from God's own self. We notice this most telling with the resurrection narratives. When the women saw the empty tomb, they did not conclude that Jesus had been resurrected. They were only perplexed, since they had expected to find Jesus's corpse but only found an empty tomb. It was through the angels at the tomb, through God's messengers, that they were informed that Jesus "has risen" (Luke 24:5). Then they believed and told others about it. Yet there is still another facet of divine providence in which humans play an important role—namely, prayer.

Prayer

In our considerations of God's care for humanity, we do not want to leave the impression that God's preserving and promising activity relegates humans to inactivity. If such were the case, it would violate our position as God's governors in the world. Once we turn to the impact of prayer on God's providential care, we will soon notice that we are encouraged to be actively involved in this providential work. We could even say that the experience of God who hears and answers our prayers is at the heart of the question of providence.[132] If God did not interact with us in a dialogical way, we would be confronted with an impersonal "it," as in the Stoic worldview, with the laws of nature or with a merciless fate. Prayer would be nothing but an attempt to calm our nerves. It would just be an attempt to obtain self-control, analogous to Far Eastern meditation exercises. Yet prayer is based on God's invitation to dialogue with God and to bring in our fervent desires and wishes concerning the future of personal lives and of the world in general.

The hymn "Lord, Teach Us How to Pray Aright" provides us with a very good introduction in the act of prayer:

Lord, teach us how to pray aright, with rev'rence and with fear.
Though dust and ashes in your sight, we may, we must draw near.
We perish if we cease from prayer; oh, grant us pow'r to pray.
And when to meet you we prepare; Lord, meet us on our way.
Give deep humility; the sense of godly sorrow give;
A strong desire, with confidence, to hear your voice and live;
Faith in the only sacrifice that can for sin atone;
To cast our hopes, to fix our eyes on Christ, on Christ alone.
Give these, and then your will be done; thus strengthened with all might,
We, through your Spirit and your Son, shall pray, and pray aright.[133]

The New Testament is full of exhortations to pray that leave no doubt that an actual I-Thou relationship between God and humanity is envisioned (cf. Matt 7:7; 21:22; John 15:7). Since God is God and not a human person, we should remember that such a relationship is not one between equals. It is not without significance that in the Lord's Prayer (the prayer Jesus taught his disciples), the assertion of the holiness of God's name comes first (Matt 6:9).[134] For once, even in addressing God as our Father, we dare not address God in a carefree, casual attitude. Neither should we pray in a boastful manner, convinced that God has no choice but to agree with the contents of our prayers (Matt 6:5–7). Instead, a prayer should be precise and made in humility.

This emphasis on God's holiness informs not only how we pray but also what we pray for. For instance, according to the Gospel of John, Christ promises, "The Father will give you whatever you ask him in my name" (John 15:16). This promise does not imply that God will grant us anything for which we ask him. Bonhoeffer

---

132. Cf. Georgia Harkness, *The Providence of God* (New York: Abingdon, 1960), 121, who also reminds us that this is the place at which many people's faith in providence is shipwrecked.
133. ELW, hymn 745.
134. Cf. Joachim Jeremias, *The Lord's Prayer*, trans. John Reumann (Philadelphia: Fortress, 1969), 21–22.

captured the meaning of prayer well when he said, "God does not give us everything we want, but he does fulfill all his promises."[135] Prayer is not a frivolous attempt to discover how far-reaching God's power is. For example, one should not ask God to reverse the sequence of winter and spring in order to see if God can change the order of the seasons. Such a request will remain unfulfilled. Rather, the intent is to rely, for Christ's sake, on the promise expressed in the Psalms: "Call on me in the day of trouble; I will deliver you, and you shall glorify me" (Ps 50:15). Since Christ has overcome the destructive anti-Godly powers, we, as his followers, are encouraged to walk beside him and call upon God to deliver us and others from the impact of these powers and the evil they bring with them.

Martin Luther was right when he said that "God's order or command and the prayers of Christians [. . .] are the two pillars that support the entire world" and without which the world would disintegrate.[136] God promises to consider the content of our prayers in his preserving, sustaining, and creative activity. Through our prayers, we express our solidarity with God, cooperating with him and dialoguing with him concerning the future of the world. Prayer therefore can have many purposes. Its content will express these purposes. First of all, we must mention adoration and praise of God. Again, Luther reminds us that we should not only call upon God in our plight. We should also thank him for his help and rescue, remember his acts of kindness, and praise him for them because "He is the Creator, the Benefactor, the Promiser, and the Savior."[137] Luther can rightly say that it is sinful if we cease to pray to God. A life without prayer is no longer in tune with God as the creative source of all life; it mistakenly presumes that our world is self-sufficient. Prayer serves here as a reminder for us to recall the one from whom we have everything that is. Therefore, we should ask God even for things that we seemingly take for granted, such as good weather or a good harvest.[138] With this last sentence, we have already touched upon the large category of petitions that seem to form the content of most prayers.

Luther also encourages us to bring before God all our anxieties, such as personal afflictions like poverty and sickness or even sinfulness. He asserts that we should not exclude any petitions whether they contain "temporal or spiritual things."[139] The American Methodist theologian Georgia Harkness (1891–1974) rightly prioritizes this all-inclusive scope of petitions when she says that "to seek God's forgiveness for past and present sin, and thus to find hope for the future, is an essential part of Christian prayer."[140] If we do not include in our prayers the plea for forgiveness of sin, our dialogue with God will always be disturbed, since we continue to distance

135. Bonhoeffer, *Letters and Papers*, 206, in a letter of August 14, 1944.
136. Martin Luther, *Sermons on the Gospel of St. John* (1537–1538), in LW, 24:81, in his explanation of John 14:12.
137. Martin Luther, *Lectures on Genesis* (1534–1545), in LW, 3:117, in his explanation of Gen 17:7.
138. Cf. Martin Luther, *Predigten des Jahres 1534*, in WA, 37:425.2–8, in a sermon on Ps 65.
139. Martin Luther, *Instructions for the Visitors of Parish Pastors in Electoral Saxony*, in LW, 40:279.
140. Harkness, *Providence*, 128.

ourselves from God. Both in our prayers and in our expectations, we would act out of our own sinful and selfish interests and not out of conformity with God. Petitions are therefore concerned first with inner strength and renewal. Of course, petitions will include more than asking for forgiveness. They will also be prayers for inner peace in times of conflict, for clarity of outlook, for new strength at moments of fatigue, and for power to cope with the daily demands of life. The following stanza from the Gospel hymn "What a Friend We Have in Jesus" expresses this kind of prayerful attitude very appropriately:

Have we trials and temptations?
Is there trouble anywhere?
We should never be discouraged—
take it to the Lord in prayer.
Can we find a friend so faithful
who will all our sorrows share?
Jesus knows our ev'ry weakness—
take it to the Lord in prayer.[141]

From the acknowledgment of God's benevolent activity in Jesus Christ, new strength and peace of mind are gained. God as the ruler of the universe does care about us little unimportant beings. He cares so much that he has come to us in the human form of Jesus Christ. This God who cares is also the one who gives strength to the weary and lifts up those who are in low esteem (Luke 1:52).

In our consideration of petitionary prayer, we dare not forget the frequent petitions for physical health and healing. Since prayers are not intended to be a substitute for work, petitions for recovery from physical illness should never replace appropriate medical care. However, the two are not mutually exclusive. The same insight must guide our attitude toward so-called faith healing. Though each case of a miraculous healing must be subjected to careful scrutiny, we know that unusual and unforeseen recoveries from grave illness do occur. There is also no doubt that some people have the gift of healing.[142] We have seen, however, that this power need not stem from God. It could also be obtained from anti-Godly seductive powers.

Again, we are confronted with the fact that a miraculous event is silent; it does not disclose its originator. However, in prayer, we have a means with which we can "discern the spirits."[143] If we are existentially involved in an event of so-called faith healing or in any other miraculous event, we are able to discern the source of this healing power. The existential involvement will usually assume one of three

141. ELW, hymn 742.
142. Cf. also the following entries: "Healing, Psychic," "Healing by Faith," and "Healing by Touch," in *Encyclopedia of Occultism & Parapsychology*, ed. Leslie Shepard, 2nd ed. (Detroit, MI: Gale Research, 1984), 2:596–602.
143. This has been pointed out very convincingly by Karl Heim, *The Transformation of the Scientific World View*, trans. W. A. Whitehouse (London: SCM, 1953), 192–193.

forms: (1) we may be the one who has the gift to heal, (2) we may be the one who has been healed, or (3) we may be an immediately involved bystander (relative). If our relationship with God in prayer is strengthened, we may safely assume that the healing power was a gift from God. It will then not become commercialized and used for self-promotion and self-exaltation contrary to what we see in some healing services. Following the example of Jesus, it will rather be used to illustrate the Christian Gospel and humbly and gratefully further the human good. If however the relationship with God in prayer is weakened, we can hardly attribute this power to God. Its source must be anti-Godly powers that help perform seemingly divine miracles to seduce people, often even accompanied externally with Christian symbols. If the relationship in prayer however remains unaffected, we may simply regard this healing power as an unusual, "natural" gift of God, similar to the superior healing gifts of some medical doctors.

Since the latter part of the twentieth century, we have increasingly realized that a human being is a psychosomatic unity. We notice that psychic disturbances, such as depressions and neuroses, can bring about physical ailments, problems with the digestive system, malfunctioning of the glands, and heart and kidney diseases.[144] Psychic disturbances are frequently intertwined with spiritual crises. Regaining psychic and spiritual strength and balance is often accompanied by a physical healing process. The strengthening, alleviating, and comforting impact of prayer cannot be underestimated. Prayer can indeed be effectively "used" to calm our nerves. Such use however does not result in a dialogue with God but moves on the meditative level of our own psyche. We should refrain from calling it prayer but term it more appropriately as *meditation*. Though it dare not become a substitute for prayer, it serves a rather useful function in our turbulent times. It can help us attain a state of tranquility and peace of mind. Of course, we should not expect that the dialogue with God, which is found in true prayer, is followed by an automatic physical improvement. Restoration of psychic and spiritual health is usually a very slow process, and occasionally, it will not be attained at all. If we take seriously the dialogical character of prayer, we must also be ready for God's noncompliance with our petitions.

When we come to petitions concerning natural events, we must bear in mind that this is primarily the realm where we will affirm the natural protective divine orders. Yet it is part of our task as God's administrators to remind God of those who are especially exposed to the dangers of the forces of nature, such as miners, travelers, pilots, and sailors. Again, prayers are intended not to replace protective measures but to accompany and perhaps enhance them. Similarly, it is our prerogative and duty to pray in adverse conditions, such as during storms, floods, and other disasters, that their impact will be softened or averted. Since a prayer is

144. Cf. Harkness, *Providence*, 135–137; see also Paul Tournier, *The Healing of Persons*, trans. E. Hudson (New York: Harper, 1965).

never uttered in selfish interest, we will pray for the well-being of ourselves as well as of others. This means the same adoration, praise, and petitions that we extend on our behalf, we extend also on behalf of others.

In all our prayers, we always conclude with the expressed or tacit admission that God's will—not ours—be done. When Jesus prayed in Gethsemane—the most fervent prayer ever uttered—he included the explicit admission, "Yet not what I want but what you want" (Matt 26:39). This provided a model for us to follow. A Christian prayer is not a demand for God's surrender but rather the prerogative and duty of a dialogue with the one who has "formed the earth and the world" and who has been "our dwelling place in all generations" (Ps 90:1–2).

When we reflect once more on divine providence, it should be clear that God cannot be understood as the primary cause that works in and through all second-ary causes in nature and history.[145] If it were so, humans would only execute God's will without having any responsibility of their own. Also, the idea has its limits that we use two different perspectives or languages, the language of the natural sciences and the language of faith. Of course, we can always explain scientifically events in nature and history without referring to God's existence and activity or present a theological interpretation of these events that explicitly refers to God's existence and working. Yet many events that are scientifically described, such as the spin of electrons, do not even call for a theological interpretation so that both ways of perceiving reality are not exactly parallel to each other. Perhaps one could side with process theology and say that God acts in all events through influence or persuasion. But again, there are many events that have nothing to do with God's activity even though they do not occur without God's knowledge. For instance, when one person murders another, then this cruel event cannot be traced back to God's influence or persuasion. Here destructive and anti-Godly powers are at work.

To do justice to God's providence, we must first recognize that through all the accidents, through all the different contingent events, ultimately something develops that in retrospect can be seen as the result of divine providence.[146] There emerges a certain order that allows life to originate and to develop. Therefore, we cannot agree with Jacques Monod when he writes that "a *totally* blind process can by definition lead to anything; it can even lead to vision itself."[147] Monod how-ever concedes that once chance has worked its effect, it is bound to that which it brought forth. Therefore, one cannot deny the possibility "that there is a divinely

---

145. Cf. Owen C. Thomas, ed., *God's Activity in the World: The Contemporary Problem* (Chico, CA: Scholars, 1983), 231–233, who at the end of this collection of papers lists five different ways of God's activity in the world.

146. Cf. to this D. J. Bartholomew, *God of Chance* (London: SCM, 1984), 143.

147. Jacques Monod, *Chance and Necessity: An Essay on the Natural Philosophy of Modern Biology*, trans. Austryn Wainhouse (New York: Alfred A. Knopf, 1971), 98.

ordained general direction, in which the process of the world is moving."[148] Though there existed no necessity that the world developed in such a way as it shows itself now, it is evident that it has developed in such a way and therefore made life possible. The question is unimportant whether God was more "in a narrow curve" or on the "long stretches" of the evolutionary process. We should affirm with the priestly creation narrative that it was not chance and evolution that brought us about but God's will. Without God, there would not have been possible an initial contingent event nor any other singular development. God is the one who is behind everything and who made possible the whole process. In a comprehensive way, God is the creator and sustainer of everything that is. God is synonymous with life and its preservation.

But how shall we regard the hindrance or destruction of that which is, be it through natural catastrophes, death, or human interference? While God counteracts these destructive tendencies in his special providence, we cannot talk about providence in a selective or manipulative way. We always must consider the whole picture. For instance, if in a railroad accident I was "miraculously" spared but others were not, then it borders on blasphemy to talk about providence. Saying that I was providentially spared would remove from God's providence those who died. Both nature and history are always "a mixed bag." There is always good and bad. The bird enjoys the worm, but the worm does not enjoy to be devoured. The confession that God wants our best does not mean that in every moment the optimally best is occurring. We dare not dissect history atomistically in its individual components and interpret them without regard to the overall picture even if we are often tempted to do this. History only makes sense in its unity because we know and confess its eventual direction, the new creation and the kingdom of God. Up to that final point, however, it is always endangered by events of nature, human malice, and plain human incompetence and negligence. The whole can only be interpreted appropriately from its end, this means eschatologically.

But where is God in the individual events? After God has appointed us humans to his cocreators and representatives, God will not treat us like puppets. We are free to shape the course of history largely in an autonomous way. Yet God has not retired from history. In his general providence, God grants stability and preservation. In this preserving activity, God can also interact in a special way, as the human experience of God's special providence shows. The secondary causes are not simply suspended so that God would interfere in the world machinery as an external force. In most cases, it is sufficient that the appropriate constellations occur at the right time and place. "The Christian understanding of providence steers a course between a facile optimism and a fatalistic pessimism."[149] As Christians, we can trust that God will ultimately have everything in his hands, though we know that God

---

148. John Polkinghorne, *Science and Providence: God's Interaction with the World* (Boston: Shambhala, 1989), 40.
149. Polkinghorne, *Science and Providence*, 44.

will not frivolously change the process of nature and history. The comprehensive change of nature and history is only envisioned at the completion of creation.

Nevertheless, the haunting thought remains that after nearly two millennia since Jesus was resurrected, we have received "the Spirit as a guarantee" that the completion is coming (2 Cor 5:5). But it still has not come. Similarly, we celebrate in the Eucharist the heavenly feast but are still earthbound. Similarly, we pray "your kingdom come," but it is still not here. What shall we make of this? Was Feuerbach perhaps right when he claimed that heaven is a projection of our desires but not an actual reality?

9 Under God's Guidance

A recent survey in Germany showed that 47 percent of all citizens in that country believed that after this life on earth, nothing will follow.[1] While 17 percent of the young adults between the age of eighteen and twenty-four believe that there is eternal life after death, as people get older, they consider life after death as more and more improbable. Only 6 percent of those persons who are sixty-five and beyond believe in life eternal. We should interpret this as meaning that as people get closer to the end of life, they think twice about whether there is nothing beyond, and in one way or other, they cling to a straw of hope. That at least does not seem to be the case in Germany. Older persons have less confidence that there is indeed something beyond this life that would make everything come out all right. There is no confidence in an eschatological perfection and an assurance that there is someone beyond who is really in control. As people get older, they become more sober and lose faith in a God almighty who will in the end provide what the seer in the book of Revelation announced: "God himself will be with them; he will wipe every tear from their eyes. Death will be no more; mourning and crying and pain will be no more, for the first things have passed away" (Rev 21:3–4). But is it realistic to believe that there is no future perfection? Is there in the end really no redemption from death and misery, and will history simply peter out, or will there be an endless repetition of the same? To answer these all-important questions that get to the essence of the God question, we must ask ourselves in what kind of God we believe.

God the Creator, Sustainer, and Redeemer

We have mentioned previously that usually God is understood to be almighty, all-knowing, all-present, and eternal. Yet these so-called attributes of God are philosophical attributes, accorded to God on account of our thinking who God should be. They are hardly found in the biblical writings that document God's history with his chosen people—the Israelites—and later, the life and mission of Jesus, God's human face. The God whom we encounter there is first of all the creator of everything that is: God created heaven and earth. This means that there is nothing prior to God. He is from eternity to eternity, and through a creative act, God made everything that is. This means that the whole world is dependent on God for its existence. Since God gave the command "to bring forth," this would imply that

---

1. Cf. to the following magazine article: "Mit dem Alter schwindet der Glaube ans ewige Leben" (idea-Umfrage), *Idea Spektrum*, November 14, 2018, 9.

there is a certain independence of the created to allow for development. Although God provided the basic material, we do not hear that God was involved in every evolutionary detail as creation unfolded. God is more the overseer of the created order than the one who would plan and execute every minute detail.

Yet God is also the sustainer of everything that is. We see this most prominently with the biblical concept of covenant. The two sections of the Bible, the Old Testament (the old covenant) and the New Testament (the new covenant), indicate that covenant is the major metaphor that is used to describe the relation between God and Israel or God and the people of God. God as the major power initiates a covenant with Israel as the lesser power. The biblical tradition informs us that the text of the covenant between God and Israel established at Mount Sinai was the Decalogue. The Ten Commandments indicate the future action that is expected from Israel as a consequence of the preceding prologue: "I am the Lord your God, who brought you out of the land of Egypt" (Exod 20:2).[2] Then we have the Davidic covenant, which refers to God's promise to David—the king—to preserve his dynasty forever (Ps 89:4; 2 Sam 23:5). The covenant at Mount Sinai, which is made with the whole people of Israel, gives Israel its distinct identity and is dependent on their obedience for its durability. The Davidic covenant is rooted in God's faithful promise to David and is unconditional. The so-called covenant with Abraham involves God granting Abraham's descendants land and making him "the ancestor of a multitude of nations" (Gen 17:4; cf. 15:18–21). With these covenants, God demonstrates that he is the Lord of history. When we look at the covenant God made with Noah, we also see God as the Lord of creation granting the steadfastness of nature and its seasons (Gen 9:8–17).

Then we hear from Jeremiah: "The days are surely coming, says the Lord, when I will make a new covenant with the house of Israel and the house of Judah. It will not be like the covenant that I made with their ancestors when I took them by the hand to bring them out of the land of Egypt—a covenant that they broke" (Jer 31:31–32). Again, the assurance is given that God will be their God, and they will be God's people. The end of the old covenant brings with it the Babylonian captivity and the dispersion of the Israelite people. There is no historical prologue anymore, as it was with the covenant on Mount Sinai but only the prediction of future acts of God. They consist not of the promise of land or of offspring but rather of the restoration of the broken relationship with God. While at Mount Sinai and later on with the prophets such as Jeremiah, the covenant community was perceived as a unity of diverse tribes or peoples based on shared values; in early rabbinic Judaism, as we can see with the Pharisees, the emphasis was then on ethnic exclusivity.[3] The issue of ethnic exclusivity was still highly debated in early Christianity. For instance, we read that certain individuals taught that "unless you are circumcised

2. Cf. to this and the following George E. Mendenhall and Gary A. Herion, s.v. "Covenant," in ABD, esp. 1:1184.
3. So Mendenhall and Herion, 1:1196.

according to the custom of Moses, you cannot be saved" (Acts 15:1). Yet as Luke tells us, the decision at the Council of Jerusalem was different. The apostle James announced, "We should not trouble those Gentiles who are turning to God" (Acts 15:19). Gentiles can become Christians without being circumcised, which means without first becoming Jews. The ethnic exclusivity was no longer valid for the Christian community; it was to become cosmopolitan.

This significant change becomes clear when we read the New Testament text recounting the Last Supper. In all the New Testament traditions concerning the Eucharist, with the exception of John, we are told that Jesus gave a cup of wine to his disciples, identifying it as the "covenant" or the "new covenant." "Here the NT tradition seems to be making some deliberate and conscious connection with older covenant traditions (especially Jer 31:31–34)."[4] According to Paul, the new covenant is founded in the blood of Jesus, and therefore, the wine in the cup depicts the new covenant (1 Cor 11:25). Since Jesus was familiar with the prophet Jeremiah, connecting Jeremiah 31 with Jesus's announcement of the new covenant sounds convincing. In a similar way, the covenant at Mount Sinai following the Exodus from Egypt was also constituted through the blood of the firstborn.[5] The "new covenant" is correlated with the term *kingdom of God*. While the former shows God as the absolute Lord of the time of salvation, the latter is an expression of the divine sovereignty that indicates the goal of completion. The New Testament continues in form and content the covenant concept of the Old Testament, but now the Old Testament stage of promise is supplanted by the New Testament stage of fulfillment. "Covenant is the thoroughgoing decree of God, the mighty announcement of the sovereign will of God in history, through which God shapes the relationship between himself and humans according to his intention of salvation, the authoritative divine decree which brings about a corresponding order of things."[6] In contrast to rabbinic Judaism, early Christianity understood that the old ethnic bases of social solidarity and cohesion had to be replaced with a larger vision of the human community. This tenor was initially set by Jesus himself, who sought relationships with people who were outside the proper ethnic boundaries. Yet it was through his self-sacrifice that he visibly instituted a new covenant as foreseen by Jeremiah. His action was then verified by his resurrection.

The resurrection of Jesus as the Christ is the central core of the Christian faith and therewith of the whole New Testament. Even the claim of a new covenant would make little sense without the resurrection of Jesus Christ. Then the Last Supper would indeed be a farewell dinner, and Jesus's blood would have been shed in vain. The apostle Paul therefore emphatically claims, "If Christ has not been raised, your faith is futile and you are still in your sins. Then those also who have died in Christ

---

4. Mendenhall and Herion, 1:1197.
5. Cf. Johannes Behm, "*Diatheke*," in TDNT, 2:136.
6. So very persuasively Behm, 2:137.

have perished. If for this life only we have hoped in Christ, we are of all people most to be pitied" (1 Cor 15:17–19). The resurrection of Jesus as the Christ connects the present to the past as well as to the future. First of all, the claim of Jesus is vindicated that he stood in the place of God. Jesus is now called the Christ and the Lord. Even the veneration that is reserved only for God is now extended to Jesus against all Jewish sensibilities. Whatever Jesus claimed in the name of God, such as the inbreaking of the kingdom, is now substantiated through his resurrection to new and imperishable life. Jesus was not an imposter but the human face of God through whom God showed what he had intended for all of humanity.

Anticipation of a New Creation

The significance of Christ's resurrection becomes especially evident when we consider it in the context of God's creative activity. The Bible suggests in many places that God's salvific activity must be seen in analogy to God's creative activity in the beginning. For instance, Deutero-Isaiah, the book that proclaims that salvation is offered through the sacrifice of the servant of Yahweh, intimately connects the creation in the beginning with salvation as the goal of history (cf. Isa 42:5; 44:6; 45:8).[7] And in the opening sentences of the Gospel of John, the author interprets the coming of Christ from the perspective of the creation in the beginning. Paul too points out a clear correspondence between the appearance of the first Adam and the appearance of Christ as the last Adam (Rom 5).

It is wrong to interpret this perspective of creation as if the resurrection were to open the opportunity for us to return to an ideal state of the past. Such an interpretation would force us into the cyclical view of history represented by most religions and mythologies: after the cataclysmic end dawns a new beginning, the wheel of world history moves on to a new revolution. A very different course of history is indicated by Paul when he writes, "For in him all things in heaven and on earth were created, things visible and invisible, whether thrones or dominions or rulers or powers—all things have been created through him and for him" (Col 1:16). This means that everything is created toward Christ. When Paul calls him the firstborn of all creation (Col 1:15), he wants to emphasize that Christ, being equal to God, does not stand only at the beginning of creation. Since Christ has been resurrected, he is also the goal toward which creation moves.[8] Clearly, such an understanding cannot condone a static view of creation that often sounds like the following: God created the world; through the fall, this good and perfect creation was distorted; then came Christ and enabled its restoration; and in the final Parousia, the creation will be returned to its original beauty. Against this cyclical view, we must assert that the "very good," which God pronounced over his creation

---

7. Cf. also Werner Foerster, "Ktizo," in TDNT, 3:1012–1013.
8. This has been pointed out especially clearly by Walter Künneth, *The Theology of the Resurrection*, trans. James W. Leitch (London: SCM, 1965), 164–166.

in the beginning, does not mean that it is complete and unsurpassable. There lies the fallacy of Leibniz to understand our world as the best possible one.[9]

Our present world, of course, is good, but as a fallen creation, it is marred by sin and its consequences. To deny this is to belittle the facts of evil and death. Moreover, creation is a beginning point and not the endpoint. To understand Christ as the goal toward which creation moves also requires a radical reorientation concerning the fall of humanity and our sinful state. The fall of humanity can no longer be viewed as a jump from a God-provided basis to some kind of lower level—namely, a state of constant sinfulness. The fall is the initial denial of the Christ line. Union with God is the intention for the whole of creation from its very beginning. Each sinful act is a reaffirmation of the initial denial and thus a rejection of God's plan for us and of his redemptive act in Christ (cf. Heb 2:1–4).

God is continually with his creation, even in its alienated or fallen state. Nothing is farther away from the biblical understanding than a deistic God who dispassionately observes the predestined course of the universe. Even after the fall, God does not angrily withdraw from the first humans, but in an act of compassion, he provides them with necessary clothing (Gen 3:21). And the church's attempt to detect in the words of the curse a primal Gospel (Gen 3:15) or the endeavor of a Gospel writer to trace the ancestry of Jesus back to Abraham (Matt 1:1) and finally to God himself (Mark 1:1) witness to the fact that God's acts in the beginning and in Jesus Christ are seen as a unity. Paul attests to this too in pointing to Christ as the antitype of Adam. Through Christ in antithetical manner, law is superseded by grace, sin by justification, and death by life.[10]

Death is not superseded by life to restore the original state. For the resurrected Christ, death is no longer a possibility. In a similar way, grace is not the opposite of law and justification or the reverse of sinfulness. Jesus Christ's resurrection does not indicate the fulfillment of a restorative process that had started with the Old Testament covenant community. His resurrection is rather the first point of a *new* creation, a creation in perfection. Could it be just an accident that Paul in his letter to the Romans progresses from declaring Christ as the new Adam (Rom 5) to our participation in the new creation through baptism (Rom 6), to the tension within us as being citizens of a new world yet still living in the old one (Rom 7), to the implications for the whole creation of God's creative act in Christ's resurrection (Rom 8)? God's creative act in Christ's resurrection goes beyond this present creation. It witnesses to the new creation that replaces this present creation at

---

9. Cf. Gottfried Wilhelm Leibniz, "Vindication of God's Justice Reconciled with His Other Perfections and All Actions" (41 and 144), in *The Monadology and Other Philosophical Writings*, trans. and with an introduction and notes by Paul Schrecker and Anne Martin (Indianapolis: Bobbs-Merrill, 1965), 122, 145, where he states "that among the infinite numbers of possible series God has selected the best, and consequently this best universe is that which actually exists." But then he continues to say, "But the most magnificent part of the world, the City of God, is a sight to which we shall at last be admitted some day." This means our present world is the best this side of heaven.

10. Cf. Otto Michel, *Der Brief an die Römer* (Göttingen, Germany: Vandenhoeck & Ruprecht, 1957), 121, in his explanation of Rom 5:12–21.

one specific point.[11] This inauguration of the new creation at one specific point, in and with the one who stood in God's place as his representative, inspired Paul and all Christians who came after him to hope for the inauguration of a new creation on a universal scale.

The resurrection of Jesus Christ cannot be isolated from the rest of world history and be treated as one event among others. It is the presupposition of the Christian existence as a community of people who participate proleptically in the newness of life, and it is the foundation of Christian hope in the final realization of this new life. Nevertheless, the full implication of Christ's resurrection is only disclosed to us when we consider it in the context of apocalyptic hopes. Only in relation to the apocalyptic view of history, with its conviction of a resurrection at the end of time, can the resurrection of Jesus Christ be understood as the anticipation of this end.[12] Even the very fact that the disciples could recognize their once familiar leader in their post-Easter experiences—in something entirely different from the possibilities of this life—and that they called the reality behind these experiences resurrection can only satisfactorily be explained in the context of apocalyptic hopes. Otherwise, it would have been interpreted as an encounter with a spirit or a phantom (cf. Luke 24:37).

In the context of apocalyptic hopes and expectations, the disciples realized that God had confirmed the authority that Jesus had claimed already in his earthly life. They also realized that in the destiny of Jesus as the Lord, the end had already occurred in proleptic anticipation, and God had already disclosed himself fully in Jesus as the Lord. In other words, through the resurrection of Jesus Christ, the apocalyptic *idea* of a common resurrection was transformed into the Christian *hope* in the resurrection. Thus the New Testament proclaims Jesus not only as "the first to rise from the dead" (Acts 26:23), "the beginning, the firstborn from the dead" (Col 1:18) but also as the one in whom we shall be united "in a resurrection like his" that we too "might walk in newness of life" (Rom 6:4–5). And we trust in God who "raised the Lord and will also raise us by his power" (1 Cor 6:14). Apocalyptic ideas provide the background material for a full understanding of the implications of Christ's resurrection; still, our hope in a resurrection is not based on these ideas but depends solely on Christ's resurrection.

Christ's resurrection connects the past of Jesus's own life with the future of the life of all creation. It indicates not only the claim of Jesus who he was but also the hope that he inaugurated with his announcement of the kingdom of God the

---

11. This is where the question of the empty tomb becomes important, not as a proof for the historicity of the resurrection of Jesus Christ, but as an indication that this present creation has no permanence, that it will be replaced by and transformed into something new. Not even the first Christian community used the story of the empty tomb as proof of Christ's resurrection (cf. Matt 27:62–28:15, esp. 28:15).
12. Cf. to the following Wolfhart Pannenberg, *Revelation as History*, trans. David Granskou (London: Macmillan, 1968), 146; and his *Jesus—God and Man*, trans. Lewis L. Wilkins and Duane A. Priebe, 2nd ed. (Philadelphia: Westminster, 1988), 81–82.

establishment of a new covenant. This also shows that God has not withdrawn from his creation but stays with it against all attempts to destroy it through death and sinful behavior. We could still ask, as have done many others, why God has gone this route and why God has not speeded up the elimination of evil, be it in nature or among human individuals.

Discerning the Mind of God

Immanuel Kant rightly cautioned that theodicy would require that we penetrate to the intelligible world in which our sensible world is grounded. Or in other words, we must be able to read the mind of God. Yet such an attempt is both frivolous and futile. Therefore, attempts in theodicy often border on speculation. We construct a God according to our imagination and deduce from such projection why God condones the world the way it is. Small wonder that so far not one theodicy has won universal approval. At most, such attempts provide the basis for further discussions. So what should we do? Should we simply give up and remain silent? No! The biblical account can at least provide us with some indication about God's doing.

The first tenet that we learn from the Bible is that God is creator, sustainer, and redeemer. This means that from beginning to end, God is in control. Initially, the Israelites even thought that God metes out both good and evil. Only gradually did they learn that evil must come from another source that stands in direct opposition to God yet without the ability to dethrone God. But no answer is given by God as to why he would condone such an anti-Godly power and why God would not simply do away with it. Occasionally, the idea advanced, as for instance with Martin Luther, that this anti-Godly power is God's devil, who God uses to punish us for our sins. Yet as the book of Job already discerned, bad things even happen to good people. Therefore, this idea of punishment answers the question of why there is evil only in some cases. The extension of evil both with regard to time and space and also with regard to whom it affects is not completely answered in the biblical accounts. At the most, we could side with Job, who admitted that it was foolish for him to question God's doings even if he had to suffer under them. Yet already in the Old Testament there are indications that the present situation will not continue forever.

In the New Testament, we then read that Jesus established a new covenant meaning that God extends his benevolent rule over all humanity. Through the resurrection of Jesus as the Christ, the apostles and many others experienced that a new creation has dawned though proleptically and only confined to Jesus. Since Jesus however was not just a human being but God incarnate, this resurrection has universal significance as the down payment for the yet coming new creation. With this new creation, all evil and imperfection including its sources in the anti-Godly powers will be eliminated. Of course, this is still an eschatological hope yet well founded in Christ's resurrection. Therefore, we know that there will be an end to everything that impairs and threatens life. But the Bible does not tell us when the eschatological fulfillment will occur. Whenever people looked for signs and were sure that they had been able to read God's mind, they were deluded. And those who thought of themselves are high enough to bring about the end-time perfection as self-styled messiahs only increased human misery and evil.

We should rest assured that God is indeed in control even if from our vantage point we sometimes wonder whether this is true, since we only see in a mirror dimly, as Paul reminded us, and because God's ways are not our ways. Furthermore, we have the assurance that there is a fulfillment of creation and of our personal lives. Yet we know as little about the date when the fulfillment will commence as we know about the date when our own lives on this earth will cease. As Jesus reminded his disciples, "But about that day or hour no one knows, neither the angels in heaven, nor the Son, but only the Father" (Mark 13:32). The answer to these questions belongs to God alone. Since we are not on the same level as God is, it makes little sense and even is sheer blasphemy if we were to accuse God of being unjust. Even if we do not always understand God's ways, we must concede with Job that God is in control, and whatever God does is right. And furthermore, we have the assurance that in the end, everything will come out all right.

We have now concluded our investigation on theodicy. In so doing, we noticed that the issue of evil is one that pervades the whole of the religious history of humanity. As soon as humans were aware of something or someone above and beyond themselves, they wondered how this power relates to them. In most instances, the recognition was that there is a benign power that rules the world. At the same time, humans have become painfully aware that not everything in the world is rosy. There is something destructive and evil, be it in nature or in humans themselves. The then often arduous and tricky question arose of how to correlate the good with the bad or evil that humans experienced. It was the thoroughgoing conviction of humanity, with few exceptions, that the bad or the evil did not just originate from the human sphere. It had a magnitude that transcended humanity.

But should evil then be located in those higher powers or gods or in the one supreme God itself? In some religions, the conclusion was reached that there is indeed a plurality of gods, some being evil and others being benign. For instance, in Manichaeism, we find a bad creator god and a good redeemer god. Some gods could even show themselves as benign at one time and evil at other times, as we notice, for example, in Hinduism. When we peruse the Judeo-Christian religion, we get the impression that initially, God metes out both good and evil. Only gradually did the Israelites understand that God is intrinsically good and that evil must come from some other source. This source does not just make human life at times miserable, but in its anti-Godly direction, it attempts to thwart God's plans, which are directed toward the perfection of the world God. Especially in the intertestamental period and in the New Testament times, there is a veritable battle going on between God (who is the creator and preserver and perfecter of creation) and those powers that are under the prince of this world, as the Gospel of John tells us. Yet through the life and destiny of Jesus the Christ, these ugly evil powers, though still active in this world, are dethroned. God's working toward fulfillment and perfection of creation is, so to speak, on the home stretch. Nevertheless, the evil forces in both nature and humanity should not be taken lightly.

Evil is not simply a deficiency of the good, as Augustine once thought. There is an actual power in and behind evil that is destructive. Since our world is still on the course from creation in the beginning to perfection and fulfillment at the end, it cannot simply be called the best possible world, as Leibniz once claimed. On the other hand, we cannot consider God as being weak or even having withdrawn from this world even when we face the atrocities that humans inflict upon each other. God is not a divine jack-out-of-the-box who comes to our help whenever evil threatens us. Since the beginning of creation, God has given us the responsibility to take care of ourselves and of our environment. Nevertheless, there are certain parameters within creation that introduce order and predictability in nature, and there are guidelines for human conduct that allow for the preservation of humankind. Furthermore, God has not withdrawn from the world but upholds it at each individual moment. Though often humans assume that the world proceeds at its own terms, we should not forget that the world is contingent. As even scientists tell us, it has a beginning, and it will have an end. Therefore, the attainment of perfection is not contained in the world itself but rests in God alone. God is creator, sustainer, and redeemer.

Since God's redemptive scheme was not finished with Jesus's crucifixion and death but climaxed in the resurrection of Jesus as the Christ to new and everlasting life, we can be assured that in principle the destructive and evil forces are overcome. God is indeed in control. Yet why God has not yet eliminated the forces of evil and inaugurated the promised new world remains an enigma that can only be answered by God. We may call this "delay" unjust. But this is our evaluation. The final answer to why the kingdom of God has not been established can only be answered by God. As the philosopher Immanuel Kant rightly reasoned, a theodicy surpasses the possibility of the human mind, and if executed, it would be a result of arrogant human reason. However, with this injunction, we need not resign ourselves. We can still face the future optimistically in the knowledge that in the end, God's kingdom will triumph.

Selected Bibliography

Aquinas, Thomas. *The Summa Theologica*. Translated by Fathers of the English Dominican Province. New York: Benziger Bros., 1947.

Baldwin, Dalton DeVere. *A Whiteheadian Solution to the Problem of Evil*. PhD diss., Claremont Graduate School, 1975.

Barrow, John D., and Frank J. Tipler. *The Anthropic Cosmological Principle*. 2nd ed. Oxford: Clarendon, 1988.

Barth, Karl. *Church Dogmatics*, 3/3. Translated by G. Bromiley and R. Ehrlich. Edinburgh: T&T Clark, 1960.

———. *Church Dogmatics*, 4/1. Translated by G. Bromiley. Edinburgh: T&T Clark, 1956.

Bartholomew, D. J. *God of Chance*. London: SCM, 1984.

Berkouwer, C. G. *The Providence of God*. Translated by L. Smedes. Grand Rapids, MI: William B. Eerdmans, 1952.

Bonhoeffer, Dietrich. *Ethics*. Edited by Eberhard Bethge. Translated by N. H. Smith. New York: Macmillan, 1965.

———. *Letters and Papers from Prison*. Edited by Eberhard Bethge. Rev. and enlarged ed. New York: Macmillan, 1968.

Boyce, Mary. *A History of Zoroastrianism*. Vol. 1, *The Early Period*. Leiden, Netherlands: E. J. Brill, 1975.

Braun, Herbert. *Jesus of Nazareth: The Man and His Time*. Translated by Everett R. Kalin. Philadelphia: Fortress, 1979.

Brueggemann, Walter. *Reverberations of Faith: A Theological Handbook of Old Testament Themes*. Louisville: Westminster John Knox Press, 2002.

Brunner, Emil. *Justice and Social Order*. Translated by M. Hottinger. New York: Harper, 1945.

Bultmann, Rudolf. "New Testament and Mythology." In *Kerygma and Myth*, edited by Hans Werner Bartsch, translated by Reginald H. Fuller, 1–44. London: SPCK, 1953.

———. *Theology of the New Testament*. Translated by Kendrick Grobel. New York: Charles Scribner's, 1955.

Calvin, John. *The Institutes of the Christian Religion*. Translated by Henry Beveridge. Grand Rapids, MI: Eerdmans, 1957.

Cobb, John B., Jr., and Clark H. Pinnock, eds. *Searching for an Adequate God: A Dialogue between Process and Free Will Theists*. Grand Rapids, MI: William B. Eerdmans, 2000.

Cranston, Ruth. *The Miracle of Lourdes*. Updated and expanded ed. by the Medical Bureau of Lourdes. New York: Doubleday Image, 1988.

Darwin, Charles. *The Correspondence of Charles Darwin*. 8 vols. Edited by Frederick Burkhardt. Cambridge: Cambridge University Press, 1985–1993.

———. *The Works of Charles Darwin*. London: Pickering, 1986.

Dator, James Allen. *Soka Gakkai, Builders of the Third Civilization: American and Japanese Members*. Seattle: University of Washington Press, 1969.

Dionysius the Areopagite. *On the Divine Names and the Mystical Theology*. Translated by C. E. Rolt. New York: Macmillan, 1951.

Elert, Werner. *The Christian Ethos*. Translated by Carl J. Schindler. Philadelphia: Muhlenberg, 1957.

Esposito, John L., ed. *The Oxford History of Islam*. Oxford: Oxford University Press, 1999.

Fadiman, James, and Robert Frager, eds. *Essential Sufism*. San Francisco: HarperSanFrancisco, 1997.

Fretheim, Terence E. *The Book of Genesis*. In NIB. Vol. 1.

Friedrich, Carl J., ed. *The Philosophy of Kant: Immanuel Kant's Moral and Political Writings*. New York: Random House, 1949.

Friedrichsen, Anton. *The Problem of Miracle in Primitive Christianity*. Translated by Roy Harrisville and John S. Hanson. Minneapolis: Augsburg, 1972.

Fromm, Erich. *The Heart of Man: Its Genius for Good and Evil*. New York: Harper, 1966.

——. *You Shall Be as Gods: A Radical Interpretation of the Old Testament and Its Traditions*. New York: Holt, Rinehart and Winston, 1966.

Glassé, Cyril. *The Concise Encyclopedia of Islam*. With an introduction by Huston Smith. San Francisco: HarperSanFrancisco, 1991.

Greaves, Ron. *Aspects of Islam*. Washington, DC: Georgetown University Press, 2005.

Griffin, David Ray. *God, Power, and Evil: A Process Theodicy*. Philadelphia: Westminster, 1976.

Harkness, Georgia. *The Providence of God*. New York: Abingdon, 1960.

Hegel, Georg Friedrich Wilhelm. *The Philosophy of History*. Translated by J. Sibree. 1st ed. New York: Dover, 1956.

——. *The Philosophy of History*. With a preface by Charles Hegel. Translated by J. Sibree. Kitchener: Batoche Books, 2001.

Hick, John. *Evil and the God of Love*. London: Macmillan, 1966.

Hume, David. *Dialogues concerning Natural Religion*. In *Selections*, edited by Charles W. Hendel, 284–401. New York: Charles Scribner's, 1927.

——. *A Treatise of Human Nature*. Edited by L. A. Selby-Bigge. Oxford: Clarendon, 1896.

Hunter, Cornelius G. *Darwin's God: Evolution and the Problem of Evil*. Grand Rapids, MI: Brazos, 2001.

Kant, Immanuel. "On the Miscarriage of All Philosophical Trials in Theodicy." In *Religion and Rational Theology*, translated by Allen W. Wood and George Di Giovanni, 24–37. Cambridge: Cambridge University Press, 1996.

——. *Religion within the Limits of Reason Alone*. Translated and with an introduction and notes by Theodore M. Greene and Hoyt H. Hudson and with a new essay by John R. Silber. New York: Harper, 1960.

Kenny, John P. *The Supernatural: Medieval Theological Concepts to Modern*. Staten Island: Alba House, 1972.

Kluger, Rivkah Schärf. *Satan in the Old Testament*. Translated by H. Nagel. Evanston, IL: Northwestern University Press, 1967.

Leibniz, Gottfried Wilhelm. *The Monadology and Other Philosophical Writings*. Translated and with an introduction and notes by Paul and Anne Martin Schrecker. Indianapolis: Bobbs-Merrill, 1965.

———. *Theodicy: Essays on the Goodness of God, the Freedom of Man and the Origin of Evil.* Translated by E. M. Huggard. La Salle, IL: Open Court, 2005.

LeMahieu, D. L. *The Mind of William Paley: A Philosopher and His Age.* Lincoln: University of Nebraska Press, 1976.

Locke, John. *An Essay concerning Human Understanding.* Edited by Alexander C. Fraser. Oxford: Clarendon, 1894.

Maier, Paul L. *Eusebius: The Church History; A New Translation with Commentary.* Grand Rapids, MI: Kregel, 1999.

McSorely, Harry J. Luther. *Right or Wrong? An Ecumenical Theological Study of Luther's Major Work, "The Bondage of the Will."* Minneapolis: Augsburg, 1969.

Moltmann, Jürgen. *The Coming of God: Christian Eschatology.* Translated by Margaret Kohl. Minneapolis: Fortress, 1996.

———. *The Crucified God.* Translated by R. A. Wilson and John Bowden. London: SCM, 2009.

———. *God in Creation: A New Theology of Creation and the Spirit of God; The Gifford Lectures 1984–1985.* Translated by Margaret Kohl. Minneapolis: Fortress, 1993.

———. *The Trinity and the Kingdom of God.* Translated by Margaret Kohl. London: SCM, 1981.

Monden, Louis. *Signs and Wonders: A Study of the Miraculous Element in Religion.* New York: Desclee, 1966.

Newsom, Carol A. *The Book of Job.* In NIB. Vol. 4.

O'Flaherty, Wendy Doniger. *The Origins of Evil in Hindu Mythology.* Berkeley: University of California Press, 1976.

Outler, Albert C. *Who Trusts in God: Musings on the Meaning of Providence.* New York: Oxford University, 1968.

Paley, William. *Natural Theology: Or, Evidences of the Existence and Attributes of the Deity, Collected from the Appearances of Nature.* Illustrated by James Paxton and with additional notes and vocabulary by John Ware. Boston: Gould und Lincoln, 1860.

Pannenberg, Wolfhart. *Jesus—God and Man.* Translated by Lewis L. Wilkins and Duane A. Priebe. 2nd ed. Philadelphia: Westminster, 1988.

———. *Revelation as History.* Translated by David Granskou. London: Macmillan, 1968.

Peacocke, Arthur. *Theology for a Scientific Age: Being and Becoming—Natural, Divine, and Human.* Minneapolis: Fortress, 1993.

Peterson, Michael L., ed. *The Problem of Evil: Selected Readings.* Notre Dame, IN: University of Notre Dame Press, 1992.

Pinnock, Clark H. *Most Moved Mover: A Theology of God's Openness.* Grand Rapids, MI: Baker Academic, 2001.

Pinnock, Clark H., Richard Rice, John Sanders, William Hasker, and David Basinger, eds. *The Openness of God: A Biblical Challenge to the Traditional Understanding of God.* Downers Grove, IL: InterVarsity, 1994.

Polkinghorne, John. *Science and Providence: God's Interaction with the World.* Boston: Shambhala, 1989.

Pollard, William. *Chance and Providence: God's Action in a World Governed by Scientific Law.* New York: Charles Scribner's, 1958.

Rahner, Karl. "Why Does God Us Allow to Suffer?" In *Faith and Ministry*, translated by Edward Quinn, 194–208. Vol. 19 of *Theological Investigations*. New York: Crossroad, 1983.

Reimarus, Hermann Samuel. *The Goal of Jesus and His Disciples*. Translated and with an introduction by George W. Buchanan. Leiden, Netherlands: E. J. Brill, 1970.

Rubenstein, Richard L. *After Auschwitz: Radical Theology and Contemporary Judaism*. Indianapolis: Bobbs-Merrill, 1966.

Saddhatissa, H. *Buddhist Ethics: Essence of Buddhism*. London: George Allen & Unwin, 1970.

Schwarz, Hans. *Creation*. Grand Rapids, MI: William B. Eerdmans, 2002.

——. *Evil: A Historical and Theological Perspective*. Minneapolis: Fortress, 1995.

——. *The Trinity: The Central Mystery of Christianity*. Minneapolis: Fortress, 2017.

Sölle, Dorothee. *Christ the Representative: An Essay in Theology after the "Death of God."* Translated by David Lewis. London: SCM, 1967.

Suchocki, Majorie Hewitt. *The End of Evil: Process Eschatology in Historical Context*. Albany: SUNY, 1988.

Suzuki, Beatrice Lane. *Mahayana Buddhism: A Brief Outline*. With a foreword by Ch. Humphreys. New York: Macmillan, 1969.

Thiselton, Anthony C. *Doubt, Faith, Certainty*. Grand Rapids, MI: William B. Eerdmans, 2017.

Thomas, Owen C., ed. *God's Activity in the World: The Contemporary Problem*. Chico, CA: Scholars, 1983.

Thompson, Cargill. *Studies in the Reformation: Luther to Hooker*. Edited by C. W. Dugmore and Philip Broadhead. London: Athlone, 1980.

Voltaire. *Candide*. With an introduction by Philip Littell. New York: Boni and Liveright, 1918.

——. *Toleration and Other Essays*. Translated by Joseph McCabe. New York: G. P. Putnam's Sons, 1912.

West, Martin Litchfield. *The Hymns of Zoroaster: A New Translation of the Most Ancient Sacred Texts of Iran*. London: Bloomsbury, 2010.

Wickler, Wolfgang. *The Biology of the Ten Commandments*. Translated by D. Smith. New York: McGraw-Hill, 1972.

Wilson, Edward O. *On Human Nature*. Cambridge, MA: Harvard University Press, 1978.

Index of Subjects

Adam, 9, 24–25, 27, 41–42, 51–53, 58, 188–89
Adam and Eve, 9, 27, 44
Ahura Mazda, 5–7
anthropic principle, 144
anti-Godly powers, 1, 42–44, 67, 70, 74, 81–82, 100, 108, 129, 150, 160–61, 175–77, 179–82, 191–92
arhat, 18
atheism, atheists, 1, 110–11, 115, 118, 161
Auschwitz, 109, 112–13, 118, 143
Avesta, 6–7

Babylonian (captivity), 37, 40, 186
Babylonian Theodicy, 34, 40
Balaam, 37–38
benevolent (creator), 88, 90, 93, 99, 101, 103–4, 143, 180, 191
Brahman, 14–17

chance, 52, 59, 66, 96, 103, 122, 144, 148–49, 182–83
coercive (power), 122–23, 135
complementarity, 173
covenant, 50, 55, 107, 132, 134, 140, 147, 165–67, 186–87, 189, 191
COVID-19 pandemic, 80

death of God, 112–13, 117, 163
demons, 15–16, 43, 67, 91, 107–8, 170–71, 177
dependability, 147–48, 150
determinism, deterministic, 12, 76, 85, 164
devil, 26, 28, 38, 43–45, 48–49, 62, 67–70, 72, 77–81, 107–8, 154, 161, 191
dualism, dualistic, 1, 3, 6–9, 26, 36, 39, 41–42, 44–45, 48, 57, 59–60, 63, 67, 74, 108, 146

eschatology, eschatological, 7, 48–50, 52, 78, 81, 93, 111, 113, 115–18, 126, 128, 135
Eve, 9, 23, 27, 44
evolution(ary), vii, 1, 25, 101–4, 119, 122, 125, 127, 142, 144, 147–49, 158–59, 167, 171, 177, 183, 186

faith healing, 180
fall, 23–28, 38, 41–42, 46, 57, 92, 124–25, 133, 155, 188–89
fate, 16, 24, 26, 68, 87–88, 130, 142–43, 146, 164, 178
free will, 6, 10, 12–13, 33, 42, 57–58, 60–62, 67, 70, 85, 91

Gathas, 5–6
German Christians, 162
Gnostic(ism), 7–9, 26, 45, 57
God, hidden, 72, 75, 141; revealed, 71–72
God's judgment, 28, 30, 34, 53, 70, 76, 165, 174; suffering, 111, 114, 116, 118; will, 37, 53, 70, 75–76, 79, 97, 118, 132, 152, 164, 182–83

hadith, 12
Holocaust, 95, 111–13
human freedom, 32–34, 46, 63, 85, 109–10, 126, 128, 133, 135, 154

incomprehensibility, incomprehensible, 72, 106, 108, 110, 124, 139
innocent suffering, 1, 18, 21, 32, 115
interference, 67, 147, 149, 170, 172, 183

karma, 15–19
kingdom of Christ, 76, 78–79
kingdom of evil, 80–81, 91–93

Index of Names

Alaric (King), 162
Al-Ash'arī, 13
Albright, William Foxwell, 42
Ali, Sayed Ameer, 12
Althaus, Paul, 141
Altizer, Thomas J.J., 112, 163
Ambrose, 59
Apollonius of Tyana, 174
Aristides, 138
Aristotle, 65, 137, 151, 153
Arouet, François-Marie, 87. *See also*
    Voltaire
Augustine, vii, 8–9, 58–63, 66, 68–69,
    74, 77, 79, 81–82, 86, 121, 143, 152–53,
    162–63, 167–68, 193

Baldwin, Dalton DeVere, 120–21
Barnard, Leslie William, 138
Barrow, John D., 144
Barth, Karl, 104–8, 122, 160
Bartholomew, D.J., 182
Bayle, Pierre, 83–84, 86
Behm, Johannes, 187
Ben Sira, 32–33
Berkouwer, Gerrit C., 163, 172
Böhlig, Alexander, 8
Bohr, Niels, 173
Bonhoeffer, Dietrich, 111, 146, 160, 163–64,
    170, 178–79
Boyce, Mary, 5
Boyd, William, 156
Braun, Herbert, 174
Brueggemann, Walter, 29
Brunner, Emil, 152, 157
Büchner, Georg, 1
Bujo, Bénézet, 153
Bullock, Alan, 162

Bultmann, Rudolf, 45, 165, 171, 174, 175

Calvin, John, 68–71, 104, 118
Celsus, 138
Charlotte of Hanover, Sophia, 83
Cobb, John B., Jr., 119, 135
Cranston, Ruth, 156, 169
Crenshaw, James L., 33
Curran, Charles E., 151

Darwin, Annie Elizabeth, 103
Darwin, Charles, 1, 96, 98, 101–4, 127, 143,
    148, 157–58
Darwin, Emma, 103
Dator, James Allen, 19–20
Descartes, René, 83, 86
Dionysius the Areopagite, 138–39, 168

Eddington, Arthur S., 171
Elert, Werner, 159
Erasmus, 71, 75, 76
Evodius, 60–61

Feuerbach, Ludwig, 94, 139, 184
Foerster, Werner, 42, 188
Fohrer, Georg, 40
Ford, Lewis, 122–23
Fordyce, John, 104
Fretheim, Terence E., 23
Friedrichsen, Anton, 175
Fromm, Erich, 24, 27

Gautama, Siddharta, 18–19
Gerlitz, Peter, 16
Gerst, Alexander, 142
Gilson, Etienne, 162
Glassé, Cyril, 11

Gogarten Friedrich, 165
Gray, Asa, 103
Greaves, Ron, 14
Griffin, David Ray, 119–21, 135
Grundmann, Walther, 51, 53

Haag, Herbert, 34, 37, 39
Hamilton, William, 112, 163
Hanifa, Abu, 12
Hare, Peter, 123
Harkness, Georgia, 178–79, 181
Härle, Wilfried, 106
Hartshorne, Charles, 119
Hegel, Georg Wilhelm Friedrich, 24, 95–98, 112, 117–18, 146, 163
Heiler, Friedrich, 6, 11
Heim, Karl, 180
Hendel, Charles, 93–94
Henry, Marie-Louise, 37
Herion, Gary A., 186–87
Hick, John, 119, 123–29
Hirsch, Emanuel, 170
Hitler, Adolf, 161, 162
Hobbes, Thomas, 152, 155
Howe, Günter, 173
Hume, David, 93–94, 156
Hunter, Cornelius G., 103

Irenaeus, 57–58, 119, 123–25, 128

Jaeger, John David, 114
Jeremias, Joachim, 50, 175, 178
Jerrahi, Sheikh Ragib Robert Frager al, 14
Job, 1, 29–30, 32, 34–38, 40, 69, 70, 90, 115, 141, 191, 192
Jung, Carl Gustav, 24–25
Justin Martyr, 138

Kamali, Mohammad Hashim, 11
Kashyap, Jagadish, 18

Keats, John, 126
Kenny, John P., 168
Kittel, Gerhard, 162
Kluger, Rivkah Schärf, 39–40
Künneth, Walter, 160, 188

Lactantius, 152
Lampert, Evgenii, 165
Lanczkowski, Günter, 6
Langford, Michael J., 145
Leibniz, Gottfried Wilhelm, 83–86, 88–89, 96, 98, 143, 189, 193
LeMahieu, D.L., 98
Locke, John, 156
Lohse, Bernhard, 77
Lorenz, Konrad, 157–58
Luther, Martin, vii, 52, 65, 71–83, 86, 107, 141–42, 145, 150–51, 154–55, 158–59, 161–64, 179, 191
Lüthi, Kurt, 37

Madden, Edward, 123
Maier, Paul L., 57, 138
Makiguchi, Tsunesaburō, 19
Mani, 7–9
Manson, William, 176
McCall, Bradford, 149
McSorley, Harry J., 74
Mendenhall, George E., 186–87
Merker, Moritz, 158
Michel, Otto, 189
Migne, J.-P., 59
Mohammed, 12
Moltmann, Jürgen, 114–18
Monden, Louis, 169
Monod, Jacques, 148, 182
Morenz, Siegfried, 158
Newsom, Carol A., 34, 36, 40

Nichiren, 19–20
Nicholas of Cusa, 169

Nicholson, Reynold Alleyne, 13
Nietzsche, Friedrich, vii

O'Flaherty, Wendy Doniger, 14–16
Origen, 114, 138, 152
Otto, Rudolf, 139
Outler, Albert C., 164, 166
Overhage, Paul, 148

Paley, William, 98–102, 104, 124
Pannenberg, Wolfhart, 190
Peacocke, Arthur, 145, 148–49, 172
Petzke, Gerd, 174
Philostratus, 174
Pinnock, Clark, 129–35
Plato, 3–5, 7, 9
Plotinus, 59, 138
Polkinghorne, John, 144, 146, 149, 182–83
Pollard, William, 143, 147–49, 173–74
Pontifex, Mark, 172
Poser, Hans, 83
Pothinus of Lyons, 57
Procksch, Otto, 51
Pseudo-Dionysius. See Dionysius

Quadratus, 138

Rahman, Fazlur, 10
Rahner, Karl, 108–11
Ravin, Arnold W., 158
Reimarus, Herman Samuel, 171
Rice, Richard, 130, 135–36
Roberts, David E., 59
Rousseau, Jean Jacques, 155–56
Rubenstein, Richard, 95, 111–15, 118, 143

Saddhatissa, H., 19, 158
Salvian of Marseille, 162–63
Sanders, John, 131

Saunders, Dale, 20
Schiller, Friedrich, 24, 163
Schimmel, Annemarie, 11
Schmitt, Gerhard, 37
Schopenhauer, Arthur, 143
Schwarz, Hans, 39, 145, 158
Sellin, Gerhard, 137
Semler, Johann Salomo, 170–71
Sergius (Patriarch), 162
Shaltout, Mahmud, 11–12
Simpson, George G., 148
Socrates, 65
Sölle, Dorothee, 95, 111–12, 114–15, 163
Spinoza, Baruch, 83, 148
Suchocki, Majorie Hewitt, 121
Suzuki, Beatrice Lane, 19

Teilhard de Chardin, Pierre, 25, 177
Thiselton, Anthony C., 141
Thomas, Owen C., 182
Thomas Aquinas, 65–68, 153–54, 168–69
Thompson, Cargill, 77, 81
Tillich, Paul, 112–13, 172
Tipler, Frank J., 144
Tournier, Paul, 181

Upadhyaya, Kashi Nath, 158
Voltaire, 83, 86–89. See also Arouet, François-Marie
von Rad, Gerhard, 38
Vriezen, Theodorus C., 24

Weinfeld, Moshe, 166
West, Martin Litchfield, 6
Wheeler, John A., 144
Whitehead, Alfred North, 119–22
Wickler, Wolfgang, 157–59
Widengren, Geo, 40
Williams, John Alden, 12
Wilson, Edward O., 158

Biblical References

Old Testament

Zechariah			3:1	39
3:1–3		38, 40	3:2	38

Extrabiblical References

Wisdom of Solomon			*Jubilees*	
2:24		26	10:5	41
			11:5	41
Sirach				
11:14		33	*2 Baruch*	
11:26		33	48:42–43	42
11:27		33	54:15–19	41
15:11–20		33		
15:11–14		33	*4 Esra*	
16:1–4		33	3:21–22	42
33:11–13		33	3:21	42
39:16		33, 34		
41:16		32	*Apocalypse of Abraham*	
50:27		32	23	41
			26	41
1 Enoch				
6		41	*Testamentum Levi*	
8:1		41	19:1	42
40:7		41		
53:3		41	*Testamentum Judah*	
56:1		41	20:1	42
69:4–5		41		
69:6		41	*Life of Adam and Eve*	
			15:3	44

New Testament

Matthew			7:12	155
1:1		189	7:18	47
2:2		73	9:13	50
5:45		48, 147	10:29	147
6:5–7		178	10:30	147
6:9		178	12:35	48
6:13		49	12:38–39	175
7:7		178	12:39	47
7:11		47	12:43, 45	48